THE CATTLEMEN'S FRONTIER

A record of the trans-Mississippi cattle
industry from oxen trains to pooling
companies, 1850-1890

by

LOUIS PELZER

President, Mississippi Valley Historical Association
Professor of History, University of Iowa

NEW YORK / RUSSELL & RUSSELL

FIRST PUBLISHED IN 1936
REISSUED, 1969, BY RUSSELL & RUSSELL
A DIVISION OF ATHENEUM PUBLISHERS, INC.
L. C. CATALOG CARD NO: 68-27077
PRINTED IN THE UNITED STATES OF AMERICA

To my favorite brands

M. W. P.

L. P. P.

H. L. P.

Contents

Illustrations

Preface

Preface

Motives in occupying and stocking the range country were fundamentally economic. Profits rather than pleasure, wages rather than excitement, interest and dividends rather than hardships, and increase of herds more than adventure must be cited as the factors in creating the cattle country. These influences constitute the principal theme of this volume and subordinate the more colorful aspects which have passed from true narrative to the haze of fiction and legends.

Unlike the forty-niners and the government surveyors, the men on the cattle ranges were not diarists or letter writers. Even the records of many self-made laws and of associations of the range have vanished. The currents of history have not kept pace with those of imagination and tradition. The characters of Ned Buntline have a wider fame than have John W. Iliff and Conrad Kohrs and their achievements.

Certain chapters of this work have been read before various historical bodies.

This sojourn in range history has been made helpful and pleasant by the companionship with various graduate students. Financial aid from the Graduate College of the University of Iowa made extended explorations possible. Grants from Armour's Livestock Bureau at Chicago are gratefully acknowledged and made possible various excursions of the highest value. Mr. John Clay of Chicago was generous in permitting use of his sources on range history and his long career on the range made him a sure guide in retracing its story. Duty and pleasure combine in acknowledging the continuing encouragement of Colonel Edward N. Wentworth of Armour's Bureau, who not only offered clues, but also the best in suggestion and advice.

LOUIS PELZER

University of Iowa
November, 1935

Introduction

Introduction

Variously called the cow country, the cattle kingdom, the range and ranch cattle area, and the range country the trans-Mississippi cattle frontier first emerged from the inpouring of cattle from Texas. Its swift spread in a quarter of a century over an area of nearly a million and a half of square miles is a phenomenon of western history. The range industry followed the conquest of the Indians of the plains and the destruction of the buffalo, but in turn it succumbed to the small ranchmen and the armies of settlers.

Ancient as cattle raising is, no quarter century of its history can surpass in enduring interest its record following the Civil War. Since the Louisiana Purchase the great plains had been visited by explorers and fur-traders. Forty-niners and Oregon immigrants had crossed them and scores of army posts had dotted the regions. Horses, cattle, and ranchmen and cowboys then took possession of the domain of free grass to create a special culture on the plains.

The range industry assumed definite form after the Civil War. Railway penetration and the establishment of packing houses and stockyards gave to it permanency. Great investments of capital followed and the business acquired a standing in the financial world. The passage of the Homestead Act, the close of the Civil War, the first Texas drives to Kansas, and the completion of the first transcontinental railroad all took place within a decade. These factors profoundly influenced not only the expansion of the cattle area but also the immigration to the West. For twenty-five years the range industry lived on the grass – at first lavishly and later sparingly. Barbed-wire fencing, overstocking, overcapitalization, storms, mismanagement, and financial crises were forces that helped to undermine the cattle kingdom of these years.

On the plains lands almost equalling in area that of Europe, the live stock industry in cattle had a development marked not so much in magnitude as by unique natural conditions and unusual methods. Standing by itself, the cow country took on a character unlike that of any other section. The East produced more cattle but the West made it the main business instead of an incident of agriculture. The East raised cattle in large, prosaic numbers – in the West the round-up was a spectacle and trail-driving became a parade.

"The Easterner, with his background of forest and farm," concludes Professor W. P. Webb, the leading historian of the plains, "could not always understand the man of the cattle kingdom. One went on foot, the other went on horseback; one carried his law in books, the other carried it strapped round his waist. One represented tradition, the other represented innovation; one responded to convention, the other responded to necessity and evolved his own conventions. Yet the man of the timber and the town made the law for the man of the plain; the plainsman, finding this law unsuited to his needs, broke it, and was called lawless. The cattle kingdom was not sovereign, but subject. Eventually it ceased to be a kingdom and became a province." [1]

1 Walter Prescott Webb, *The Great Plains*, 206. Reprinted herein by permission of Ginn and Company.

The revolution in the range cattle industry – from longhorns to Herefords and Shorthorns, from water-holes to windmills, from free grass to haystacks and pastures, from the open range to barbed wire, and from trail-driving to railroads – was the conversion of an adventure into a permanent business. Old men – now few – reflect in their wistful moods on the old ranges of their youth and early manhood. But the horseman of *The Virginian* has dismounted. "He rides in his historic yesterday. You will no more see him gallop out of the unchanging silence than you will see Columbus on the unchanging sea come sailing from Palos with his caravels." [2]

---

[2] Owen Wister, *The Virginian, a horseman of the Plains*, 2. Reprinted herein by permission of The Macmillan Company.

A Decade of Ox-team Freighting on the Plains

A Decade of Ox-team Freighting on the Plains

Caravans of ox-teams during the two decades before the close of the Civil War carried Mormon settlers, Oregon emigrants, gold seekers, and army supplies across the great plains. These animals aided by horses and mules moved over numberless trails and wagon roads in bringing the explorers, the engineers, the soldiers, and the scientists to regions of the trans-Mississippi West. The oxen in performing their work were grazed on the grasses of the plains and then driven back to winter in the corn-growing states. Some, however, became the food of Indian tribes or were converted into roasts and fillets at the various army posts.

For about eighteen years after 1848 the ox-teams of Alexander Majors, the pioneer freighter, distributed stores from the Missouri river to points in the far West. Fort Leavenworth and Nebraska City became the great depots from which trains of twenty-five or twenty-six wagons drawn by over 300 oxen departed in the spring on their 1000-mile journeys. These oxen were then sold to emigrants or driven back to be corn-fed in the states. In 1854 he gave up freighting for the New Mexican merchants in order to carry government stores to the western army posts. In the next two years the firm of Russell, Majors, and Waddell transported army supplies from Fort Leavenworth to these posts. About three hundred wagons were used and the profits of the firm rose to about $300,000. In 1857 the army stores arrived too late at the depots, the season was too far advanced and about 1000 oxen belonging to this company were sent to winter near Fort Kearney where the herd was stampeded and dispersed by Indians.[3]

Such freighting firms were numerous, the "bull-whackers" constituted an army and their oxen a host. The firm in which Majors was the dominant partner employed at its zenith 6,250 wagons and about 75,000 oxen.[4] Already Kansas City was becoming a great cattle mart. Nearly a million dollars worth of cattle from Missouri, the Cherokee country, Texas, and Arkansas were sold there in 1857. These cattle were destined for California emigrants, for the Mormons in Utah, for the soldiers at Fort Kearney and Fort Laramie, and for the home market.[5] In 1859 Captain Randolph B. Marcy's *The Prairie Traveler* was published – a handbook which contained twenty-eight detailed itineraries for emigrants, for stages, and for ox-trains bound to points in the far West.

A sudden and profitable impetus to freighting over the plains was given by the expedition of 2,500 soldiers sent to quell the Mormon disturbances of 1857 and 1858. In the spring of the latter year Russell, Majors, and Waddell contracted with the United States government to supply the "Army of Utah" with 3,500 cattle to be taken from their ox-teams and to be delivered in lots of about 250. On twenty days' notice the firm agreed to

[3] Alexander Majors, *Seventy Years on the Frontier*, 77, 103, 140-143.

[4] Charles F. Lummis, "Pioneer Transportation in America," in *McClure's Magazine*, vol. XXVI, 81-94.

[5] C. C. Spalding, as quoted in *Kansas Historical Collections*, vol. XI, 121, 122, from the *Annals of the City of Kansas* (1858), 78, 79.

increase the number to 10,000 at a price of $7.50 per hundred pounds.[6] The freighters were remarkably successful in furnishing cattle and supplies for the Mormon War and in delivering stores to Fort Kearney and Fort Laramie. Over 6,000 mules and 46,896 oxen pulled the 4,956 wagons in which these army stores were transported. A herd of 3,500 chosen by Majors to winter in 1859-1860 on the clover and wild rice of the Ruby Valley in Nevada Territory was to be delivered to the army in the spring. In November, however, there came a heavy snow with cold temperature and in forty days all but two hundred lay in starved and frozen heaps.[7]

Another contract of this firm in April, 1860, provided that it was to receive army supplies at Fort Kearney and at Fort Riley. Ox-teams were to freight the goods with all "practicable despatch" to Fort Union in the Territory of New Mexico. The rates varied according to the months of starting: a rate of $1.00 per hundred was to be paid on freight leaving in January or December but in June or July when the weather, water, and grass were more favorable, the rate was $.16 to $.20 less.[8]

In Alexander Majors's ox-trains the wagonmaster and his assistant had duties and powers equal to those of a captain of a ship or steamboat.[9] Another man looked after the cattle and two or three in addition were employed to replace those who might become sick or disabled. The "bull-whackers" trained and yoked the oxen

[6] U.S. Senate *Executive Documents*, 35th congress, first session, no. 46, vol. XII, 2-4 (April 16, 1858).

[7] *Ibid.*, 35th congress, second session, no. 1, vol. III, 797. Majors, *Seventy Years on the Frontier*, 142.

[8] U.S. House *Executive Documents*, 36th congress, second session, no. 47, vol. VIII, 9-11.

[9] Majors, *Seventy Years on the Frontier*, chap. xvi.

and day after day walked alongside the train as it trailed over the prairies. Skilled in the use of their great whips they killed the rattlesnakes which sometimes fatally struck the grazing animals. From six to eight teamsters formed a mess, "each mess selecting the man best fitted to serve as cook, and the others carrying the water, fuel, and standing guard, so that the cook's sole business when in camp was to get his utensils ready and cook the meals." The average pay for these men was $1.00 per day and expenses, and all of Majors's employees signed – if they did not keep – an agreement to abstain from treating their oxen cruelly, from gambling, from getting drunk, from using profane language, and from doing anything incompatible with the conduct of a gentleman.

Discovering that stock could be wintered on the plains was, it would seem, a gradual process. In about 1853 Seth E. Ward, a settler from Fort Laramie, began to winter cattle in the valleys of the Chugwater and Laramie rivers in what is now Wyoming. In the next year Alexander Majors's 300 oxen were driven to Fort Laramie where 100,000 pounds of freight were delivered in November. Knowing that it was too late to enable them to return to Missouri, the freighters sent their poor and sorefooted cattle out to the grazing grounds where Ward's cattle had wintered the season before. Attended by herders the oxen quickly recuperated and in the spring were in the finest working condition. For ten years Majors wintered cattle on these ranges. Although always in poor flesh when turned out in the fall the cattle grew sleek and fat on the cured winter grasses. During some winters he grazed thousands upon the ranges and the season's loss was less than half of one per cent.[10]

10 Copy of letter from Alexander Majors dated April 15, 1884, and printed in the *Cheyenne* [Wyo.] *Sun*, May 1, 1884. See also A. T. Babbitt, "The Graz-

A somewhat similar discovery was made by Captain
W. F. Raynolds while engaged in the exploration of the
Yellowstone river.[11] He arrived in the valley of Deer
Creek (in southeastern Wyoming) in November, 1859,
and turned out his seventy exhausted horses and mules
to graze during the winter. The animals did not escape
the terrific winds, the bitter cold and snowstorms of
December, but to his surprise Raynolds found the animals in the spring in as fine a condition as if grain-fed
and stable-housed all winter. They had grazed over an
area of about fifty square miles. This experience the
captain regarded as "the most forcible commentary I
can make upon the quality of the grass and the character
of the winter."

The noise and bustle of freighters at Lawrence, Kansas, in 1859, has been described by Horace Greeley who
travelled over the plains that year.[12] The contractors'
wagons, built large and strong, carried two extra axles
under the body to replace those which might become
broken on rough roads. The oxen were generally unbroken at the start but soon became tamed under the
skillful driving of the "bull-whackers." Day after day
they browsed on the free grasses of the plains but at night
were driven into the circular corrals formed by the
wagons. "The drivers are as rough and wild-looking
as their teams, though not quite so awkward at their
business."

These trains of ox-teams, as he saw them in May,
were on their way to Utah, others to Fort Hall, and still

ing Interest and the Beef Supply," dated March 10, 1884, and printed in
[Chicago] *Daily Drovers Journal,* April 10, 1884.

11 U.S. Senate *Executive Documents,* 40th congress, second session, no. 77,
vol. II, chap. iii. Contains "Captain Raynolds's Report and Journal."

12 Horace Greeley, *An Overland Journey from New York to San Francisco,*
23-25.

others to Green river. "Very few wagons or cattle ever come back; the freighting is all one way; and both wagons and cattle are usually sold at or near their point of destination for whatever they may fetch – to be taken to California or disposed of as they best may."

Successive waves of emigration toward the West crowded the frontier of settlement farther and farther beyond the farming areas and were gradually establishing the ranchmen's or cattlemen's frontier. The federal census reports of 1850, 1860, 1870, and 1880 classified cattle as "milch cows," "working oxen" and "other cattle" but it was the latter group which increased at the greatest rates. Western grazing areas were being discovered by men who saw the nutritive qualities of grasses and the opportunities of the open, free range. John W. Iliff, a former student at Delaware College, came to Colorado Territory in 1859 with a load of provisions which he sold for $100. This he invested in a herd of cattle which became the foundation of his enormous ranching interests in that country.[18]

During the Civil War food and supplies hauled by ox-teams were delivered to the western army posts and to Indian agencies. These wagons drawn by ten oxen carried about 5,500 pounds each. Over 36,000,000 pounds of grain were delivered by such wagons to the twenty-one western army posts and Indian agencies during the year ended June, 1865. "Travellers by the stage from Denver to Fort Leavenworth," reported the war department, "a distance of six hundred and eighty-three miles, in the month of July, 1865, were never out of sight of wagon trains, belonging either to emigrants or to the merchants who transport supplies for the war

[18] Hubert Howe Bancroft, *History of Nevada, Colorado and Wyoming,* 385.

department, for the Indian department, and for the
mines and settlers of the central territories." [14]

In the same year Samuel Bowles, the editor of the
Springfield Republican, visited the western frontiers
described in his volume *Across the Continent.*[15] At Fort
Kearney he noted ox and mule teams arriving from the
West with their empty wagons. Others, westbound, were
loaded with corn, machinery for the mines, food, clothing, and luxuries for the accumulating populations in
the western territories. "The wagons," he wrote, "are
covered with white cloth; each is drawn by four to six
pairs of mules or oxen; and the trains of them stretch
frequently from one-quarter to one-third of a mile each.
. . . They depend entirely upon the prairies for food
as they go along; and indeed the animals grow stronger
and fatter as they move on in their summer campaign
of work, coming out of their winter rest poor and
scrawny, and going into it in the fall, fat and hearty."

James F. Meline in June, 1866, was a witness of the
ox-trains loading at Fort Leavenworth and departing
for the Territory of New Mexico.[16] "They are remarkable," he wrote, "each wagon team consisting of ten yokes
of fine oxen, selected and arranged not only for drawing
but for pictorial effect, in sets of twenty, either all black,
all white, all spotted, or otherwise marked uniformly."
The average load of a contract ox-team ranged from
6,500 to 8,000 pounds and Meline commented on the

[14] U.S. House *Executive Documents,* 39th congress, first session, no. 1, vol.
III, part i, 112, 113, 251. Contains the report of Quartermaster-general M. C.
Meigs, dated November 8, 1865.

[15] Samuel Bowles, *Across the Continent,* 14.

[16] James F. Meline, *Two Thousand Miles on Horseback; Santa Fé and
Back; a Summer Tour Through Kansas, Colorado, & New Mexico in the
year 1866,* 3, 5, 9, 10, 22.

slowness of these teams whose average daily travel was but seven miles. In his first week of travel westward he counted 680 wagons carrying their burdens of freight and emigrants. More than half of these were bound for Denver with freight and one team was hauling an engine, a boiler, and a quartz-crushing machine. Other trains were destined for Virginia City, Empire City, Utah, and even Oregon. "The freight trains are on the road all the time, going and coming, have all their teamsters armed, and do not require the surveillance necessary for emigrants. It would be within bounds to say that one hundred and fifty wagons pass west daily, during the season."

Railway construction during the Civil War invited labor and immigration to the West. Nearly seven hundred miles of the Union Pacific Railroad had been constructed westward from Omaha at the close of the year 1868. Agricultural areas and new pasturages were thereby enabled to send their tribute to eastern markets. The Pacific Telegraph had completed its line from Omaha to Salt Lake City in 1862.

Viewing such events in western expansion the bureau of agriculture wrote in 1866 that the capacity of our whole country for producing cattle had not yet been fully tested.[17] The year 1860 was the year, it regarded, when the production of cattle had commenced on a largely increased ratio. The West had not yet received numbers commensurate for use and for feeding and the country was just beginning to get a glimpse of the enormous possibilities of the plains for cattle production. The buffalo and the Indians might retard this

[17] Lewis F. Allen, "Improvement of Native Cattle," in *Report of the Commissioner of Agriculture for the year 1866*, 294-320.

industry but with the coming of the telegraph and the emigrant, passenger, and traffic trains all obstacles would disappear.

"The rural population of the great western plains and the central basin," wrote Lewis F. Allen in this report, "will be composed chiefly of herdsmen, and their main occupation that of grazing cattle. . . The mining population which is to exist among them will, for many years, consume all other products which the farmers may have to spare, besides taking a great many of their cattle. Let there be peace throughout our borders and no foreign war to disturb our industry, and it is safe to predict that the census of 1870 will give the United States and territories forty millions, and that of 1880 sixty millions of neat cattle within their limits."

With the advent of the railroads to the West came a decline in ox-team freighting, and, after 1868 the ox became a less vital factor in pioneer transportation. After that he became less and less a westbound draught animal and more and more an article of eastbound freight. His value came to be reckoned in pounds of beef rather than in ox-power. And, in the cattlemen's frontier the cowboy rather than the teamster, the ranch rather than the freighting train, and the range rather than the wagon-trails became dominant features. On this new frontier the word "steers" rather than "oxen" became the generic term for the millions of cattle on the pastoral lands of the West.

The Texas Cattle Trails

The Texas Cattle Trails

Spanish conquerors bringing with them their Anda-
lusian cattle laid the foundations of the Mexican herds
which gradually overspread the vast pampas regions
of Texas. By 1830, it is said, about 100,000 cattle existed
in Texas and four-fifths of these living in the settled
portions of the state were of Spanish origin. In 1842
driving to New Orleans began and four years later
Edward Piper drove 1,000 Texas cattle to Ohio where
they were fed and sold. In 1850 the drives to California
began and six years later the first Texas herd entered
Chicago. Another Texas cattleman, John C. Dawson,
made in 1859 what was said to be the first drive of stock
from Texas or Indian Territory to the Territory of Colorado.[18]

Frederick Law Olmsted in 1856 counted in Texas
a drove of four hundred oxen bound for California.
Twenty-five men mounted on mules – guides, drovers,
and young men emigrating to California – were grazing
the animals.[19] Over three and one-half millions of cattle
were listed in Texas in 1860 for assessment purposes.
In 1866 about a quarter of a million long-horned Texas
cattle were started for Sedalia, Missouri, but the drovers
meeting various obstacles and objections, diverted the
herds to other points.[20]

---

[18] Clarence W. Gordon, "Report on Cattle, Sheep, and Swine" (10-31),
in *Tenth Census of the United States*, III, 965-985.

[19] Frederick Law Olmsted, *A Journey Through Texas; or a Saddle-Trip
on the Southwestern Frontier*, 274.

[20] Gordon, *op. cit.*, 21.

In the same year two young Iowans – Harvey Ray and George C. Duffield [21] – made a drive of cattle from central Texas to Iowa. In April a camp was set up near the Colorado river, pens were built, and cattle received and branded. In the northerly movement of two weeks the twenty cowboys had rough work in handling the three herds during the rains, thunderstorms, and stampedes. Then the men swam the cattle and horses over the Brazos river. Provisions and blankets were "rafted" over and with a long rope they pulled the camp wagon safely across the stream. But most of the "Kitchen furniture" such as "Camp Kittles Coffee Pots Cups Plates Canteens &&" were lost. After rounding up the cattle "all Hands gave the Brazos one good harty dam" and resumed the drive.

A whole day was required to swim the cattle across the Red river. One man was drowned and Duffield himself had a narrow escape. A few days later two men got lost and for sixty hours were without food. Cattle strayed, ponies gave out, Indians were very troublesome, and cowboys became sulky. Even the faithful oxen were detached from the camp wagon to pull cattle out of the boggy mud. "Hard Rain & Wind," noted Duffield's diary for June 12, 1866. "Big stampede & here we are among the Indians with 150 head of Cattle gone hunted all day & the Rain pouring down with but poor success. Dark days are these to me Nothing but Bread & Coffee Hands all Growling & Swearing – every thing wet & cold Beeves gone rode all day & gathered all but 35 Mixed with 8 other Herds Last Night 5,000 Beves

[21] The diary covering the period from February 17-November 7, 1866, is printed in *Annals of Iowa* (1924), third ser., XIV, 246-262.

stampeded at this place & a general mix up was the result."

Drives of four weeks across the Indian Territory brought the longhorns to Baxter Springs in Kansas. Provisions were gone when the drovers came to the Arkansas river and they were forced to live on beef and flour. Duffield went to Fort Gibson and there obtained coffee and the promise of military aid against the Indians. It took four days to cross the Arkansas river. "Worked all day hard in the River trying to make the Beeves swim & did not get one over," the young drover wrote. "Had to go back to Prairie Sick & discouraged. Have *not* got the *Blues* but am in *Hel of a fix.*" Duffield's back became blistered by exposure to the sun and when crossing the Verdigris river he was attacked by a longhorn and only escaped by diving. But pleasanter scenes came when the drovers enjoyed the fine springs and the blackberries on the Kansas prairies.

Ordered off the Shawnee reservation, Duffield moved in a southwesterly course back into the Indian Territory for about three weeks. The torrid July sun and the flies tormented men and beasts. For three days in the land of the Osages they saw no animals except a few lonely wolves. On Sunday, August 5, 1866, the men were near the Arkansas river "but we dont Know How far nor where we are now going to turn North & trust to luck."

During the remainder of August the cattle were grazed northward as far as Nebraska City. The monotonous diet of beef was relieved by vegetables and pot pies of prairie chickens. But when the cattle trampled upon the settlers' fields Duffield was visited by angry farmers and "threatened with the Law." Striking the old Santa

Fé Trail the herds passed near Lost Spring, Diamond Spring, and Council Grove. Then the cattle for the first time saw the railroad, then completed from Kansas City to Fort Riley. On September 1 the cattle were on the prairie near Nebraska City. There Duffield "lay around the wagon (for that is all the camp we have) all day feel very tired & lazy cattle all got up & stole off from the Herder while he was asleep – could not find them until morning –."

After ferrying the cattle across the Missouri river they were driven leisurely to the eastward, passing near the Iowa towns of Sidney, Clarinda, Afton, Osceola, and Chariton. The animals browsed on the prairies and meadows but occasionally invaded the ripening corn fields. Duffield "carred" the cattle at Ottumwa to be shipped to Burlington and Chicago. The exploit of the twenty-two year old trail-driver was remembered by the Texas cowboys but its stampedes and hardships were not to deter the Texas cattlemen from invading the western ranges with their great herds.

Railway construction in Kansas in the year 1866 was pushing into the grazing areas of that state and likewise connecting them with the great markets of St. Louis, Chicago, and the Atlantic seaboard. The Kansas Pacific Railroad was progressing westward in the Kansas and the Smoky Hill valleys and in July, 1866, was completed to Junction City. The completion of the Missouri Pacific Railroad to Kansas City furnished a continuous line from Topeka to the eastern seaboard. These events and the subsidence of Indian uprisings in the Southwest were the prelude to the coming of great herds from Texas in 1867.[22]

---

[22] Samuel J. Crawford, *Kansas in the Sixties*, 230.

Quick to see the commercial possibilities of this coming invasion of Texas cattle, Joseph G. McCoy, an Illinois stockman, visited Abilene, Kansas, in 1867 to which the Kansas Pacific Railroad had been completed. This small village of about a dozen log huts, four-fifths of which had dirt roofs, was chosen by McCoy as a terminal point for the Texas cattle drives. Here he constructed offices and a hotel. Stockyards and all the facilities for holding, hauling, and shipping were built and the Kansas Pacific Railroad built a hundred car switch. An agent was sent south to inform Texas drovers of these facilities and thousands of dollars were spent in advertising Abilene where, it was pointed out, Texas cattlemen would find facilities for taking care of the drives and for making eastbound shipments. Markets and profits now seemed to be assured.[23]

Thirty-five thousand Texas cattle came to Abilene in the summer of 1867 and thus established the northbound Texas cattle trail over which millions of steers were to be driven in the next two decades to be dispersed over the great plains. The first shipment of twenty cars from Abilene to Chicago was made on September 5, 1867, and netted small profit but great rejoicing. A second shipment of 900 cattle to Albany, New York, was made, but at a loss of $300.[24]

"The Texas Trail was no mere cow-path. It was the course of empire." [25] From scores of points in Texas

[23] Joseph G. McCoy, *Historic Sketches of the Cattle Trade of the West and Southwest*, 44, 50, 115.

[24] *Idem*, 51-53.

[25] Charles M. Harger, "Cattle Trails of the Prairies," in *Scribner's Magazine* (1892), XI, 732-742. Philip Ashton Rollins, *The Cowboy: his Equipment, and his Part in the Development of the West, passim*. Joseph Nimmo, Jr., "The Range and Ranch Cattle Business of the United States," in U.S. House

paths and trails converged toward the north of the state.
A great zone of travel winding and twisting was pushed
northward, now contracting, now narrowing, and then
branching as the herds grazed into the western plains.
It was a highway of commerce unlike the Oregon Trail,
which was a road of migration. Grass and water and the
avoidance of Indian dangers rather than ease of travel
had to be sought by the thousands of trail-drivers who
directed the herds.

One route – the Fort Griffin and Dodge City Trail –
began at Bandera, Texas, and lay almost due northward
for a distance of about 600 miles. This passed through
Fort Griffin and crossed the Red river at Doan's Store
in Indian Territory after which the herds swam or
forded in turn the Washita, the Canadian, and the Cim-
arron rivers. The Arkansas river was crossed to get to
Dodge City. If the drover continued northward through
Kansas he finally came to Ogallala on the South Platte
river in Nebraska. This trunk trail with its modifica-
tions was also referred to as the Chisholm Trail.

Other routes, developing into greater and greater importance as the movements of cattle were diverted by
the settlements, bore their commerce of cattle as well
as their names. The Old Shawnee Trail after running
parallel to the Chisholm Trail for about a hundred miles
then veered westwardly to strike Baxter Springs in
Kansas. Where this route touched the Canadian river
the Middle or West Shawnee Trail began its course to
Junction City in Kansas. Still another cattle route was
the West Chisholm Trail which, avoiding later settle-

Executive Documents, 48th congress, second session (1885), no. 7, vol. **xx**,
part ii. *Yearbook of the United States Department of Agriculture for 1908,*
227-241.

THE FREIGHTERS, PILGRIMS OF THE PLAINS
From a contemporary sketch drawn in 1871.

ments, penetrated into western Kansas to Ellsworth. As the receiving ends of the trails became branched byways so the other ends became frayed into various routes over which cattle were sent to cow towns and to the fattening ranges in every part of the great plains.

Among the 75,000 cattle arriving at Abilene, Kansas, in 1868 was a herd of 600 wild Texas steers driven by M. A. Withers. Leaving Lockhart, Texas, on April 1, his crew of eight drivers and the cook passed through Austin, Waco, and Fort Worth; then the Arkansas river was crossed at Fort Gibson and the stream followed to Wichita, Kansas. Another short drive brought the herd to Abilene on July 1. The animals had been valued at $8 to $10 per head in Texas, and the expense of driving had been about $4 per steer. The herd was grazed north of Abilene until fall when they were sold at $28 per head to a firm of Champaign, Illinois.[26]

Over 5,000,000 Texas cattle, it was estimated, were moved up the trail in the eighteen years ending in 1884. The greatest number, estimated at 700,000, came to Abilene in 1871. As the ends of the trail shifted to other areas, Wichita, Ellsworth, Dodge City, Junction City, Garden City, Hayes City, in Kansas, and Ogallala and Cheyenne to the north received the tribute of millions of cattle. Perhaps nowhere in the history of the world is there a record of cattle migration of such magnitude.

Eyewitnesses impressed by the northerly flow of cattle from the great Texas reservoir have recorded their estimates of numbers during the prosperous years of the trail. The *Fort Worth Democrat* of April 30, 1878, noted

[26] J. Marvin Hunter, editor, *The Trail Drivers of Texas* (second revised edition, Nashville, 1925), 96-99. This volume reproduces with minor changes the material in vol. I (San Antonio, 1920) and vol. II (San Antonio, 1923). References in this work are to the second revised edition of one volume.

the arrival of bands of 1,700, 3,200 and 2,500 and of a drive of 120 horses bound for Iowa. In that year up to that date over 18,000 cattle – one, two, and three-year-olds – had passed Fort Worth. The grass was pronounced as excellent and the cost of driving was but $.30 to $.40 per head. A few weeks later the same paper stated that 82,000 had passed northward. It estimated the drive for the season at 102,450 and stated that Snyder Brothers alone had driven 2,500 to Wyoming Territory. A Kansas editor estimated the drive to that state in this year at 200,000. "This will give to Kansas," he said, "the cream of the Texas cattle trade, and the East a superior article of beef." [27]

Over 60,000 cattle were trailed past Fort Griffin during 1880 up to May 13. The *Ford County Globe* of Dodge City, Kansas, said that in the year 1880 to June 25 fifty-four firms had registered there, and that their 200,000 cattle were bound for Dodge City, for Big Springs, and for Ogallala in Nebraska, and for Indian Territory. The herd of 7,000 of West and Brothers was to be delivered to a point on the Yellowstone river.[28] During sixteen days in 1882, according to the *Cheyenne Transporter,* 71,462 cattle owned by forty-one different firms had passed up the trail in herds varying in size from 214 to 3,750.[29]

Accounts from numerous old trail drivers have helped to preserve the history of this famous cattle highway. In 1876 ten men trailed a herd of 2,500 Texas longhorns from the Nueces river to a point on the Missouri river where government traders supplied Indian agencies.[30]

27 *Ford County Globe,* April 30, June 4, 10, 1878.

28 *Ibid.,* June 29, 1880.

29 Reported in *The Caldwell* [Kas.] *Post,* June 15, 1882.

30 James H. Cook, "Trailing Texas Long-Horn Cattle through Nebraska," in *Publications of the Nebraska State Historical Society,* XVIII, 260-268.

This, the first large herd driven through Nebraska into Dakota Territory, crossed both branches of the Platte river near Ogallala and then grazed northward over lands drained by the headwaters of the Dismal and Loup rivers. In their 1,800 mile journey the men encountered high water, stormy weather, hunger, and thirst. Stampedes of both horses and steers were other troubles. In one stampede most of one night was spent in quieting the galloping animals. After riding around or "milling" them and singing songs – effective if not tuneful – the terrified herd finally rested on the plains.

More welcome scenes came as the herders grazed their stock through the sand-hill region of Nebraska where the soapweeds were in bloom and where the ripened sand cherries afforded not to the eye alone a welcome feast. North of the Platte river game was abundant and antelope, elk, and deer were made to replenish the cook's larder. Arriving at an unnamed lake, the steers crowded into the water to quench their thirst and from it flocks of wild geese, ducks, swans, and pelicans rose in alarm before this unwelcome invasion by the Texas longhorns.

About 15,000 head of mixed cattle belonging to J. F. Ellison and John O. Dewees, two former comrades in the Confederate army, were moved up the trail in six herds during the year 1877. Eight men including the horse wrangler and the negro cook, of which none was over twenty-three years of age, left the pasture at Lockhart, Texas, with a herd of 2,500 in April. The cook drove the wagon pulled by two oxen and containing the bedding and the provisions which from time to time had to be replenished at the various scattered outposts on the trail. A stampede occurred on Onion Creek and another on Panther Creek near the Red river. Heavy work was required to reassemble the herd and then to let the cattle string out to be recounted. Drenching rains fell at night and the cattle had to swim the Red, the Washita, and the North Canadian rivers. Fifteen Indians demanding beef were appeased by a tribute of five lame steers. Dodge City was finally reached and fresh provisions were bought for the cook's wagon. A drive of three hundred miles more brought the steers to Ogallala where they were delivered to numerous buyers who distributed them to various ranches of the great grazing country.

John B. Kendrick, later a member of the United States senate, has told the story of a drive in which he took part in 1879.[31] Two weeks in March were spent in receiving steers from one to five years old from various ranches near Victoria, Texas. Placed in large pens the steers were then roped and thrown by the front feet by Mexicans and negroes who were the most skilled help at that kind of work. After all the steers were road branded the herd was started north early in April.

The average distance travelled in a day was from fifteen to eighteen miles. The foreman, J. D. Wufjen, divided his ten or twelve men into two reliefs during the day and into four during the night when each guard was to be on duty from two hours to two and a half hours. The last guard called the cook and turned the cattle from their night bed of two or three acres to graze northward until seven or eight o'clock. "Then after breakfast the foreman would go on, followed by the cook and the horse wrangler with the wagon, and locate the water and site for the noon camp. In the meantime the entire

---

[31] John B. Kendrick, "The Texas Trail," in the *Cheyenne* [Wyo.] *State Leader*, December 10, 1916.

force of men would bunch the cattle and head them toward the 'Trail.'"

Barren areas with short grass were not uncommon as were electrical storms and stampedes. Herds were in front as well as behind and care was required to avoid the areas where the grass had been cropped. When watering places were reached the steers were kept from crowding into the water and rendering it muddy. Indians visited the foreman to demand tribute for the passage of the herd over their lands. Others demanded "paper, paper," or a written statement which would recommend them to the liberality of other foremen. But a message given might merely warn the next foreman that the illiterate Indian bearing it was a thief and a scoundrel.

Kendrick was impressed by the luxuriant grass, the flowers, the songs of birds and by the huge, shadowy oak trees "hundreds of years old when the Declaration of Independence was signed." The herd was finally delivered to a ranch located on Running Water Creek, near the modern town of Lusk, Wyoming. His last trip on the trail was with a herd of steers numbering 3,470 at the start and only forty less when they were turned loose on the banks of the Cheyenne river.

Detailed figures as to numbers, costs, and profits of driving have been given by Mr. Ike T. Pryor of San Antonio, Texas, who drove fifteen herds from Texas to the northwestern states in 1884.[32] These cattle were moved in droves of 3,000 and one hundred and sixty-five men and about 1,000 saddle horses were required to handle these herds. For each herd there was a foreman and a crew of ten men who were furnished six horses

[32] Hunter, *The Trail Drivers of Texas*, 367, 368.

each. The foreman was paid $100 and the others $30
per month. To these wages he added $100 a month for
provisions which made a total expense of $500 in mov-
ing a herd of 3,000 cattle a distance of 450 or 500 miles.

"Briefly speaking," said Mr. Pryor, "in those days it
was possible to drive 3,000 cattle 3,000 miles for $3,000,
or in other words from south Texas to Montana a herd
could be driven of 3,000 head, for not to exceed $3,000.
. . . The average distance travelled by these herds was
from 450 to 500 miles per month and when I had sold
and delivered all of these cattle to Montana, Dakota,
and Wyoming ranchmen, I had lost 1,500 head or 3
per cent."

Already a sentimental haze has surrounded the adventures as recorded by the old time cowmen of the
Texas Trail Drivers' Association. And, the durable
prose of Andy Adams and Tacie Lockhart in *North of
'36* have relumed a form of pioneer cattle transportation
as earlier Bret Harte depicted the mining camps and
as more recently *The Giants in the Earth* has portrayed
the somber hues of Dakota pioneering.

The trans-Mississippi cattle trails of the sixties, seventies, and eighties led to grazing areas, shipping points,
and to the small and the great ranches. Prejudices
against Texas cattle but more especially the glacier-like
advance of the settler armies forced the trails farther
west, southwest, and northwest. Storms and uncertain
markets reduced the numbers on the trails. But the
northern ranges continued to receive the tribute from
northbound trails to about 1890. But even after that date
trail cattle were competing with the settlers' frontier
for the occupation of the Dakota plains.

The Shifting Cow Towns of Kansas

The Shifting Cow Towns of Kansas

When Abilene received the first herd of Texas cattle in 1867 the first of the great cattle marts in Kansas was established. The drovers, foremen, and cowboys whose 35,000 cattle entered Abilene in various herds that year found a frontier hamlet of log huts, saloons, stockyards, and the new shipping facilities which enabled about 1,000 cars of stock to be shipped eastward. Here too was the Drovers' Cottage, a three story hotel, where Texas drovers and northern buyers met to discuss prices and shipments as well as the progress of the northerly drives.[33]

The herd of six hundred steers from Lockhart, Texas, in charge of M. A. Withers reached Abilene after a journey of three months. A camp was established on Chapman Creek twelve miles north of the village. Four of the eight hands were then discharged and the others remained to herd the steers until fall. The cattle were in fine condition when sold at $28 per head.[34] W. K. McCoy and Bros. who purchased the herd later estimated that the Texas drives brought 75,000 cattle to Abilene in 1868. These were sold to Indian contractors, to ranchmen from the territories of Utah, Colorado, and

---

[33] McCoy, *Historic Sketches of the Cattle Trade of the West and Southwest*, 44, 50, 51.
[34] Hunter, *op. cit.*, 98, 99.

Montana, and to speculators from Iowa, Nebraska, Illinois, and other places.[35]

A great invasion of cattle estimated at 150,000 came to Abilene in 1869 and the hamlet became a scene of noisy activity. Day after day during the summer the few hundred inhabitants watched the dusty herds trailing over the prairies. At the station arose a never ending noise of hoofs and of empty and loaded cars. All day long the scales received and discharged the terrified longhorns. At the few stores there was a brisk trade in articles ranging from camp supplies to spurs and star-spangled boots. About this time four Texas cowboys and two California Spaniards roped ten buffalo which were to be shipped eastward to advertise Abilene as a shipping point. Four died of the heat, three others became sullen and died, and only three arrived in Chicago in good condition.[36]

Thousands of cattle continued to arrive at Abilene in 1870 and 1871. Sometimes from a hilltop thirty or forty or even fifty thousand head could be seen at one time. The latter year was stormy, the grass washy, and stampedes were very frequent. Freight rates were high between Chicago and the East so that Abilene became glutted with large numbers of poor stock. It was estimated that 300,000 unsold cattle were driven west to forage upon the buffalo grass. It was further estimated that a quarter of a million cattle died from cold and starvation. One firm had placed nearly 4,000 to range near the Republican river but in the spring only 110 living cattle could be found. Carcasses rotted on the plains, were devoured by the wolves or were skinned

35 McCoy, *op. cit.*, 124, 131.
36 Hunter, *op. cit.*, 99-103. McCoy, *op. cit.*, 131, 180, 181, 202.

for the hides. At one railway station nearly 50,000 hides were collected and shipped to the East.[37]

For miles and miles around Abilene almost every foot of soil was trodden by the Texas cattle. Water was a prime requisite and the valleys of Mud Creek, Chapman Creek, and Turkey Creek and their tributaries became prize camping and grazing places. Here drovers and buyers would inspect the herds and bargain over prices. The camps were scenes of well-earned rest and excusable confusion after the long drives. Here the old rickety mess wagon was relieved of its cargo – "a lot of saddles and horse blankets, a camp-kettle, coffee-pot, bread pan, battered tin cups, a greasy mess chest, dirty, soiled blankets, an ox yoke, a log chain, spurs and quirts, a coffee mill, a broken-helved ax, bridles, picket-ropes, and last but not least, a side or two of mast-fed bacon, to which add divers pieces of raw hide in various stages of dryness." [38]

During the Texas cattle trade at Abilene a carnival of crime and lawlessness prevailed. Desperadoes, thieves, gamblers, and courtesans flocked like vultures to the cattle market. The sheriff's office was indifferent but in September, 1869, the hamlet was incorporated and a local government was organized. In the next spring T. C. Henry, the chairman of the board of trustees, was clothed with wide powers and began the task of establishing law and order. Thirty-two saloons existed, firearms were carried everywhere, and vice and crime flourished. A jail was started but a crowd of cowboys tore down its walls. Then under a strong guard the place was soon rebuilt. A negro cook for a trail herd

[37] McCoy, *op. cit.*, 226-228.
[38] McCoy, *op. cit.*, 131, 132.

was the first occupant but the trail-drivers battered down the door, rescued their cook, and thereby their daily meals. One marshal after another resigned in despair and two policemen imported from St. Louis were so amazed and cowed by the lawlessness that they forsook the town on the next train home.[39]

Then Mr. Henry appointed in May, 1870, a quiet, reticent man, Thomas J. Smith, as marshal of Abilene. His tact and personal courage reduced crime and won the respect of merchants, saloon-keepers, cowboys, and gamblers. In November following while assisting a deputy in arresting a desperate character he was shot dead. He was buried with honors and with manifestations of the deepest grief among the citizens of Abilene. Thirty-four years later they erected a monument to his memory which declared him "a fearless hero of frontier days, who in cowboy chaos established the supremacy of law."

His successor was James B. Hickok, the "Wild Bill" of novels and romantic tales, and a man more proficient as a marksman than as a marshal. In 1871 the number of cattle driven to Abilene exceeded that of any previous year, and crime, disorder, and shame eclipsed the worst that had been known. The citizens of the town and the farming population then combined to resist the traffic in cattle at Abilene which in every season had trampled upon the grain and cornfields for miles around. In 1872 the "Farmers' Protective Association of Dickinson County" was formed. A circular was sent broad-

---

[39] *Prose and Poetry of the Live Stock Industry of the United States, with Outlines of the Origin and Ancient History of our Live Stock Animals*, vol. I, 509, 510. This was the only volume issued of the three projected and was prepared by authority of the National Live Stock Association. The author of the historical sections of the book is Jerome C. Smiley of Denver.

cast to Texas and to the southern range country in February requesting the drovers "to seek some other point for shipment, as the inhabitants of Dickinson will no longer submit to the evils of the trade." [40]

Meanwhile railway construction and the struggle for grazing areas were causing other cow towns to spring up. Baxter Springs and Coffeyville had a brief season of the rough cattle trade. The coming of the Atchison, Topeka and Santa Fé Railroad to Newton in 1871 created a cattle market and a shipping point for a year. Further railway construction in 1872 attracted cattle herds to Wichita and Great Bend where the harpies of former cow towns found new, though temporary havens. Other towns such as Ellsworth and Hayes City received Texas herds but never became the famous markets or the notorious towns of the earlier years. [41]

But for about ten years Dodge City was the greatest cattle market of the world. This town situated in the 100th meridian three hundred and sixty-three miles west of Kansas City was laid out in July, 1872, and the Atchison, Topeka and Santa Fé Railroad reached there in September following. Here in the next few years was the meeting place of freighters, hunters, and government teams. Enormous quantities of buffalo hides and meat were assembled here and shipped away. Hundreds of wagons blocked the streets until they departed with their cargoes to the far West and to the frontier towns and army posts. [42]

When the great cattle drives to Dodge City began in 1875 it became the great market for the southwestern

[40] *Idem*, vol. I, 509-513. T. C. Henry, "Thomas James Smith," in *Transactions of the Kansas State Historical Society, 1905-1906*, vol. IX, 526-532.
[41] *Prose and Poetry of the Live Stock Industry*, vol. I, 514, 515.
[42] Robert M. Wright, *Dodge City the Cowboy Capital*, 9, 10, 259.

frontier embracing western Kansas, eastern Colorado, and Indian Territory, the Territory of New Mexico, and Texas. In that year and the next about a quarter million cattle came to it and for the next decade it was dominated by the Texas trade. As a receiving and distributing point Dodge City became the preëminent cow town of the West.[43]

Prosperity in Dodge City came quickly. In 1877 millions of pounds of supplies were transferred from the rail trains to the hundreds of mule and ox trains which invaded it from every direction. Immense quantities of supplies went to the army posts at Fort Elliott and Fort Supply. Thousands of pounds of dried buffalo meat were bought and sold. To this village of about 1,200 there came about 250,000 Texas cattle in 1877, and its six or seven general stores, its bakeries, drug stores, butcher shops, blacksmith shops, and the nineteen gilded saloons each seventy-five to one hundred feet long vibrated with energy during the season of the drive from Texas.[44] "Dodge City," wrote a trail driver, "was then a wide-open town. Gambling and fandangoes were in full blast. While we were there two men were killed in a saloon row." [45]

Seventy-seven herds containing 168,500 cattle passed Fort Griffin during the eight weeks ending May 28, 1878. Three of these herds belonging to Woodward and Oge were destined for Dodge City but the third herd numbering 1,950 mixed cattle and driven by Virgil Johnson was finally delivered at Ogallala, Nebraska. Other notable drivers this year were James Ellison, John

---

43 *Idem*, 260.
44 *Idem*, 260-262. *Ford County Globe*, January 15, 1878.
45 Hunter, *The Trail Drivers of Texas*, 261-263.

Lytle, Dillard R. Fant, W. H. Day and Millet and Dewees.[46] Their herds would generally be grazed near Dodge City until sold and then dispersed to stock ranches and to ranges in Kansas and Nebraska. The Texas newspapers chronicled the movements of north-bound drives, giving the names of the owners and bosses, and the number and destination of the herds. In every season the editors paid tribute to Dodge City as a great western cattle market.

Although a slight decrease came in 1879 in the northerly movement of the Texas cattle Dodge City, northern Texas, and Ogallala again had their brisk cattle trade. James F. Ellison drove at least three herds northward.[47] Two herds combined and numbering 5,500 were driven to Ogallala under the direction of a foreman, Richard Withers, whose outfit contained nine cowboys, a cook, and a horse wrangler. This was perhaps the largest herd that passed through Dodge City that season. At Dodge City three additional men were employed to take the cattle on their eighteen-day journey to Ogallala. There Ellison met his herd which was delivered to a purchaser on the North Platte river.[48]

Sixty-six firms listed in the *Ford County Globe* of Dodge City of March, 1880, were expected to bring 294,000 cattle northward that season. These herds varied in size from 1,200 to 6,000 and were to be delivered to points in the Indian Territory, to the Territory of Wyoming, and to places in Colorado, Nebraska, and Kansas. Over 200,000 had arrived in Dodge City by June 25, when there were fifty-four cattle firms registered in that

[46] *Idem,* 261-263. *Commercial Indicator,* June 13, 1878.
[47] *Commercial Indicator,* July 10, 1879.
[48] Hunter, *The Trail Drivers of Texas,* 282-285.

place. The last 1,100 of Louis Oge's herd of 6,000 were sold to a man from Cass county, Missouri. A special stock train of twenty cars left Dodge City in September and after the remarkably fast run of twenty-four hours arrived at Kansas City.[49]

The rainy season of 1881, it is likely, lessened somewhat the numbers in the northerly drive of that year. Nearly thirteen inches of rain fell near Dodge City in May rendering the grass soft and washy. Five inches of rain in July likewise did not improve the grazing ranges about Dodge City. Heavier drives came in 1882 when the seasonal exodus from Texas numbered over 200,000. There fifty herds were started for Dodge City, while others went to the Territory of New Mexico, to Colorado, and to the well-known cow town of Ogallala.[50]

The *Texas Live Stock Journal* of Fort Worth, in January, 1883, estimated the drive from Texas at 220,000 for that season. Of these 140,000 were to be yearlings, 55,000 two-year-olds, and the balance three-year-olds and female cattle. It was estimated that nearly half of the drive would go to Dodge City and Ogallala to be sold for ranch purposes. On the Texas ranches the yearlings cost from $10.50 to $12.50, the two-year-olds $14.50 to $16.50 and the three-year-old steers from $18 to $19.[51]

The enormous number of 300,000 moved in 106 herds constituted the northerly procession of Texas cattle in 1884 to Dodge City. The first herd arrived on May 6,

---

49 *Ford County Globe,* March 12, April 27, June 29, July 13, August 17, September 21, 1880.

50 *Ford County Globe,* June 13, 1882. Nimmo, "The Range and Ranch Cattle Business of the United States," 213, as cited in note 25. Printed also as part III by the bureau of statistics in *Report on the Internal Commerce of the United States* (1886).

51 [Fort Worth] *Texas Live Stock Journal,* January 13, 1883.

and the last on August 15. One of the largest herds, as reported by Brand Inspectors Rhodes and Taylor, was that owned by Captain Richard King and numbering 3,965. From July 17 to December 1 of that year, 3,648 cars of beeves were shipped from Dodge City to Kansas City and Chicago.[52]

The trade in Texas cattle profoundly influenced the moral, social, and economic life of the frontier village of Dodge City as it had of Abilene a decade earlier. "There was a general pandering to the Lone Star sentiment, and lone stars abounded in all sizes and hues. Saloons, cheap-clothing shops, 'hotels,' dance-houses, and various other outfits bore the Lone Star trademark." [53]

To the firm of Wright Beverley and Company the Texans came for their jingling spurs, their carved ivory-handled Colts, or their suits of velveteen. A room thirty by fifty feet on the second floor of their store was devoted to clothing and saddlery. In the warehouse and yard from sixty to eighty thousand buffalo robes and hides could be found in 1878. A banking department was conducted and in another place jewelry and firearms were for sale. Cheyenne and Arapahoe Indians made purchases at this store and over a dozen men were employed to check off the goods to be transported in wagons.[54] The Dodge City and Panhandle Stage owned by P. G. Reynolds and the United States mail line ran between these two places in 1878.[55] And from Dodge

[52] *Western Central Kansas Cowboy,* June 28, July 19, September 6, December 13, 1884.

[53] *Prose and Poetry of the Live Stock Industry,* I, 515.

[54] Quoted from *Ford County Globe* in Wright, *Dodge City the Cowboy Capital,* 157, 158.

[55] *Ford County Globe,* November 26, 1878.

City a regular line of freighters ran to Camp Supply in Indian Territory and Fort Elliott in Texas.

Of the 2,160 people living in that county in 1878 about 648 lived in Dodge City and the others in the country. "Until recently," wrote an observer about this time, "the community has been made up in part by the class of people who properly belong to the frontier; but the prospects of agricultural advancement and the natural tendency of immigration to fill up the border counties have brought many intelligent and worthy residents into the community." [56]

"Some came to Dodge City out of curiosity;" wrote a resident, "others strictly for business; the stockman came because it was a great cattle market, and here, in the Arkansas river, was the place appointed for the cattle going north to be classed and passed on, for bargains to be closed, and new contracts made for next year; the cowboy came because it was his duty as well as his delight, and here he drew his wages and spent them; the hunter came because it was the very heart of the greatest game country on earth; the freighter came because it was one of the greatest overland freight depots in the United States, and he hauled material and supplies for nearly four hundred miles, supplying three military posts, and all the frontier for that far south and west; last but not least, the gambler and the bad man came because of the wealth and excitement, for obscene birds will always gather around a carcass." [57]

Religious organizations were neither numerous nor prominent in the frontier town of Dodge City in 1878.

[56] *First Biennial Report of the State Board of Agriculture Kansas for the years 1877-1878*, 213-216.

[57] Wright, *Dodge City the Cowboy Capital*, 154, 155.

A Baptist group contained twenty-eight members; two residents were Episcopalians; forty-five belonged to the Methodist church; a Presbyterian group numbered fifteen; but the two Catholic organizations had a membership of five hundred. "Dodge City," wrote a minister the next year, "is not noted for its virtue. Being the center of the Texas cattle trade it has all the accompaniments." But, he pointed out, the union of some of the churches was spreading the leaven among the masses.[58]

During the driving season the social and the business barometers registered high. The Cox Hotel and the Dodge House became the homes of drovers, buyers, and railroad men where the rooms reëchoed with the discussions over beeves, cows, and steers. Such talk became even more animated in those places where men forgot their worries and hardships. "The 'Alamo,'" said an observer of 1877, "is presided over by a reformed Quaker from New York, and it is hinted that the manner in which he concocts a toddy . . . increases the value of a Texas steer two dollars and seventy-five cents." [59]

Names of men notable in the Texas trade appear in the roster of visitors at Dodge City during the spring drives. James F. Ellison, who, for eleven years had driven cattle up the trail, was a Confederate veteran and in June, 1880, was waiting for his herd of 3,000.[60] In the same month appeared his Confederate comrade and his former partner, John O. Dewees. John R.

[58] *First Biennial Report of the State Board of Agriculture Kansas for the years 1877-1878,* 213-216. The Reverend Adam Holm in the *Western Christian Advocate* as reprinted in the *Ford County Globe,* June 24, 1879.

[59] Quoted in Wright, *Dodge City the Cowboy Capital,* 264, 265.

[60] Hunter, *The Trail Drivers of Texas,* 476-478. *Ford County Globe,* June 22, 1880.

Blocker while waiting for his herd of 4,500 bound for Cheyenne perhaps reminded his fellow cattlemen of his first drive in 1873.[61] Captain John T. Lytle, a veteran Confederate cavalryman, also registered in Dodge City in June, 1880, and had a record of having directed the northerly movement of thousands of Texas cattle. Four years before he had opened a trail from Fort Griffin to Dodge City, a distance of four or five hundred miles.[62] Major Seth Mabry, another drover, would spend a day in the saddle and then in the evening come to town. Then the major dressed up like a dandy, "waltzed, pirouetted, took part in every dance and was the beau of the ball." Financially he was not a success, like so many other cattlemen whose names are scattered from the Canadian line to the Gulf of Mexico.[63]

R. G. Head in June, 1880, was waiting in Dodge City for the two herds of Head and Bishop destined for Nebraska and the Territory of Wyoming. He was pointed out as an example of rising success in the cattle trade. Beginning on a salary of $30 per month he rose to the full management of the trail business of Colonel John J. Myers. For seven years he had driven cattle to Abilene, Wichita, Great Bend, Ellsworth, and Dodge City in Kansas. Other herds were delivered at Cheyenne, Salt Lake City, to points in the Territory of Nevada, to California, and to various Indian agencies in the Black Hills and on the upper Missouri river.[64]

A noteworthy shipment of cattle from Dodge City

---

[61] Hunter, *The Trail Drivers of Texas*, 319-321. *Ford County Globe,* June 22, 1880.

[62] Hunter, *op. cit.,* 319, 321. *Prose and Poetry of the Live Stock Industry,* I, 661.

[63] John Clay, "My Life on the Range," in *Live Stock Markets,* vol. XXXII, no. 32, November 16, 1922.

[64] Hunter, *op. cit.,* 212-214.

was that of three hundred and eighty-nine cars of beef
cattle by W. E. Anderson and O. H. Nelson of Bur-
lingame, Kansas, in 1881. These 7,789 cattle bought
for $291,000 were shipped over the Atchison, Topeka
and Santa Fé Railroad and sold at Kansas City. In
March of the next year another active buyer in the
Dodge City markets was A. H. or "Gus" Johnson, who
in the following year was the manager of four cattle
companies.[65]

Veteran drovers and buyers appeared among the sixty
or seventy cattlemen registered in Dodge City in 1882.
Henry Collar's ranch was located in Comanche county
where he was known as "Hi" Collar. Three Choate
brothers from Texas were still driving herds from the
south. None could fail to be impressed by the portly
frame of A. H. or "Shanghai" Pierce, a native of Rhode
Island, who in dramatic and powerful voice recounted
stories of the Texas trail or his experiences in Texas
where he had lived until grand juries had become too
vexatious. L. M. Kokernut, another trail driver, was
the son of a Jewish family of Amsterdam. After serving
in the Mexican War he engaged in the cattle business
and for many years had been delivering herds at Dodge
City. Such men constituted the solid element in the
vanishing cattlemen's frontier in the early eighties.[66]

The cattle trade created for Dodge City a reputation
for wickedness not uncommon on the frontier and not
surpassed by that of other cow towns. While there was
much of life that was orderly, respectable, and even
prosaic there were reasons why visitors left lurid ac-

---

[65] *Ford County Globe*, March 28, 1882.

[66] *Ford County Globe*, June 6, 1882. McCoy, *Historic Sketches of the Cattle
Trade of the West and Southwest*, 141-143. *Texas Live Stock Journal*, October 14, 1882.

counts of "The Beautiful, Bibulous Babylon of the Frontier" and of the "Wickedest Town in America." A citizen of the town wrote: "There were women, dance halls, music, saloons and restaurants, equipped with every luxury, while gambling in every conceivable form, and every gambling device known at that time was in full blast." [67] Like other frontier towns Dodge City had its "Boot Hill" where lay buried men and women of violence and sin.

Other visitors saw the beginnings of a better state of things in Dodge City. The town was defended by its newspapers whose news items and descriptions of the trade carefully crowded out many a sensational, violent event. "But, in extenuation of the conduct of her early inhabitants," wrote the historian of this cow town, "I plead the newness of the territory, the conditions of life, the dangers and associations of a western frontier, and the daring and reckless spirit that such conditions engender." [68]

In November, 1877, Bob Shaw and Texas Dick, alias Moore, engaged in a desperate battle of six-shooters with Marshal Edward J. Masterson in the Lone Star dance hall. All were wounded, but the marshal, transferring his weapon from his wounded, paralyzed right arm to his left held the cowboys at bay until help came. "Nobody was killed," said the local paper, "but, for a time, it looked as though the undertaker and the coroner would have something to do." [69]

In the following April six cowboys were dancing and drinking in a saloon – likely the one called the "Old

---

[67] Wright, *Dodge City the Cowboy Capital*, 155.

[68] *Idem*, 6.

[69] *Idem*, 305, 306, as quoted from the *Dodge City* [Kas.] *Times*, November 10, 1877.

House." Masterson attempted to disarm Jack Wagner and a scuffle ensued. A quick volley of shots was fired and the cowboys then rushed from the dance hall. Wagner had been shot through the lungs and twice through the arm but was able to run into Peacock's saloon. When dying he confessed that he had shot the marshal. Four cowboys were arrested but after a full and fair investigation before Judge R. G. Cook were discharged, being blamed only for having been in bad company.

Masterson, mortally wounded, was carried to his brother William's room. There the wounded man told his story and bade his brother an affectionate farewell. During the funeral ceremonies the stores of Dodge City were closed, a mournful procession marched to his grave and the city council and other civic organizations passed resolutions extolling his character and services.[70]

But such scenes, although only too numerous, can hardly be said to represent more than the roughest days of the frontier cattle town. Visitors, residents, and cowboys were privileged to witness pleasanter scenes. President Hayes came to Dodge City in 1879 and with him General W. T. Sherman whose speech drew rousing cheers from an audience of which Southern partisans made up over one-half. A cowboy band was organized in 1881 which soon gained a national reputation as much from the uniforms worn as the melodies rendered. The next year it furnished the music at a cattlemen's ball at which, it was estimated, the stockmen represented wealth equal to $50,000,000.[71]

A unique entertainment at Dodge City on July 4, 1884, was witnessed by trail outfits of John R. Blocker,

[70] *Idem*, 307. *Ford County Globe*, April 16, 1878.
[71] *Idem*, 292, 293, 322, 323.

Dillard R. Fant, and the Snyder Brothers whose herds had arrived during the first few days of that month. On that day the town was crowded with cattlemen and cowboys who, temporarily at least, forsook the gambling houses, dance halls, and saloons to witness a real Mexican bullfight in a specially prepared arena of forty acres.

Cowboy Killer, Lone Star, Rustler, Iron Gall, Ku Klux, and seven other untamed bulls were to meet five famous bullfighters from Mexico. When the matadors and picadors entered the arena, the first bull was shot full of darts, showing considerable fight but was finally driven out. The second was a coward, and the third, fourth, and fifth in turn were not much better.

Then a vicious bull was brought in to meet Captain Gregorio Gallardo who was descended from a famous Spanish bullfighter and carried a Toledo blade one hundred and fifty years old. The Mexican's escape from the long horns became narrower and narrower. Finally the band played for the swording. Gallardo then took his blade and after several attacks and counter attacks stabbed the bull in the right shoulder. The bull died slowly as noisy cheers and the crash of music sounded over the plains. "Take it all in all," said the local editor, "Dodge City considers its worth of keeping the Fourth a great success." [72]

But symptoms of the waning greatness and glory of Dodge City as a cow town were already apparent in 1884. The Kansas granger was pushing westward and seizing the live water. Early the next year a quarantine law against Texas cattle was passed. The extension of railroad lines was affording other places for loading and

---

[72] *Idem*, 243. A full account is reprinted from the *New York Herald* in the *Kansas Cowboy*, July 12, 1884.

for the eastward shipments of stock. In 1885 Ford county, of which Dodge City was the county seat, was checkered with fields of barley, wheat, corn, millet, oats, and numerous orchards – many of which were enclosed by wire fences. Its 47 school districts, 17 church organizations, 17 post offices, and the 6 civil divisions containing a population of 7,778, are the prosaic proof of the passing of a rough and perhaps romantic cattlemen's frontier at Dodge City. Two years later each section of land contained nearly seven people.[73]

The youth of Texas who had come to Dodge City in their saddles were, like birds of the plains, unaccustomed to the restraints of the invading grangers. The Texan, "a child of the frontier handy with his gun, did not understand the changing days west of the 100th Meridian and he died hard." [74] Today wheatfields, stacks of hay, and grain elevators occupy old bedding grounds of Texas herds and mark the settlers' conquest of the plains. Where noisy horsemen galloped in Abilene and Dodge City and where longhorns trailed over dusty roads are now paved streets and homes. Only a few residents remain who can recall Joseph G. McCoy, Wild Bill, the Drovers' Cottage, the Dodge House, and the oceans of grassy, Kansas plains.

[73] *Fifth Biennial Report of the State Board of Agriculture Kansas, 1885-1886,* vol. x, 224-229. *Sixth Biennial Report of the State Board of Agriculture Kansas, 1887-1888,* vol. XI, 156-161.

[74] Clay, "My Life on the Range," in *Live Stock Markets,* vol. XXXII, no. 32, November 16, 1922.

Cattle Pools and Associations

Cattle Pools and Associations

The rapid rise of the cattle industry of the plains in the seventies exhibited a freedom and an individuality that became somewhat diminished in the next decade. Increasing numbers of cattle, the invasion of the farmers, larger investments, new business methods, and an inevitable tendency toward coöperation induced the ranchmen of the eighties and even during the seventies to combine into local and territorial pools and associations. Such organizations, born in customs, supplemented or even anticipated territorial laws and regulations. At the same time they register the changing methods and problems of the cattlemen's frontier.

Common misfortunes drew together the stockmen of the Territory of Colorado in 1867. These men sustained regular losses when the migratory herds of intruders passed over their ranges and when petty thieving of hides taken from dead cattle became common. A meeting of stockmen appointed a committee to draw up a constitution and by-laws. On November 3 of that year these were adopted by the "Stock Growers' Association" assembled at the Planters' Hotel in Denver. This became the leading association of the territory and the parent of similar pools and associations.

Legislation for the stockmen was discussed at once. In 1868 a committee was directed to wait upon the Denver commissionmen and butchers to acquaint them with the work of the association. The president, A. G.

Reed, was authorized to employ detectives for the "use and bennifitt of the Association." In 1871 all live stock came under the protection of this body. The secretary, William Holly, was required to keep a full record of the brands and the ranges used, and all members were required to report strays to this officer.[75]

The change in name to the "Colorado Cattle Growers' Association" in 1876 is a symptom of the growing rivalry between cattlemen and the other live stock interests. President J. M. Wilson stated that sheepmen and cattlemen had nothing in common save "grazing on the same grass." The idea that the range was unlimited and could not be overstocked he denied as "simply nonsense." Joseph P. Farmer, the president the next year, urged that round-up captains be paid from county funds and brand inspectors from state funds. Chandler Smith and William Brown were appointed as inspectors on the Kansas Pacific Railroad with instructions to scrutinize only such brands as should be reported to them by the officers of the association.[76]

Eighty-eight names appear on the membership roll for this year. "We represent," ran an optimistic estimate of President Farmer, "nearly 600,000 head of cattle, with a capital of nearly $10,000,000 giving employment to 2,000 men." A detective at Las Animas was discharged and one appointed for Denver. A strong resolution was adopted urging a state live stock commission and the association voted to refuse inspection privileges to those delinquent in their dues.[77]

[75] *Minute Book* (Colorado Cattle Growers' Association), 45-50, 80, 81. This unprinted document covers the years 1867-1883 and was found in the office of the *Daily Record Stockman* at Denver, Colorado.

[76] *Idem*, 62-67. Supplement to *Colorado Farmer and Live Stock Journal*, September 13, 1877.

[77] *Colorado Farmer and Live Stock Journal*, January 17, 1878.

Year after year the minutes record the names of round-up captains appointed and the hopeful addresses of the presidents. The pinch of hard winters, diminishing pastures, low prices, and sharper competition are reflected in the "Minute Book" of this pioneer cattle organization of the eighties. Long speeches describe pleuropneumonia, and "wholesale stealing and mavericking" are condemned. In 1881 charges appeared that there was a custom among "a goodly number of stockmen" to violate the maverick laws by inducing cowboys to steal mavericks, to brand them, to alter brands, and to rebrand cattle which had been dimly branded. It was urged that more elaborate and stricter rules should govern the round-ups; captains should be required to round up mavericks first and brand them on the first day; all cowboys should be required to work in their districts only, and, there should be a "follow-up round-up" for the various districts.[78]

Winter losses came to the members but the association raised its protest against stories and rumors of hard winters and lean years on the Colorado pastures. Rewards were voted for the capture of cattle thieves and an active committee was named to raise more money — "which," reported the minutes, "they did and if you don't believe it ask Jim Wilson." [79] In 1884 the association had twelve brand inspectors and five hundred and eighty-six strays were reported. Its seventy-one "paid members" and the absence of further minutes indicated, however, a decline in the work and vigor of this association.[80]

Near Pueblo during the seventies was located the

---

[78] *Minute Book* (Colorado Cattle Growers' Association), 105-111.
[79] *Idem*, 116-120.
[80] *Idem*, 141.

Green Horn Association which carried out the seasonal round-ups. At the meeting of the Southern Colorado Cattle Growers' Association in 1878 a representative of a Kansas City commercial house was present to discuss rates and service. It corresponded with the Colorado Cattle Growers' Association and requested that it offer a reward of $150 for the detection of cattle thieves. Other groups of cattlemen recognized the services of the larger body. In 1879 the cattlemen of North Platte in Nebraska representing 140,000 cattle valued at $4,500,000 elected W. P. P. St. Clair president, drew up a code of laws for cattlemen, and appointed a committee to urge them upon the legislature.[81]

In southwestern Kansas the Smoky Hill Cattle Pool was established in Lane county in the fall of 1882. About seventeen firms belonged to it in its prosperous days. Each member had his own cattle and herd but the stock ran together on the range. The pool hired the necessary range riders, made assessments, and assumed charge of the principal watering places in the Smoky Hill river, on Indian Creek, and at other places. Officers were elected, a constitution was adopted, and the brands of the pool were advertised in the *Dodge City Cowboy*. In 1883 fifteen hundred calves were branded and the cost of keeping cattle for a month was but twelve and one-half cents per head. Its fifteen hundred cattle in 1884 ranged over lands claimed by the pool and extending twelve miles north and south of the Smoky Hill river for a distance of thirty miles. In that year one hundred and forty Shorthorn bulls were purchased. A drift fence of oak posts and galvanized wire forty miles long was constructed by the pool.[82]

---

[81] *Commercial Indicator*, July 11, August 15, 1878, January 23, 1879.
[82] W. P. Harrington, *History of Gove county, Kansas, to the Organization of the county in 1886*.

The Forrester Pool of Gove county, Kansas, was formed in the fall of 1884. Its six members or partners owned 4,000 cattle and in that year set up twenty miles of fence. Two thousand calves were branded in that year and seventy-four carloads of cattle from its ranges were shipped to eastern markets.[83]

Both pools suffered several losses in the winter of 1884-1885. A pool cowboy was frozen to death on Salt Creek in January. But the next winter was one of severe and continued intense cold and blizzards. Great numbers of the carcasses of cattle froze on the plains and hundreds of weakened survivors died in the spring. "Anyone who has not lost 25% of his cattle or sheep may well congratulate himself," wrote a local editor. "We do not blame anyone not a Christian for getting 'excited' at least." A resolution of one of the pools declared that "the range cattle business is played out." Snow and rain had done great havoc. Fences were sold to ranchmen and a final round-up was ordered to wind up the affairs of the pool.[84]

But other troubles came in July when the members of the two pools were arrested for illegal fencing in of the public lands. At the federal court in Leavenworth, however, the defendants showed that other cattlemen had not been kept out of their ranges. At the request of the prosecuting attorney the case was then dismissed.

Urgent need for cattle pools and associations appeared at other places in the Southwest. The Texas drives with their attendant problems gave rise to many such organizations which served until the cattle areas were pushed farther west. In February, 1882, the stockmen of southwestern Kansas and of the Cherokee nation in Indian

---

[83] *Idem.*

[84] *Idem. Grainfield* [Kas.] *Cap Sheaf,* April 2, August 6, 1886.

Territory formed an organization of 100 and adopted a constitution and by-laws. Membership fees of $5.00 were to be used to capture and to prosecute cattle thieves. It was voted to publish a pamphlet containing marks and brands. The members further urged that in driving a distinction be made between wintered cattle and the through cattle from Texas carrying the Texas fever. Inspectors were to be appointed at Cheyenne, Kansas City, St. Louis, and at Indian agencies. The Cherokee strip was to be divided into three round-up areas and riding was to commence on March 18th. Another resolution declared that the "six-shooter is not an absolute necessity" for cowboys in the Cherokee strip except against outlaws and Indians. "But," continued the resolution, "we deprecate carrying of six-shooters in all cases while visiting the towns along the border." [85]

Under the direction of Wilmot Proviso Brush of the Kansas City *Commercial Indicator* the association published a book containing the brands of 125 members and 55 brands of the Comanche County Pool, the Barbour County Stock Growers' Association, and other cattlemen's groups. One of the brands was that of William W. and Valentine B. Dickey, two brothers, whose herds ranged in the valley of the Canadian river.[86] In 1882 their 20,000 cattle marked them as one of the leading members of the Southwestern Cattle Growers' Association. But the two men soon suffered reverses in forsaking the active management of their ranges to taste "the golden fruit of city life" in Kansas City or to mingle among the "crimson poppies" of Chicago. To this neg-

[85] *The Caldwell* [Kas.] *Post*, February 23, March 9, 1882. *Brand Book containing the Brands of the Cherokee Strip* (1882).

[86] Clay, *My Life on the Range*, 88-92. This volume contains the articles published by John Clay in *Live Stock Markets* referred to in previous footnotes.

lect came the allied misfortunes of drouth and storms
to deplete the herds of Indian Territory.

In the Southwestern Cattle Growers' Association established in March, 1882, a resolution provided for six
captains of designated round-up districts where work
was to begin on May 8th. It authorized the employment
of inspectors at Kansas City and another in the Indian
Territory. Another resolution urged the removal of the
cows and calves and an inspection for strays before cutting out or driving away the steers. The cattlemen also
condemned the turning loose or "boarding" of cattle
when the increase of the stock would infringe on the
rights of neighboring ranchmen. In the same month the
Turkey Creek Pool near Caldwell, Kansas, appointed
a committee to prepare for the pool round-up, and
another committee was to cause fire guards to be plowed
around the pool range and "to oversee the burning of
them out." [87]

About forty-five stockmen formed the Western Central Kansas Stock Association in the spring of 1883
when a constitution of twenty-one articles was adopted.
A reward of $500 was offered for the arrest of any person
killing or stealing the stock of members. Another reward
of $200 was voted for the arrest of any culprit who ma-
liciously set fire to the range. Stray stock was to be herded
until the owner could be notified, but no aid was to be
given any persons who might turn their stock on the
ranges of others. Another rule required that descriptions of ranges be filed with the secretary of the association.[88]

An executive committee was empowered to settle dis-

---

[87] *Caldwell* [Kas.] *Post*, March 9, 1882. *Brand Book containing the Brands
of the Cherokee Strip.*

[88] *Western Central Kansas Cowboy*, September 1, 1883, July 12, 19, 1884.

putes as to brands, ranges, and damages. The association also voted to own, manage, and publish a paper.
The *Western Central Kansas Cowboy* under the management of S. S. Prouty at Sidney became the active
organ of the association. After Dodge City became the
capital of the cow country the newspaper was removed
to that point in 1884. The faith and zeal if not the best
judgment of the association was voiced in the editor's
declaration that: "Today in the United States grass is
king." It also published eighty-one brands of the Western Kansas Stock Growers' Association at Dodge City
whose membership included cattlemen from Kansas,
Texas, Indian Territory, Missouri, and Colorado.[89]

Prior to the coming of the Northern Pacific Railroad
into the Territory of Montana, the cattlemen of the
Northwest sent their stock to southern shipping points.
Those who were members of the Wyoming Stock Growers' Association secured inspection through that body
at various stations on the Union Pacific Railroad. An
early union of cattlemen in the Territory of Montana
was the Shonkin Stock Association formed near Fort
Benton in July, 1881. Leading cattle growers from the
Belt, Highwood, Arrow Creek, and Shonkin ranges
met at a range, elected Jack Harris president, chose an
executive committee, and adopted regulations and by-
laws. The association resolved to protect the cattle
ranges against Indians and to share the expenses of building corrals. Anyone refusing to become a member was
to be denied the privileges of the corrals and the
round-ups.[90]

The Eastern Montana Live Stock Association had

[89] *Idem,* July 12, 1884.
[90] *The Benton Weekly Record,* August 4, September 1, 1881.

its beginnings at Miles City in October, 1883.[91] T. J. Bryan became the first president and J. W. Strevell the secretary and treasurer. The latter was instructed to get a copy of the rules and regulations of the Wyoming Stock Growers' Association which, after being explained by a representative from that body, were adopted. A list of the ninety-five cattlemen owning cattle in "this vicinity" was read by the secretary. Such firms as the Marquis de Mores from Dakota Territory, Granville Stuart, the McKenzie Cattle Company formed a few weeks before and ranging in the Territory of Dakota, and the Montana Cattle Company of the Musselshell Valley constituted the solid element of the range cattle industry and could furnish the backbone of an association. Other cattlemen represented the Territory of Wyoming and Iowa.

In the directors' room of the First National Bank of Helena, the Montana Stock Growers' Association was conceived in April, 1884. Conrad Kohrs, the most famous cattleman of the Northwest, was the principal originator and became a powerful member. At the organization meeting of April, 1885, T. J. Bryan was elected president and the new body was then combined with the Miles City organization. Sixty-three of the ninety members were present at this meeting and the executive committee of twenty-five represented not only the thirteen counties of the territory but also the Territory of Dakota. A long list of applicants for membership included the name of Theodore Roosevelt.

At the Macqueen House crowded beds afforded hospitality if not comfort. Meetings of the association were held in a skating rink but after the sessions the cowmen

---

[91] *The Yellowstone Journal,* October 13, 20, 1883.

convened more informally at the Miles City Club where "we all met, ate roast pig, hard boiled eggs, cheese and bread and drank more than was good for us." In other places a genial host in white apron and with a diamond stick-pin dispensed to the broad-hatted thirsty horsemen a hospitality not enjoyed on the ranges or around the mess-wagon. From Fort Keogh, a nearby army post, came a band to blare forth a musical welcome to the guests of the little frontier cow town on the Yellowstone.

Although patterned after the Wyoming association the Montana group never equaled it in power and initiative. In the Territory of Montana the Board of Live Stock Commissioners, created in 1884, recorded and issued brands and settled disputes among cattlemen over such brands and marks. The board likewise appointed brand inspectors at the principal markets and shipping points and had the right to name stock detectives for each county. It appointed a stock inspector for each county who had the power to quarantine or exterminate diseased stock. It devised and recommended legislation and exercised a general supervision over the cattle interests of the territory.

At the meeting of the Montana association in 1886 the members subscribed over $1,000 to assist a committee on legislation at Washington to promote the work of the Bureau of Animal Industry. Seventeen round-up captains were appointed. At the next meeting an unsuccessful attempt was made to condemn the Interstate Commerce Commission. And here as in other associations the absorbing topics for debate were the Texas fever and the overstocking of the ranges. In 1887 Joseph Scott became president and held office for several years.[92]

---

[92] Clay, *My Life on the Range*, 346-355. Hermann Hagedorn, *Roosevelt in the Bad Lands*, 392-395, 444-446.

Some of the strongest personalities of the Northwest were members of this association. Theodore Roosevelt had recorded his cattle brands representing a triangle and an elkhorn as early as July, 1884. By the next year he had invested over $82,000 in his Dakota ranches. In the meeting of 1886 he was appointed one of the round-up captains and placed on the executive committee. A few weeks later he was directing sixty cowboys in the spring round-up on the Little Missouri ranges and working from fourteen to sixteen hours daily. At the next meeting he defended the Interstate Commerce Commission in the debates at Miles City. A few days later after viewing the winter destruction of his cattle he wrote: "for the first time I have been utterly unable to enjoy a visit to my ranch." [93]

John T. Murphy was the manager of the Montana Cattle Company. Benjamin F. Potts had served the territory as governor. Conrad Kohrs had migrated from Germany and had witnessed the gold rushes to the territory. His extensive ranches and his great success in the cattle business made him the preëminent cattle king of the Northwest.

The killing storms of 1886-1887 not only marked a sinister factor in the cattle range business but they also marked a decline of the old pools and associations. Stricter business methods and more individual initiative were required to meet the changing conditions and the new demands in raising and fattening cattle on the plains. The pools and associations, however, had per-

[93] *Brands and Marks,* Book A, 427, in the office of the Live Stock Commission, Helena, Montana. Hagedorn, *Roosevelt in the Bad Lands,* 482. Roosevelt to Henry Cabot Lodge, June 7, 1886, April 20, 1887, in *Selections from the Correspondence of Theodore Roosevelt and Henry Cabot Lodge, 1884-1918,* Henry Cabot Lodge, editor, 41, 42, 54.

formed distinct functions on the ranges and a service to the cattlemen of the West.

Describing the origin of the Colorado Cattle Growers' Association, the oldest on the ranges, a prominent stock paper in 1879 said: "It has given Colorado cattle growers, individually and collectively, a well deserved prominence; it has attracted marked attention to Colorado-raised cattle in eastern markets; it has secured in a great measure the repression of crime as against cattle on the range, and given the association standing in business and political circles." [94]

Eight years later, H. M. Taylor, an agent of the Bureau of Animal Industry, wrote of this association: "Its usefulness has grown with every year of its existence. The record it has made stands as an unanswerable argument in favor of associated effort. The cost of maintaining it has been merely nominal to its members, and it has profited the industry hundreds of thousands of dollars. Its members would go out of the business if they could not have the benefits obtained through its agency." [95]

[94] *Commercial Indicator,* January 23, 1879.

[95] *Third Annual Report Bureau of Animal Industry for 1886* (dated February 22, 1887), 105-124 at pp. 115, 116.

A Cattlemen's Commonwealth on the
Western Range

A Cattlemen's Commonwealth on the Western Range

From successive frontiers of our American history have developed needed customs, laws, and organizations. The era of fur-trading produced its hunters, its barter, and the great fur companies; on the mining frontier came the staked claims and the vigilance committees; the camp meeting and the circuit rider were heard on the religious outposts; on the margins of settlement the claim clubs protected the rights of the squatter farmers; on the ranchmen's frontier the millions of cattle, the vast ranges, the ranches, and the cattle companies produced pools and local, district, territorial, and national cattle associations. The greatest of these in membership and influence was the Wyoming Stock Growers' Association which has completed over a half-century of existence and which for about fifteen years was a cattlemen's commonwealth on the pastoral lands of the West.

Confederate veterans in Texas in 1866 began to drive their surplus cattle northward to be dispersed over the northern ranges. In that year the Kansas Pacific Railroad entered Junction City in Kansas and the Union Pacific Railroad was completed to Cheyenne in 1867.[96] From then on the vast grazing areas received their tribute of millions of Texas cattle, which, after being ma-

---

[96] Crawford, *Kansas in the Sixties*, 230. McCoy, *Historic Sketches of the Cattle Trade of the West and Southwest*, 44, 50, 115.

tured and fattened on the range grasses, were freighted in ever increasing streams to the eastern markets. A surplus of cattle in Texas, free grass, and an outlet for matured cattle ushered in the dominant decades of the range and ranch cattle business.

About 350,000 cattle from Texas were herded northward in 1869.[97] In 1871 over half a million Texas cattle, it was estimated, were moved northward and bought by the cattlemen of the western states and territories.[98] The ends of these drives at Abilene, Ellsworth, Hayes City, and Dodge City in Kansas, and Ogallala in Nebraska were the great cow towns from which the cattle were dispersed to the ranches and the ranges.

Thus the cattlemen's domain was established. Territorial laws, courts, and local governments were inadequate to minister to a business which had grown so swiftly, which was spread over an area of nearly a million square miles, and for which there was no guide or pattern in the world's history. The Territory of Wyoming, centrally located in the range country, was the heart of the cattlemen's domain and Cheyenne became not only the capital of the territory but likewise the administrative and social metropolis of the immensely larger cattlemen's range.

The five formative years of the Wyoming Stock Growers' Association began on November 29, 1873, when a group of stockmen of Laramie county met in the county clerk's office in Cheyenne and organized the "Stock Association of Laramie." At the next meeting on February 23, 1874, twenty-five persons and firms

---

97 Nimmo, "The Range and Ranch Cattle Traffic . . . of the United States," in *Report on the Internal Commerce of the United States,* part iii, 122.
98 *Idem,* 122.

signed the membership roll. Laws and regulations were adopted, the annual meeting was fixed in April of each year, and it was resolved to hold regular meetings on the first Monday of each month. Admission fees were fixed at $5 and the regular dues at $.50 a month.[99]

Thirty-one names were added to the membership roll in the next four years; money receipts lagged behind dues and assessments; and the great distances to be travelled caused many absences at the annual meetings. A set of laws to govern the annual round-ups was adopted, two hundred copies were ordered to be printed, and an equal number of handbills were to be sent out to inform the stockmen of Laramie county of the commencement of the annual round-up. The round-up for 1874 was set for May 15 but later postponed to June 1. An assessment based on the amount of stock held was levied to raise money for the "payment of detectives." The next year N. J. O'Brien, the sheriff of Laramie county, was elected a member of the association.[100]

A special committee of three in 1876 secured $150 per month for two months from the county commissioners for "detective work," and the association voted that none but "said committee shall know [the] detectives." Alexander H. Swan succeeded M. V. Boughton as president and Thomas Sturgis began his long career as secretary of the association.[101]

W. C. Lykins was appointed a detective in 1877 and

[99] *Laramie Stock Association Minute Book,* 3, 4. These records begun by the secretary of the association, W. L. Kuykendall, are preserved in the office of the Wyoming Stock Growers' Association at Cheyenne. The name "Laramie County Stock Association" is also used in these official minutes. Volume II of these records is unpaged and has the title of *Minute Book Wyoming Stock Growers' Association.*

[100] *Idem,* 5-22.

[101] *Idem,* 14, 16, 19.

also became one of the four round-up foremen the next
year. An offer of a reward of $200 was voted for the
capture of persons killing or stealing the stock of members. The next year the work of the detective bureau was
endorsed because it was surely reducing crime in the
territory.[102] A famous criminal, Middleton, once declared that "if the Wyoming Stock Growers' Association would let up on him, he did not care for all the
sheriffs in Nebraska." [103] With the aid of Lykins the
association finally landed him behind the bars. In 1884,
Judge Charles W. Wright was retained as an attorney
for the association and ex-Sheriff N. K. Boswell as its
detective made several arrests in Texas and Arkansas.[104]
Two years later the expenses of the detective bureau
had grown to over $15,000 a year.[105] Another sheriff,
F. M. Canton of Johnson county, in 1884 was voted the
thanks of the association for his work in capturing crimi-
nals on the range.[106]

In 1879 the association drew up a petition for reduced
freight rates on the Union Pacific Railroad, copies of
which were sent to similar stock organizations of Colorado and Nebraska. Later a "transportation committee"

[102] *Idem,* 20, 22, 30.

[103] Quoted in a letter of William Sturgis, a former secretary of the association, to Harry E. Crain of Cheyenne, under date of April 11, 1915. In 1914
the association appointed a committee to gather "all memories and available
data, that they may be able to properly commemorate the pioneer history of
Wyoming." Twelve letters from old Wyoming ranchmen were received,
copies of which are preserved in the office of the secretary of the association
at Cheyenne. In 1923 these letters, containing valuable data and reminiscences,
were published under the title of *Letters from Old Members and Friends of
the Wyoming Stock Growers' Association.* The Sturgis letter is on pages 42
and 43 of this fifty-five page pamphlet.

[104] From the annual report of Secretary Thomas Sturgis dated April, 1884,
and recorded in the *Minute Book Wyoming Stock Growers' Association.*

[105] *Idem,* in Annual Report of April, 1886.

[106] *Idem.*

was created, which by securing lower rates in 1885 effected a saving of about $72,000 to the members of the association.[107]

An expanding and varied array of business is recorded in the brief minutes of these cattlemen's congresses. On March 28, 1879, an executive committee of three residents of Cheyenne to be elected for one year was created. Joseph M. Carey, Thomas Sturgis, and E. Nagle were the first members of this committee which, for the next decade exercised almost imperial control over the cattlemen's domain.[108]

The change of name of the "Stock Association of Laramie" to the "Wyoming Stock Growers' Association" on March 29, 1879, indicated the expanding importance of the cattle industry on the plains.[109] A committee of fourteen was appointed in 1880 to consider the increasing dangers from range fires. A resolution of 1882 deploring the carrying of firearms "except in the immediate presence of Indians" leaves to be imagined the number of personal tragedies in the cow towns and on the range.

The not infrequent mention of the non-payment of dues revealed human nature in not a few members, some of whom the "association" in 1879 threatened to bar from participation in the annual round-ups. The next year the annual dues were fixed at $10 and soon after an admission fee of $15 was voted. Fifty-three new members were elected that year and seventy new names added in 1883 swelled the membership roll to one hundred and eighty-seven.[110] A glow of pride shines in Secretary

[107] *Idem. Laramie Stock Association Minute Book, 25. Minute Book Wyoming Stock Growers' Association.*
[108] *Laramie Stock Association Minute Book, 31.*
[109] *Idem, 32.*
[110] *Idem, passim.*

Thomas Sturgis's report of 1885. Recalling that in 1873 the association had ten members representing 20,000 cattle worth $350,000, he said: "Today we have 400 members." Their 2,000,000 cattle, their houses, plants, and real estate he valued at $100,000,000.[111]

Consolidation with other cattle associations was attempted in 1881. A committee of three proposed Cheyenne as a central meeting place and a government vested in an executive committee. Invitations were sent to the Weld County Stock Association of Colorado, to the associations of Lincoln, Keith, Cheyenne, and Sioux counties in Nebraska, and to the associations at Rapid City and Deadwood in the Territory of Dakota. In May of that year the associations of Cheyenne and Sioux counties in Nebraska and Albany county in the Territory of Wyoming were admitted to the association and were each apportioned two members on the enlarged executive committee of eleven. In 1883 the associations of Unita, Carbon, and Johnson counties in the Territory of Wyoming were admitted to membership.[112] In 1885 the members from the Territory of Montana withdrew from membership to enter an association in their own territory and about the same time the Nebraska members resigned to enter the Nebraska Stock Growers' Association.[113]

As the number of brands increased and as the volume of eastbound shipments of range cattle grew, an elabo-

---

111 *Minute Book Wyoming Stock Growers' Association.*

112 *Idem. Laramie Stock Association Minute Book, 57, 64, 66, 88.*

113 *Minute Book Wyoming Stock Growers' Association.* Thomas Sturgis, "Report of the Wyoming Stock Growers' Association, 1886," in *List of Members, By-Laws, and Reports of the Wyoming Stock Growers' Association, and the Laws of Wyoming, for the Protection of Stock Growers, as Amended by the Ninth Assembly.*

rate system of brand inspectors was devised by the association. Such inspectors or detectives detected illegal
brands as well as marks and brands that had been "re-
touched" or altered. These men supervised the sales
of thousands of strays and mavericks at railway termi-
nals and at stockyards. Indeed, from the time that the
animals left the range until they were slaughtered they
were under the alert espionage of the range detectives
and brand inspectors.[114] The proceeds from the sales of
strays were finally turned over to the owner of the brand
but the treasury of the association became enriched
from the sale of the mavericks.

During the year beginning April, 1884, the inspectors
of the association supervised the sale, the transportation
by rail, and the passage by trails of about 1,000,000
cattle. In 1883 at Council Bluffs, Iowa, over 110,000
cattle were inspected and over a thousand strays were
discovered. Other inspectors were maintained at Valentine in Nebraska, at the Rosebud Indian Agency, at
Pine Ridge, at Custer, Camp Clark, Deadwood, St.
Paul, Ft. Fetterman, and at other points. Later inspections were made at Boone and Missouri Valley in
Iowa, at Miles City in the Territory of Montana, at
Mandan in the Territory of Dakota, and at various
Indian agencies.[115]

These inspectors possessed a remarkable knowledge
of the thousands of brands of the western ranges. Their
keen eyes would swiftly sweep over a trainload of steers
and detect the brands of animals which had intruded
from another range or cattle which had never felt the

[114] Philip Ashton Rollins, *The Cowboy: His Characteristics, his Equipment,
and his Part in the Development of the West*, chap. xii.
[115] *Minute Book Wyoming Stock Growers' Association.*

branding iron. In the year ending April, 1886, the work of inspection at about thirty-five different points and areas was done at an expense of over $26,000, but the 2,276 mavericks sold that year netted the association the sum of $25,605.[116] As new railway lines became built inspections became more urgent because of the illegal butchering of cattle for the construction and grading camps.

Vital questions relating to the public domain and to the increasing use of the grazing lands early burdened the meetings of the association. The Public Lands Commission in 1879 submitted a series of twenty-eight questions on agriculture to the ranchmen and other citizens of the West. A special meeting of the Wyoming Stock Growers' Association was called for November of that year and the meeting was attended by the representatives from the Territory of Wyoming and from Colorado and Nebraska. Both houses of the Wyoming territorial legislature were present at the session. After an elaborate debate a resolution was drawn up for transmittal to the commission.[117] This resolution strongly urged the continuation of the existing system which permitted the securing of title to only small tracts of lands. If congress, however, were to enact any legislation it was urged that provision should be made for a maximum purchase price of $.05 per acre, for a long term of payment of the principal, and for the sale of land only to actual occupants of the soil.

Five reasons, urged the association, strongly sup-

---

116 *Idem.* "Report of the Wyoming Stock Growers' Association, 1886," 61-67, in *supra* note 113.

117 U.S. House *Executive Documents*, 46th congress, second session, no. 46, 544-548. This is the report of the public lands commission on the resolutions and the testimony of the association.

ported the plea for the existing system of the disposal of the public lands: cash entry and gradation would be conducive to monopoly and work hardship to the owners of small herds; there was a greater gain from the widely spread stock industry of numerous prosperous owners than from any sums to be realized from land sales; the uncertainty of the supply of grass for feeding rendered it unwise to invest more than one-sixth in property which in a few years might be a barren waste; the confining of cattle in any "positive and impossible limits" would prevent them from seeking adequate food and shelter during the blizzards and storms of the ranges; and finally, the association believed that self-interest would prove a safeguard against overstocking the range and that any system of sale would excite quarrels and a bitter feeling of injustice among the stockmen.

Secretary Thomas Sturgis, ever alert to the interests of the association, submitted an additional memorandum against any change in the existing land system: "That the territory is young, its settlement covering but ten years; that the cattle business is in its infancy, a large majority of the herds having more or less indebtedness upon them; that to clear this off and to acquire a surplus for investment in land must be a work of time; that to open the lands they graze over to general entry at the end of a year would injure them greatly; that under the present system our population is rapidly increasing, because owners of small herds find grazing facilities; and that under a changed system, permitting entry of large tracts, this increase would cease, and population might even diminish."

At other meetings Secretary Sturgis continued to defend the rights of ranchmen and the executive committee of the association continued its work of sending memorials which, however, did not raise the question of fencing large areas by the cattlemen. It urged, however, the preservation of their rights free from civil or penal liability and their privilege of building corrals and cabins in the business which annually brought $5,000,000 into the territory. Recalling that the Easterners called the stockmen "bullock barons and aristocrats of the plains," Secretary Sturgis retorted that the government would neither sell nor lease lands, eighty per cent of which could never produce grain.[118]

The pressure of settlement is reflected in another protest of the association in 1886.[119] Emphatic denial is made against the accusing opinion of the East that cattlemen were obstructing and preventing by violence and intimidation the settlement by farmers of the grazing lands. The association further declared it would welcome any "fair and equitable adjustment" looking toward the sale or lease of these lands.

But for years bitter protests from settlers and small ranchmen had been made against the large cattle companies. "The large cattleman," wrote a farmer from Horse Shoe in the Territory of Wyoming in 1883, "owns no lands and makes no improvements, is opposed to the settling up of the country, is in fact a bitter enemy to the homesteader. . . Every foot of the territory is now claimed by the large cattle companies." [120] Another let-

118 Report of Secretary Sturgis of April, 1884, in *Minute Book Wyoming Stock Growers' Association.*

119 "Report of Wyoming Stock Growers' Association, 1886," 34, 35, in *supra* note 113.

120 Letter from Robert Walker to Secretary of the Interior Henry M. Teller, dated Horse Shoe, Territory of Wyoming, March 9, 1883, and preserved in the records of the commissioner of the general land office at Washington, D.C.

ter accuses a cattleman of having fenced in 100,000 acres of choice hay land, of refusing to move his fence, and (he thinks) of having bribed the "land agent." [121] In 1887 another letter charged that the Frontier Land and Cattle Company had inclosed land on the north fork of Powder river and that impediments and fraud were preventing persons from settling on their range.[122]

A most important and a regular order of business of the association was the planning and the execution of the spring and the fall round-ups of the thousands of cattle on the ranges. As early as February, 1874, a committee of five was directed to draft laws for the government of round-ups. Two years later the telegraph line between Cheyenne and Ft. Laramie was designated as the boundary between "the upper" and "the lower" round-up. In 1878 foremen were appointed for the round-ups designated "the Southwestern," "Pole Creek," "Northwestern," and "Lower Horse Creek." [123] Thirty-one round-ups were laid out in 1884 and two horse round-ups were organized two years later.[124]

A statute of the Territory of Wyoming in 1884 made it the duty of the association to provide for a "general spring round-up" and a "general fall round-up." At the spring meeting the entire territory was to be divided into districts. It was to appoint a foreman for each district, to fix the time and place for the beginning of the round-up, and to determine in what manner and in what

[121] Letter from S. F. Sanders to Secretary Henry M. Teller, dated Laramie, Territory of Wyoming, April 9, 1883, and preserved in the records of the commissioner of the general land office at Washington, D.C.

[122] Letter from Alexander C. Cable to Commissioner of the General Land Office William A. J. Sparks, dated Riverside, Territory of Wyoming, February 4, 1887.

[123] *Laramie Stock Association Minute Book*, 5, 18, 22.

[124] *Minute Book Wyoming Stock Growers' Association.*

order the various districts were to be worked. These foremen were elected for a year and each was clothed with full power in his district. All persons working in the district were required to obey all orders of the foreman under penalties of fine and imprisonment. A similar penalty was provided for any person who should engage in any illegal round-up. The law, furthermore, specifically recognized the "by-laws and rules" of the association.[125]

A diligent committee laid out these areas for gathering cattle and reported the arrangements to the general meeting on large sheets of paper. The various districts completely covered the territory, hundreds of handbills and newspaper notices informed ranchmen, so that every owner could perfect his plans and mobilize his forces.[126] Then for weeks hundreds of cowboys would ride in valleys, over canyons, gulches, and ravines, across meadows and over the plains where any stock had been feeding during the summer or browsing on the cured grasses during the winter. When the galloping herds were finally assembled and placed under control the foreman could determine the various brands, count the strays and mavericks, and estimate the losses from stealing, from wolves, and from the Wyoming winters. To determine the extent of the calf crop was another task of the foreman and a matter of prime importance to the owners of the herds.

In the meeting of April, 1882, the association provided for twenty-two round-ups from which were gathered

[125] "An act to further encourage and protect the interests of stock growers," approved March 6, 1884, and printed in *Session Laws of Wyoming Territory*, 147-152.

[126] Clay, "My Life on the Range," in *Live Stock Markets*, November 23, 1922.

AMONG THE COWBOYS BREAKING CAMP

From a contemporary sketch drawn by W. A. Rogers in 1880.

cattle that had been ranging over at least 100,000 square miles.[127] In the previous year five or six weeks were required in doing the work designated in round-up number one and the mere linear distances between the camping places designated in it totalled over four hundred miles.[128]

No subject generated more wordy warfare and heated discussions at the meeting than that of the maverick – the unbranded or motherless animal running at large. He was the pariah of the plains, an outcast of unknown origin, a homeless intruder among cattle respectably branded, and a foundling trespassing upon the range. On one round-up a foreman gathered one hundred and fifty mavericks – some of them four-year-old steers and cows with calves at foot – and without a brand or ear slit on them.[129] "This was the hour," wrote a member of the association,[130] "when an adventurous man could start a herd of cattle if he was able to register a brand as his mark and property. Many of them did and not

[127] Report of Governor William Hale of the Territory of Wyoming, dated November 10, 1883, and printed in U.S. House *Executive Documents,* 48th congress, first session, no. 1, part v, 559-625.

[128] *Tenth Census of the United States* (statistics on agriculture), III, 62. The following was the plan for one round-up: "Round-up no. 1 shall begin at Fort Laramie on May 23, shall proceed up the south side of the Laramie river to the mouth of Sabile Creek, up the Sabile to the Black Hills divide; thence to the head of the Chugwater; down the Chugwater to Kelly's ranches; thence to the head of Richard's Creek; down said creek to its mouth; thence to Houston's Creek; thence to the Bear Creeks, up said Bear Creeks to their head; thence to the telegraph road, where it intersects Horse Creek; thence up said Horse Creek to Horse Creek lakes; thence to the head of Pole Creek, and down Pole Creek to the telegraph road; thence across the country to Big Crow Springs; thence up Big Crow Creek to its head; thence across to the bend of Lone Tree Creek; thence down Lone Tree to Charles Terry's ranch; thence to Jack Springs; thence to Box Elder."

[129] Clay, "My Life on the Range," in *Live Stock Markets,* November 23, 1923.
[130] *Idem.*

a few respectable citizens of today made a beginning, adding on to it by other devious methods not necessary to explain."

Numerous sections in the two territorial statutes of 1884 and 1886 [131] are attempts to settle the perplexities of the maverick question. The foreman of every round-up was required to brand all mavericks on the side of the neck with an M – the official brand of the Wyoming Stock Growers' Association. A full written report as to the sex, color, and grade was to be made at the close of every round-up. All mavericks were to be sold on the day of their discovery to the highest bidder in lots or as individuals. In the presence of the foreman the purchaser was then required to place his brand on the animals. Within thirty days after the sale the foreman was required to transmit the proceeds of such sales, less ten per cent as his commission, to the Wyoming Stock Growers' Association.

Six months were allowed to any person to establish proof of ownership over any mavericks thus sold. Upon satisfactory proof the claimant would be reimbursed but the animal would remain the property of the purchaser. The proceeds of the sales of all mavericks were to go to the treasury of the association unless ownership should be proved within the six months. No person could lawfully brand a maverick except under the supervision of a foreman.

Only fragmentary data reveal the workings of these statutes, and violations of them were left unrecorded. The branding irons of the association were prepared in

[131] Acts of March 6, 1884, and the amendatory act of February 27, 1886. See *Session Laws of Wyoming Territory passed by the Ninth Legislative Assembly*, 62, 63; and *Revised Statutes of Wyoming in Force January 1, 1887*, 868-871.

1884 and all foremen were directed to return them after the fall round-up to the custody of the association. In that year the 1,900 strays were valued at $76,000.[132] Two years later, however, 2,276 mavericks were sold at an average price of $12.50 which, after deductions for commissions, netted the association over $25,000.[133] The next year 3,446 mavericks were sold at prices varying from $10 to $1. During that year when the association had suffered great reverses and was in need of funds, A. T. Babbitt, a prominent member, proposed that all members enter into a binding contract to bid at least $10 for each maverick sold at the auctions.[134]

Fears over the Texas fever or splenic fever or pleuropneumonia are found lurking in the minutes of the association as early as 1881. This disease was carried northward by Texas cattle and levied a destructive toll upon the herds of the Western ranges. A communication from Colorado cattlemen on the subject of diseased cattle from Texas was endorsed and forwarded to the territorial delegate in congress. The association urged its members to report promptly any shipments destined to the Territory of Wyoming and to Nebraska in order to afford an opportunity for sending a competent veterinarian to examine cattle suspected of such a disease.[135] A stringent law prohibiting the importation into the Territory of Wyoming of diseased stock was enacted by the legislature in 1882,[136] and in the next year Secre-

---

[132] Report of Secretary Sturgis in 1884 in *Minute Book Wyoming Stock Growers' Association.*

[133] *Idem,* for Secretary Sturgis's report in 1886.

[134] *Idem.*

[135] *Laramie Stock Association Minute Book,* 58, 59.

[136] "An Act to Suppress and Prevent the Dissemination of Contagious and Infectious Diseases among Domestic Animals," approved March 8, 1882, amended March 12, 1886, and printed in *Report of the Wyoming Stock Growers' Association, 1886,* 110-118.

tary Thomas Sturgis reported that "bovine scourges" did not exist in the territory.[137]

A proclamation issued on April 7, 1885, by Governor Francis E. Warren of the Territory of Wyoming prohibited the importation of cattle from known infected regions and imposed certain restrictions upon all cattle brought into the territory.[138] Over 54,000 cattle from seventeen states and territories entered Cheyenne in the year following. A heavy burden was imposed on the territorial veterinarian and his assistants in the work of enforcing the quarantine laws. The quarantine also became a matter of ceaseless and anxious care to the executive committee of the association. The importers of blooded cattle and of the Texas cattle entering by rail exerted a tremendous weight against the quarantine barriers. Not a week passed without a meeting of the committee which mitigated the annoyance to importers while rigidly safeguarding the interests of the stockmen of the Territory of Wyoming.[139]

The territorial legislature of 1885 had adjourned without making adequate provision for the isolation and quarantine of cattle imported from regions where contagious diseases existed. In this emergency the territorial veterinarian appealed to the executive committee of the association which then generously supplied the means for the construction of the territorial quarantine yards. These were located near the railroad a mile east of Cheyenne. Twenty-nine acres inclosed by a wire

---

[137] Letter from Thomas Sturgis to E. S. Morgan, secretary and acting-governor of the Territory of Wyoming, dated June 11, 1883, and printed in U.S. House *Executive Documents*, 48th congress, first session, no. 1, part v, 586.

[138] *Second Annual Report of the Bureau of Animal Industry* (1885), 550-552.

[139] Annual Reports of Secretary Sturgis and the territorial veterinarian, Jas. D. Hopkins, dated April, 1886, and printed in "Report of the Wyoming Stock Growers' Association, 1886," in *supra* note 113.

fence and containing nine corrals furnished accommo-
dations for 3,000 cattle. Sheds on the north provided
shelter and each corral was supplied with abundant
water from Cheyenne. A comfortable home for the
watchman was built nearby and the quarantine yards
were connected with the Union Pacific Railroad by a
switch from which cattle could be unloaded directly
into the corrals.[140]

Nineteen states are represented in the membership
of four hundred in the Wyoming Stock Growers' Association of 1886.[141] Of these, two hundred and sixty-
seven were residents of the Territory of Wyoming, and
to relume their careers is to furnish a picture of the
territory as seen by *The Virginian* of Owen Wister.
Charter members like Joseph M. Carey, John F. Coad,
and A. H. Reel had known the territory when it was
a province as wild as Virginia had been in the seven-
teenth century and later when settled law and population had rendered it eligible to statehood.

John H. and T. F. Durbin were the managers of
the Durbin Land and Cattle Company and as early as
1873 their brand J-D had been recorded in Laramie
county.[142] For ten years or more their horses and cattle
had ranged the valley of the Sweetwater river from
which they were finally driven by the sub-arctic winters.
Lower down the valley was Tom Sun, a swarthy French-
Canadian, who was a type of the pioneer, scout, trapper,
and cattleman. Another member, Frank Wolcott, was
a Union veteran, a former United States marshal, and

---

[140] *Idem,* in report of Jas. D. Hopkins.

[141] The membership list for the association for 1886 is printed in the
"Report of the Wyoming Stock Growers' Association, 1886," 5-20. See *supra*
note 113.

[142] *Record of Brands,* Book A, 95.

later a successful cattle owner and hunter of bull elk on Deer Creek. John Sparks, whose cattle ranged in Nevada and Nebraska, had been trained in Texas in all branches of the business. He rose on the flood tide of the cattle industry and later attained the governorship of Nevada.[143]

To A. T. Babbitt, F. E. Warren, and Philip Dater was given the task of preparing the first brand book of the association. As published in 1882 the little volume contained the names and brands of one hundred and sixty stockmen.[144] Mr. Babbitt was the manager of the Standard Cattle Company whose numerous cattle fed on various ranges. F. E. Warren for many years represented his state in the senate of the United States. Philip Dater had emigrated from New York. "Old Phil" as the cattlemen loved to call him was a man of imposing appearance but contributed more to the social life of Cheyenne than to the work on the range. "Boys," he once said in a speech at the Cheyenne Club, "hold onto your books and you will have no difficulty in selling your many wintered cows – though dead – at satisfactory figures." [145]

A passion for big game and for adventure had brought a colony of Englishmen to Laramie City, where J. H. D. Willan, a stout jolly Britisher, and a member of the Douglas, Willan, Sartoris Cattle Company, represented the association at Cheyenne. Robert Marsh and Frank Cooper, another English firm, ranged their cattle on

143 Clay, "My Life on the Range," in *Live Stock Markets,* September 14, 1922.
144 *Cattle Brands owned by Members of the Wyoming Stock Growers' Association.*
145 Quoted in a speech by Joseph M. Carey in the *Proceedings of the Adjourned Meeting of the Wyoming Stock Growers' Association,* 62, held at Douglas, Wyoming, April 15-16, 1915.

Rock Creek where they carried on a struggle until the terrible winter of 1886-1887.[146] Moreton Frewen whose address was 18 Chapel Lane, London, was interested in the Powder River Cattle Company. In 1884 he proposed a new route for cattle shipments to England. Such cattle were to be transported by rail from Cheyenne to Duluth. Then shipments were to be made by steamer over Lake Superior and Georgian Bay and then by rail to Quebec. Steamers were then to carry the stock to Liverpool. The plan was intended to avoid pooling interests in Chicago and to save six hundred miles of land and nine hundred of ocean travel. Horace Plunkitt, the Irish reformer, was representing the Frontier Land and Cattle Company but lived too far in the northern part of the territory to attend the meetings of the association at Cheyenne.[147]

Another and more notable member of the association was Hubert E. Teschemacher, the son of a California argonaut and a Harvard graduate, who typified the movement of those unique characters from Europe and the Eastern states to the Western ranges. Coming to the territory in about 1879 he helped to advertise its latent wealth and imbued the spirit of its ranges. Before him was the life of the cowboy, the morning cup of coffee, the long rides to circle around the cattle, the noisy round-ups, the branding in the afternoon, and then sleep under clear Wyoming skies. After the spring work he returned to his bachelor's quarters in Cheyenne were an old servant served coffee and rolls in the morning. By merit he rose to a place on the executive committee of the association. Like hundreds of others he was almost finan-

---

[146] Clay, "My Life on the Range," in *Live Stock Markets,* July 26, 1923.
[147] *Minute Book Wyoming Stock Growers' Association.*

cially ruined by the killing storms of 1886-1887 which, however, left unimpaired his personal and social charm.[148]

His brother Arthur, Richard Trimble, later the secretary of the United States Steel Corporation, and F. O. de Billier were other members of high standing. Retreating from the social comforts of Cheyenne they repaired to the head of Cottonwood Creek where they met the stinging cold and blizzards of that region. But their log hut, their youthful optimism, a great supply of wood, and a glowing fireplace enabled them to endure one of the coldest winters on record.[149]

The president of the Wyoming Stock Growers' Association in 1876 was Alexander H. Swan, a native of Pennsylvania and a former merchant of Indianola, Iowa, from which he had migrated to Cheyenne in 1876.[150] His career aptly illustrates the meteoric rise of the cattle business on the range as well as its tragic decline. Under his spell and magnetic personality a considerable faction of cattlemen were soon worshipping at his feet. In 1883 he went to Scotland and there floated the Swan Land and Cattle Company of which he became the manager in America and its misguiding spirit. Of the 120,000 cattle acquired in 1883 and of the 11,000 sold that year not a hoof was counted but all transactions were by book count.[151]

An old *Record of Brands* which lists the nine herds of horses and cattle acquired by his company in the next two years reveals how debts were recklessly pyramided

---

148 Clay, "My Life on the Range," in *Live Stock Markets*, October 19, 1922.

149 *Idem*, October 12, 1923.

150 *Warren* [Indianola, Iowa] *Record*, September 10, 1874.

151 Clay, "My Life on the Range," in *Live Stock Markets*, September 28, 1922, and September 6, 1923.

by the manager.[152] The purchase of lands, houses, stables, and corrals, expenditures for miles of ditches, the manager's salary, losses of cattle on the range, and Mr. Swan's practice of accepting book counts rather than making actual enumerations, caused ever larger demands upon the Scottish shareholders as well as shrunken dividends.

When Mr. Swan resigned as manager in 1887 his successor Finlay Dun from Scotland at once repaired to the Territory of Wyoming. He at once proceeded to make a count of the cattle – not by the usual custom of branding – but by painting them. But the summer rains and heat soon compelled Mr. Dun to admit that the paint was not "sufficiently adhesive and permanent" which gave circulation to an amused laugh and a couplet on the range:

> "Daddy Dun's a dandy
> But his paint won't stick." [153]

A stinging rebuke to Mr. Swan's management bristles in the annual report of the company in December, 1887. Funds of the company to the extent of $19,000 were appropriated by the manager, and, after making and endorsing as manager a note of nearly $11,000, he discounted the paper and placed the funds to his own credit. "The company will sustain a certain amount of loss by these defalcations," ran the report, "but it has suffered still more seriously from the late manager's neglect and extravagance." [154]

One of the thirty men from Nebraska holding membership in the association was John F. Coad whose stock

---

[152] *Record of Brands,* Book A, *passim.*

[153] Clay, "My Life on the Range," in *Live Stock Markets,* September 13, 1923.

[154] *Annual Report of the Swan Land & Cattle Co. Ltd.,* for the year ending December 7, 1887.

browsed on the North Platte river. Another was Charles
F. Coffee, an old Texas trail-driver, who had borne the
name of "Chalkeye" because he showed so much white
in his eyes. Locating in Hat Creek Valley he remained
there until 1885. "Then," he has recorded, "the Northwestern Railroad came poking in and brought the fes-
tive granger. Then trouble did begin. It was not like
the Indians for one couldn't shoot and the only way I
could do to get even was to go into the banking business . . ."[155]

But the sober and official minutes of the Wyoming
Stock Growers' Association are not animated by the
fellowship and the social delights of its annual meetings.
Besides the owners of great herds and the small ranchmen with a few hundred cattle, there were present a
goodly number of cowpunchers fresh from the range.
Managers and general freight agents brought with them
their live stock agents, and the cheery smiles of Colonel
Hooker of the Rock Island and the genial comradeship
of Jake Hardin of the Burlington were long remembered. Chicago commission men and managers of feed
stations were there while still others were seeking to
find jobs or to indulge their curiosity. Foremen were
busy arranging round-ups for their various districts.[156]

But at the Cheyenne Club all comers were welcome
and the warm cheer from cold bottles helped to close
many a contract. Here men dined generously, sang songs,
debated politics, planned horse races and tennis matches,
described their travels in foreign lands, discussed the

[155] Letter by C. F. Coffee to Harry E. Crain dated Cheyenne, Wyoming,
March 31, 1915, and printed in *Letters from Old Friends and Members of the
Wyoming Stock Growers' Association*, 25-29. See *supra* note 103.
[156] *Idem*, 5-7, for letter by John B. Thomas, March 12, 1915.

cattle business, and recounted the twice-told tales of losses, profits, and hardships on the ranges. In the evening came speeches, and, if not the flow of reason at least the flow of soul – and other things. "Cow punching, as seen from the veranda of the Cheyenne Club," reflected an Englishman, "was a most attractive proposition." [157]

Luke Murrin's saloon likewise extended a warm welcome during these meetings. It was this man who coined an epigram on the custom of the range in buying and selling cattle by book count rather than by an actual tally or enumeration. When the cattlemen leaned against his bar for their noon dram and as the snowstorms and blizzards swept over the ranges or howled through the frontier town of Cheyenne their faces grew long and downcast over the prospect of losses on the range and unpaid notes in the fall. Then Murrin wiping the bar or pouring another glass would console the cattlemen: "Cheer up boys, whatever happens the books won't freeze."

Containing the ablest men of the territory and having its headquarters at the territorial capital, the association became a power in law-making. In 1875 the secretary of the association and three other members were also members of the legislature of the territory and two years later the president, Alexander H. Swan, sat in that body. In 1881, Secretary Sturgis and two other members were legislators and the next year six members also sat in the council and house of representatives. In 1883, Dater, Warren, W. C. Irvine, Babbitt, Coad, and Teschemacher were members of both the association and the

---

[157] *Idem.* Clay, "My Life on the Range," in *Live Stock Markets,* November 23, 1923.

legislature. The next year a group of seven members of the association made up one-sixth of the house membership and one-third that of the council.

Secretary Sturgis in 1886 named eight bills which had been drafted by the executive committee of the association [158] and which had become statutes of the territory. These ranged from amendments to the maverick law and to the veterinary and contagious disease law to the legislation which required railway companies to plough and to maintain fire-guards. The secretary also drew an analogy between the structure of the state governments and that of the association. Efficient governing and law-making were necessary at the centres. And, as the administration of the state was vested in hundreds of local units so the members of the executive committee were to administer the laws of the association in the various districts where they might reside.

In each of the fourteen executive districts in 1886, explained the secretary,[159] was at least one member. The duties of the members were to attend at least one committee meeting at Cheyenne annually, to consult in person or by letter with the cattlemen of their districts as to the inspector to be nominated, to supervise and direct the work of inspectors in the districts, to report to the headquarters at Cheyenne any crimes which might require additional inspectors or a detective, to give notice of incompetency in any inspector, and finally, to represent the association before the county officials. In brief, the faithful committeeman was a delegate or represen-

[158] "Report of the Wyoming Stock Growers' Association, 1886," 47-52. See *supra* note 113.

[159] *Idem.*, 56-59.

tative of a vast cattlemen's province the wants and complaints of which he made known to their annual congress at Cheyenne.

Referring to the "disinterested and unselfish" character of the association, Secretary Sturgis declared it was the agent of the many and not of the few. "To this end," he reported, "all are given free access to reports and records, all information asked by letter is carefully collected from the lists and forwarded, and small bodies of stockmen in distant localities are informed that if they will send a single representative to our annual meeting to express their views about round-ups and round-up foremen, they will be regarded with respect and attention." In the same report the association was likened to a vast commercial business: members as well as other stockmen were absolutely relegating to its care many of the most important problems of the cattle ranges.

The wintry purgatory on the ranges in 1886 to 1887 closes the history of the formative period of the Wyoming Stock Growers' Association and marks the end of an era in the cattle business of the range. The parching summer of 1886 had been followed by blizzards, low temperature, and a snowfall of unprecedented depth. Thousands upon thousands of cattle froze, starved, or were smothered as they stumbled into the deep snows of the coulees and ravines. A mournful array of figures only partly told the story of the winter tragedy. The spring thaws disclosed thousands of carcasses, and skeletons and staring skulls were harvested by agents of fertilizer factories. A great many bones of the herds of Theodore Roosevelt were left on the plains near the Little Missouri river. Here and there the bark of trees had been peeled off by the cattle in their desperate search for food.[160]

A herd of about 5,000 steers of the Worsham Cattle Company was almost completely lost and the Swan Land and Cattle Company gathered about 100 three-year-old steers from a herd of 5,500 placed on the range. Mismanagement, recklessness, and greed and a bitter winter were the evil factors which had conspired against the range cattle from southern Colorado to the Canadian line and from the 100th meridian to the Pacific slope.[161]

A tragic gloom pervaded the fifteenth annual meeting of the Wyoming Stock Growers' Association in April, 1887.[162] The president, the vice-president, and the secretary were absent; Swan, Sturgis, and other leaders were ruined; Eastern men and Britishers deserted their ranges and the territory; the old-time cattlemen had begun to disintegrate. "The old love of the open range, the burning fires of old-days smouldered," wrote a prominent member thirty years later, "sometimes flashing into flames but the old regime passed away. The wide-open days were closed. The hard drinking, rollicking youngster who turned himself loose when he struck town gradually evaporated or changed his methods, and in their place there grew up a careful, economical, rigid owner, who possessing nerve and experience, made a success . . ."

The cattlemen's commonwealth had ruled the western range, and on the whole had ruled beneficially, when the West was still wild. The old Cheyenne Club where

---

160 Hagedorn, *Roosevelt in the Bad Lands*, chap. xxv. Clay, "My Life on the Range," in *Live Stock Markets*, August 16, October 18, 1923.

161 Clay, *loc. cit.*, August 16, 1923.

162 *Idem*, October 18, 1923.

echoed the romance and the prose of this cattlemen's domain still stands in the shade of old cottonwoods. But its rooms have been commercialized and to a degree vulgarized. A copy of an old picture of Paul Potter's bull shows the hole bored through the foreleg by John Coble's six-shooter. Pictures of racing cups and horses still adorn the walls and the chance visitor can gaze upon the steel engraving of Albert Bierstadt's "In the Heart of the Big Horns." As at Abilene, its memories of frontier days are fading into traditions and incomplete historical legends. Who are there to recall the great cattle companies, Alexander H. Swan, the social delights of Cheyenne, the anxious seasons of the Texas fever, and the days of unfenced ranges?

The Boom in Cattle Companies
in the Eighties

The Boom in Cattle Companies in the Eighties

The solid foundations of the range industry as laid by men like Iliff, Carey, Kohrs, Stuart, and Murphy before 1880 were to be strained and broken during the cattle boom of the eighties. In these years of frenzy for cattle companies the wild financing, mismanagement, and overstocking of the ranges produced a collapse of ruin and almost total destruction of the cattle business of the range. But, tempered by these disasters, there emerged saner methods and management for the cattle business of the plains.

Varied causes generated this boom and gave it momentum. The heavy prosperity of the eighties illustrated Walter Bagehot's phrase that, "At particular times a great many stupid people have a great deal of stupid money." Blind capital was large and craving. It sought for someone to devour it. It found hungry investors and there was speculation. When the capital had been devoured there came the ills of panic and depression.[163] Money was plentiful and its reckless use kept pace with the extravagance of ideas.

Feverish railroad building invaded and crossed old buffalo ranges. Traffic receipts fell and in quick order reflected low prices in bonds and stocks, terrified investors, and railway receiverships. The "boom" town of

---

[163] Walter Bagehot, "Edward Gibbon," in *The Works and Life of Walter Bagehot,* edited by Mrs. Russell Barrington, vol. II, 127, 128.

the West blossomed as the "queen of the prairies." Cities and towns were platted along the railway lines and land promoters hawked the sale of lots.

For about four years after 1880 the boom rose and reëchoed over the West. Bureaus of immigration sent out a literature of alluring tracts – not always signed or copyrighted by the authors. Railroads bore thousands of settlers to the West and long lines of covered wagons of "movers" jolted from old homes in the East to "settle" in the West. About two hundred years were required for effective settlement to spread from Jamestown to the Missouri river but a few decades were sufficient for the occupation of the rest of the area to the Rockies.

Great advances in the prices of ordinary stock cattle for range purposes up to 1882 were due to several causes. The favorable winter season of 1881-1882 had left range stock in good condition. Old Texas cattlemen increased the numbers and the movement of their trail herds. The contagion of mounting prices spread from Texas to the West. "Texas cattlemen," observed a live stock journal, "have been crowding forward their shipments, the volume and quantity of which have been a 'caution' to Northern owners." The editor's estimate that the year 1882 would bring 100,000 more Texas cattle to Chicago than in 1881 was wrong. Some 200,000 more Texas cattle came to Chicago in 1882 than the previous year. But nothing so electrified cattlemen everywhere as did the Chicago sales of "grass-fed" Texas cattle in 1882 at $6.80 per hundredweight.[164]

Free grass, abundant cattle, excitement, a buying stampede, high prices, and a clamorous demand for

---

[164] *Daily Drovers Journal*, August 22, 1882; *Prose and Poetry of the Live Stock Industry*, 663, 664, 666.

money were some of the elements of the range boom. Money lenders stiffened and interest rates of one and one-half and two per cent with personal security were given by men who could still see the glow of the prosperous years. The few notes of warning were falsetto but the New York banker who refused a loan to a Texan with 3,000 cattle was not so cautious as he was ignorant of the range. Learning that there were no fences in Texas he looked horrified at the cattleman: "No fences! Why good Lord, young man, I'd as soon take a mortgage on a school of codfish off the banks of Newfoundland." [165]

Week by week prices of stock on the range mounted, "soon reaching $30 per head; and before the summer closed $35 was planked down for such stock in many parts of the range country." Swift Brothers and Company and Armour and Company slaughtered 344,000 cattle in 1882. "Cattle production," ran a hopeful estimate, "has just begun." [166]

Prosperity was abroad in the land and people were demanding more beef. At Chicago, Kansas City, and elsewhere the great packing firms had been established. Their canned meat and their refrigerated half carcasses of dressed beef were invading the foreign markets. The Texas drives and the shipment of cattle from the corn belt areas added to the boom – if not to the values – in the cattle kingdom. The phrases, "cattle barons" and "cattle kings" – neither coined in the West nor graciously accepted by it – inflated the popular notions of range profits and prosperity. These became the magic

[165] *Prose and Poetry of the Live Stock Industry*, 667; *Daily Drovers Journal*, March 1, 1882.

[166] *Prose and Poetry of the Live Stock Industry*, 667; *Daily Drovers Journal*, December 27, 1882.

words which tempted the small investors to embark upon the new but alluring business of cattle raising in the West and which unlocked the money chests of eastern and European capitalists.

The Evans-Jackson Live Stock Company, an early firm of seven incorporators, had been organized at Council Bluffs, Iowa, on June 15, 1877. On the assessment rolls of Laramie county in the Territory of Wyoming for that year their lands and implements were valued at $400. Their 300 beef cattle were valued at $5,700 and their 1,200 yearlings and two-year-olds at $8,500. Five years later its name was changed to "Bay State Live Stock Company" and its place of business transferred to Cedar Rapids, Iowa.[167] In May, 1880, the Montana Cattle Company was incorporated at Helena for a period of ten years. A few months later the Montana Cattle Company with a capital of $50,000 was organized to operate in the "Musselshell Valley" in Meagher county.[168]

A quick crop of cattle companies was produced in the office of the secretary of state of the Territory of Montana from 1879 to 1884. The corporate form continued to be the favorite one for raising capital and for conducting the business on a large scale. The Territorial Stock Growers' Association was incorporated at Helena for twenty years and with a capital stock of $20,000. The five trustees of the Benton and St. Louis Cattle Company were to have charge of a capital stock of $500,000. The company was chartered for twenty years

---

[167] *Assessment Book for Laramie county for 1877* (Territory of Wyoming), 24; *Records of Incorporations* in the bond and investment division of the secretary of state, Des Moines, Iowa, Book H, 534.

[168] *Records of Incorporations* (office of secretary of state at Helena, Montana), Book B, 50, 51, 74, 75.

and from its headquarters at Fort Benton on the Upper Missouri river was to direct its herds on the Teton ranges. The Colorado and Montana Live Stock Company, incorporated in 1882, was capitalized at $200,000. Its seven trustees presided over the company at Denver whose operations extended over Arapahoe county in Colorado and in the Territory of Wyoming. The Green Mountain Stock Ranching Company of 6,000 shares had its place of business in Minneapolis. The River Falls Live Stock Company, a Wisconsin company, was incorporated at Helena in 1883. In the same year the Northwestern Cattle Company was formed. In this company Ethan H. Cowles of Pine Bluff in the Territory of Wyoming subscribed for 100 shares, and the other 131 shares were bought by 14 investors in Concord, New Hampshire. Another firm was the McKenzie Cattle Company having its headquarters at Bismarck, in the Territory of Dakota and dealing in cattle, horses, and sheep. Other records have preserved the incorporations of the Wisconsin and Montana Cattle Company, the Keystone Cattle Company, and the Blackfoot Horse and Cattle Company located in Deer Lodge county.[169]

Walter Baron von Richthoven, a European nobleman, published his *Cattle Raising on the Plains of North America* in 1885, giving a list of seven Scottish companies then operating in the far West. The capital stock of these companies ranged from 42,000 shares at £5 each as in the Hanford Land and Cattle Company to 9,000 shares at £10 each in the Wyoming Cattle Ranche Company. He quoted with approval the president of the Cattle Growers' Association of Colorado who, in 1883, had extended an urgent invitation to for-

[169] *Ibid., passim.*

eign capitalists to embark in the cattle industry of the plains.[170]

The Powder River Cattle Company was formed in August, 1882, and was under the guidance of Moreton Frewen, an Englishman from London. The official brand for the cattle was "76," and the herds ranged along the Powder and Tongue rivers and Rawhide Creek in the Territory of Wyoming. The twelve herds purchased in 1882 made the holdings of the company 28,488 by January, 1883, and in the fall of that year its cattle numbered nearly 50,000. The herds in 1885 contained 57,917 cattle and produced a calf crop of 6,655. But the record of its purchases and sales became mute for 1886. The last entry in its records is that of a meagre list of cattle sold in 1886 to firms in Chicago, Superior, Omaha, and at Newman in Nebraska. No inventory was made for the thousands of its cattle lost, frozen, or starved during the Wyoming blizzards of 1886 and 1887.[171]

Officers, directors, or shareholders of over eighty cattle companies held membership in the Wyoming Stock Growers' Association in 1886.[172] The names of these corporations and the addresses of the various directors or officers indicate a widespread interest and financing in cattle companies. A. T. Babbitt, representing the Standard Cattle Company, had his post office at Ames, Nebraska. Another member gave his address as London. Other members and representatives came from

---

170 Walter Baron von Richthoven, *Cattle Raising on the Plains of North America*, 54, 55.

171 *Powder River Cattle Co. Cattle Book.* Found in the office of J. M. Carey and Sons, Cheyenne, Wyoming.

172 *List of Members, By-Laws, and Reports of the Wyoming Stock Growers' Association.* . . See *supra* note 113.

Pennsylvania, Colorado, Illinois, Iowa, and Connecticut. The Middlesex Live Stock Company was represented by O. W. Mead whose address was Boston. Oscar Pfeiffer, representing the Des Moines Cattle Company, was from Brooklyn, New York. Other members belonging to the Bay State Live Stock Company resided in Boston and Omaha.

An American firm of bankers, Underwood, Clark and Company, of Kansas City, introduced the western range business to the financiers of Edinburgh in 1880. To them the prairies were a land of romance teeming with grass in which fattening cattle brought high profits. "These profits," ran the original prospectus, "had been not less than from 25 to 40 per cent per annum, and under more favorable conditions have exceeded 50 per cent. Such profits are not surprising when it is kept in view that to raise a three-year-old steer worth $25 to $30 costs only from $6 to $10." Accordingly in January, 1881, the Prairie Cattle Company was formed with a capital of £100,000.[173]

Optimistic statements from Underwood, Clark and Company, who continued to control the company, excited the Scottish shareholders. "The financial officers of that conservative old city had found a new mine to exploit. The drawing rooms buzzed with the stories of this last of bonanzas, staid old gentlemen who scarcely knew the difference betwixt a steer and a heifer discussed it over their port and nuts."

High prices for cattle and excellent climatic conditions favored the company in its first few years. Dividends of twenty and one-half per cent were paid in 1883

---

[173] The sketch of this company is based on Clay, *My Life on the Range*, chap. xviii.

but this sum was largely realized from the sales of the
original herds – the capital of the company – rather than
from the annual increment of the herds. Indeed, the
first six years of the company netted large profits. "Dividends were paid from capital, shares were boomed, the
slick ones slipped, the promoters stole, then bullied the
directors and forced outrageous settlements. No wonder
the Scotch shareholders were tired, sick, disgusted."

A. H. Johnson, the first manager of the Prairie Company, was also the manager of three other companies
until his death in 1882. W. R. Green, the second manager, was succeeded by R. G. Head, who served from
1884 to 1886. The annual report of the company for
1884 gave warning that the ranges were overstocked.
A settlement was then made between the promoters and
the company whereby the bankers received $100,000 in
shares and $300,000 in cash. In this way promoters and
managers reaped an undeserved harvest for which the
Scottish shareholders paid.

"The report of the company for 1886," writes Mr.
John Clay, "is a most pathetic document. The calf crop
drops off, the number of cattle are apparently short. . .
Aside from shortages comes a great drop in prices. From
about $35 per head realized for their sale cattle in 1882,
they accept $17.90 in 1886, many of the latter, however,
being young cattle. There is another crushing admission.
It is discovered that in a purchase of 6,742 cattle and
125 horses in 1881, Underwood, Clark & Co. had collected twice. The sum involved was $100,863. It de-
veloped to be a pure and simple steal. The matter
was compromised by Underwood, Clark & Co. paying
$65,000 in notes which were, we believe, eventually
collected. The bright spot in the report is that the mana-

ger and cashier decreased expenses nearly $30,000 in the year."

The remarkably successful years of 1882 and 1883 in the cattle business attracted into the West swarms of shrewd speculators, promoters, swindlers, and financiers. English and Scottish syndicates, incorporated companies from the East, and individuals of abundant means invaded the range country. Their managers and agents swarmed to the West to purchase ranches, cattle, horses, water sites, and ranch buildings and equipment.

An epidemic of cattle companies raged with vigor in London. In March, 1882, the Cattle Ranche and Land Company [174] began its career. The ranch and cattle of Rufus Hatch, Earl W. Spencer, and Francis Drew were located on the Kiowa river mainly in Indian Territory. Their cattle numbered 7,000 and other purchases were made. After making various sales the number of cattle held by the company in November, 1882, amounted to 26,000. The expenses of promoting and organizing the company had been over $10,000 but out of the fall sales amounting to $128,000 the London office had figured profits of $85,000. This was equivalent to a dividend of fifteen per cent. The shareholders were elated but their optimism over their property over 5,000 miles away was to have a short season.

An alluring prospectus ushered in the flotation of the Wyoming Cattle Ranche Company, known on the range as the "Seventy-one Quarter Circle Ranche." Fourteen men assembled at Edinburgh in June, 1882, and issued a circular which described the property located in Carbon and Sweetwater counties in the Territory of Wyoming. The 4,000 square miles of grazing lands contained

[174] *Idem,* chaps. iv, xxii.

19,000 improved cattle, including 150 Shorthorn and
Devon bulls. The circular also listed 150 saddle and
work horses, dwellings, storehouses, ranch equipment,
and branch establishments. The owner, John T. Stewart
of Council Bluffs, Iowa, was offering to sell this property
for $400,000.

The prospectus cited the advantages of healthfulness,
abundant water, shelter, grass, and low mortality. "The
locality of this Ranche was, until lately, the favorite
winter range of the buffalo, deer, and antelope, whose
unerring instinct secured here every requirement of a
natural home, *viz.*, a pasturage relieved by the shelter
of hill, bluff, and cañon from winter storms, an extra-
ordinary dryness of climate, which neutralized the cold
of the severest seasons, and an abundance of rich standing grain – like hay . . ."

Another section of the prospectus dealt with "profits."
Cattle raising in the West was regarded as "one of the
most lucrative enterprises in the world." It was hope-
fully stated that, through the calf increment, the herd
would double in value and number every four years.
Extracts from Governor J. W. Hoyt's "Pastoral Re-
searches of Wyoming," a charming and equally truthful
and optimistic account of the territory, was the bene-
diction to the prospectus.

Mr. John Clay was immediately sent out to examine
the ranch in the summer of 1882. With Stewart and Cap
Haskell, the foreman, he rode over the ranges to observe
the grass, water, and cattle, and later he also examined
the books and schedules of David Street, the ranch
superintendent. A favorable report was sent to Scotland,
and a contract of sale, the cause of a sharp lawsuit later,
transferred the property to the new Scottish company.[175]

---

175 Stewart *v.* Wyoming Cattle Ranche Company, 128 U.S. 383.

Another project, promoted by a firm of London barristers, gave rise in October, 1882, to the Western Ranches, Limited, a British company, generally called the "VVV Outfit." [176] Two men, John Clay, and the managing director, Robert Pringle, had made a visit earlier in the fall to the Belle Fourche ranges in the Territory of Dakota. After a preliminary inspection of the herds owned by Duncan Plumb and Dorr Clark a favorable report was sent to the board in Scotland. A remarkably strong board of directors, such as Thomas Nelson, Sir George Warrender, and John Wilson, an Edinburgh merchant, piloted the company in its early policies. Dorr Clark became the first range manager and directed the Texas cowboys in the range work.

Mr. John Clay, who became the agent and superintendent of the company, was instructed to stock the ranges at an expense not to exceed £92,000. A heavy demand for range cattle caused brisk bidding. In March, 1883, a contract was signed for the purchase of 5,659 cattle to be paid for after actual counting, branding, and delivery. On the Goschen Hole and Cheyenne river ranges the firm of Sturgis, Goodell, and Lane had assembled a motley assortment of Iowan cattle – heifers, steers, and half-starved milch cows, two, three, and four years old. These cattle delivered at Valentine, Nebraska, cost $166,568 and the expense of driving them to the Belle Fourche ranges amounted to $3,512.

Another lot was a purchase of 4,774 Texas steers from Grimes and Thornton which were branded W.G. These three, four, and five-year-old cattle had wintered in the Cheyenne River Valley and were also driven to the Belle Fourche ranges. The total price of the cattle there delivered was $129,127.29. Other purchases costing

[176] *Annual Reports of the Western Ranches, Limited.*

$22,972 included 246 bulls, 11 Canadian cows, and four heifers. The total expenditure in stocking these ranges in 1883 was $322,180.30. An additional outlay of about $9,000 for land, houses, and ranch equipment completed the transactions for 1883.

The company began the year 1884 with 13,547 cattle. During the year the herd was augmented by 9,400. Bulls were purchased in Illinois; a lot of 1,000 Texas steers was purchased for $15,000 at Dodge City, Kansas; other additions of about 7,000 yearlings and two-year-old steers from Charles Francis, the Dickey Brothers, and from C. C. Sugg plus the calf crop of 1,224 made the total holdings of the Western Ranches, Limited, about 23,000. About 2,000 steers were left on ranges of the Indian Territory until they were transferred to the company's ranges in 1887. The sale of 4,241 two-year-old steers in 1884 and the estimated losses of only 400 justified a dividend of 7s per share.

Another foreign company – the giant among the western cattle corporations – had meanwhile been spreading stock over the ranges and its stocks and debentures among Scottish investors. Its herds and pastures were extensive and the administration extended from its Edinburgh offices to the round-up captains and foremen on the plains. The man whose name it bore not only rode on its prestige but also gave it several years of tragic range mismanagement.

"The Swan Land and Cattle Company, Limited" conceived in 1882 was a Scottish company whose unbroken but checkered history extends to the present. Thomas Lawson, a Scottish farmer, Colin J. Mackenzie of Portmore, and George Prentice, another Scotchman, had been investigating three range properties in the Terri-

tory of Wyoming during the year. These were the Swan
and Frank Live Stock Company, the National Cattle
Company, and the Swan, Frank and Anthony Cattle
Company. Their report on these holdings was favorable
and Alexander H. Swan and John Donnelly visited
Scotland. There to the Scottish investors the western
lands of promise were portrayed, and figures, prospectus, and imagination united to form a picture of profits
and dividends.[177]

A contract of sale dated November 27, 1882, and
signed by the vendors and by James Wilson representing
a limited company, launched one of the most famous
cattle companies of the West. The largest item, $2,187,-
675, was the price of 87,507 cattle and another item of
$124,000 was for 1,660 bulls. The sum of $41,650 was
paid for 833 mules. The sale included also all lands,
water rights, improvements on lands, houses, barns, corrals, stables, live stock brands, tools, one hundred and
twenty miles of fencing, implements, wagons, harnesses,
outfits for ranch, camp, and round-up, office and fixtures
in Cheyenne, and branding irons. A further clause stated
that the herd books listing the acquisition, increase, and
disposition of the herds "had been correctly kept." [178]

An able board of seven directors was chosen and for
years in the office at 130 George Street the tragedies and
difficulties of this company were debated. Colin J. Mackenzie presided. James Wilson, another director, had
been a merchant importer from China. James Shepherd
was a manufacturer, Lord Douglas Gordon was a mem-

---

177 Clay, *My Life on the Range,* 201, 202.
178 Swan Land & Cattle Co., Limited *v.* Frank et al. 39 *Federal Reporter,*
456; report of directors to first general meeting of stockholders dated April
2, 1884, and found in *Annual Reports of The Swan Land & Cattle Company,
Ltd., 1883-1912.*

ber of parliament, and Alexander H. Swan, besides
being a director, was the manager in America. One of
the banking firms of the company was in Edinburgh
and others were located in New York, Omaha, and
Cheyenne. A firm of Edinburgh lawyers represented
the company in Scotland and another of Cheyenne its
American interests. Finlay Dun, whose honesty was
much greater than his knowledge of the range, became
the secretary. Of the 60,000 shares at $50 each, 3,545
were paid up and $30 were paid on each of the remain-
ing shares. Debentures were issued to the extent of
$1,125,000 and made a capital outlay of $3,000,000 for
the company.[179]

Purchase upon purchase in the southeastern part of
the Territory of Wyoming marked Swan's management
in 1883. Over 12,000 cattle were added to the original
herd. Under the desert, the homestead, and the timber
culture acts about 21,000 acres were acquired. The Clay
Ranch and the Rehmeyer Ranch were added. A part of
the Muleshoe Ranch in the Sibylee Valley consisting of
640 acres of meadow lands and its stone house, barn,
fencing, and ditches cost nearly $40,000. Three home-
steads of 1,762 acres formed another purchase at $52,000.
House and stabling in Cheyenne, implements, and the
telephone line from Cheyenne to the ranches made a
further outlay of $4,000. Later the sum of $280,000 was
paid on the balance due on the Muleshoe Ranch. Its
headquarters was about eight miles below the Two-Bar
Ranch, the Swan headquarters on the Sibylee river.
The transfer involved 5,000 acres of fenced lands, nearly
9,000 cattle, 180 horses, corrals, and a two-story masonry

---

[179] Report of directors, dated April 2, 1884, and found in *Annual Reports
of The Swan Land & Cattle Company, Ltd., 1883-1912.*

house. This purchase gave the company entire control of the Sibylee Valley for a distance of thirty miles.

The laconic phrase, "market slow and weak," of October, 1883, epitomized not the extent but the condition of the range cattle industry. Texas cattlemen were preparing for the eighteenth northerly drives. Everywhere the next year – in Texas, in the cow towns, on the ranges, at the shipping centers, at round-ups, at the various stockyards, and in the directors' rooms of packing firms – men were watching drooping markets and the changing industry on the ranges.

Cattle at $1.80 per Hundredweight

Cattle at $1.80 per Hundredweight

Early warnings and even back sets were swept aside in the rise and momentum of business of the early eighties. The voices of optimists drowned the warnings of the prophets of evil. One editor early in 1882 spied "the demon of speculation" riding on the high tide of prosperity. Beware, he cautioned, of a widespread catastrophe – "a thing that has happened many a time in the world's history." The arrival at Chicago of 175,000 cattle in October, 1882 – the largest number on record – did not prevent another warning, that during the past two or three years there had been "a vast amount of overtrading done all over the country, in different branches of trade, and for all this a day of settlement must come." [180]

Railway construction had declined in 1883, mercantile failures had almost attained five figures, business had recoiled from the buoyancy of 1879, and financial papers were soon to torture readers with vocabularies of "depression," "passed dividends," "defaults," "receiverships," and "failures." But on the ranges the bull market for steers still rose. Buyers besieged sellers. Railroads dumped "skimmed" cows and heifers from the corn belt upon the ranges. Young bulls, suitable for feeding and marketing as beef steers were, instead, shipped to the ranges.

---

[180] *Daily Drovers Journal,* February 2, November 3, December 5, 1882.

An "annual round-up" [181] of facts and figures gave a picture of range conditions in 1883. The average losses of two and one-half per cent were chiefly among the old cows. Ten per cent more of bulls had been imported. The range grass was not so good as the previous year. An average advance of $5.80 per hundredweight was noted in range sales. Extensive fences were being built in the Southwest and there was a growing policy of putting up winter feed.

"Range cattle" appeared on the classified market quotations in Chicago on June 4, 1883, and the sales of thirty cars of cattle ranged from $4.70 to $5.37½ per hundredweight. "The immense influx of cattle into the business," wrote Horace Plunkett that month, "has been to [us] a good deal of blind and illegitimate speculation." Brain and muscle were taking hold of the business. "But let them not be too credulous." [182]

A minority element – the old conservative cattlemen – possessed foresight as well as hindsight. Seeing but not experiencing the speculative fever in cattle, they brought to their aid agents and salesmen. These with pencil and well-thumbed memorandum books quickly conjured up figures of increase, dividends, profits, prices, and expanding range rights. What would prevent prices of range cattle from going up to $40? Or, of rising to $45 "with a strong probability of selling for $50 in the not very distant by-and-by?" [183]

The report of the directors of the Swan Land and Cattle Company to the shareholders on April 2, 1884, recommended an increase in the proportion of bulls,

---

[181] *Idem,* May 14, 1883.

[182] *Idem,* June 4, 14, 1883.

[183] *Prose and Poetry of the Live Stock Industry,* 668.

fresh purchases of Hereford, Polled Angus, and Shorthorn bulls, the fencing in of the bulls to prevent calving
in the spring, and the policy of keeping heifers fenced
in until two years old. The snowstorms and the rainfall
of the previous spring had impaired the fattening quality of the grass and thereby had delayed the maturing
of the steers for three weeks. Of the steers 1,651 of the
poorest had been sent to Omaha to be fattened on distillery grains, hay, and oil cake at an expense of $24,000.
For the year 1883 the total calf brand was 19,334 and
the sales from cattle brought $385,000. But in this Sahara
of figures the shareholders were happy to discover an
oasis in the dividend declared payable on April 4.[184]

Sullen gloom and clouds of distrust overhung the
commercial and financial horizons in 1884. A severe
storm broke in the New York stock market in the middle
of May. Ugly rumors were adrift in the cattle country
that the ranges were overstocked, that there were out-
breaks of pleuropneumonia, that the Texas Trail was
to be closed, and that barbed-wire fences were cutting
up the open range. In November the price of range
stock at Chicago dropped to $2.50. "If you have steers
to shed," advised one stock journal, "prepare to shed
them now." [185]

In that same month at St. Louis the "National Cattle
and Horse Growers' Association of the United States"
was organized.[186] The captains of the industry were
present and the sorrows of the past year were, for a time,
forgotten in many speeches and much wassailing. But
the long title of the newly formed body belied its short

---

[184] Report of directors, dated April 2, 1884, and March 11, 1885, and found
in *Annual Reports of The Swan Land & Cattle Company, Ltd., 1883-1912.*
[185] *Daily Drovers Journal,* September 20, 1883, December 10, 1884.
[186] [St. Louis] *Daily Globe-Democrat,* November 18, 1884.

existence and sobered and unsobered cattlemen returned to face the changing conditions on the range.

Another report of March 11, 1885 – heavy with dull figures – told the Scottish shareholders of the Swan Company of the operations in 1884.[187] Receipts of sales from 8,400 cattle rose to nearly $400,000; the calf brand to nearly 21,000; and the inventory at the close of the year showed the number of cattle to be nearly 1,000 more than at the beginning of the year. A dividend of ten per cent again invested the management with confidence and high hopes from the shareholders.

But other facts in this financial report revealed symptoms of mismanagement, gross carelessness, and evasion. The manager, Alexander H. Swan, although receiving an annual salary of $10,000, was active in floating other cattle companies. A program of vast purchases in 1884 required an outlay of nearly $600,000. On the Laramie plains 549,423 acres were bought from the Union Pacific Railroad Company for $460,900 to be paid for in ten annual installments. This purchase permitted uninterrupted grazing over an area of over 1,000,000 acres. The ranches of H. B. Kelly and E. W. Whitcomb aggregating 4,743 acres and costing $196,000 included a hotel, a store, dwelling houses, barns, and sheds. These "conterminous properties give us irrigated and well sheltered meadows, extending for ten miles on both sides of the Chugwater, along which our freehold runs with scarcely a break for thirty-five miles."

A lot of 9,764 Texas steers caused another outlay of $172,000. A herd of grade and thoroughbred cattle was bought from Kelly and Whitcomb for $100,000. Other

---

[187] Report of the directors dated March 11, 1885, and printed in *Annual Reports of The Swan Land & Cattle Company, Ltd., 1883-1912.*

expenditures for buildings, materials, ditches, irrigation, telephone extensions, lands, and ranch furnishings required about $42,000. The taxes for the year were $15,357 or $.12 2/3 per head while the running expenses of the range – salaries of managers and foremen, wages, "board and feeding" of cowboys amounted to $67,966 or $.56 per head of cattle.

An undertone of warning and apology came from another part of the report. Mr. Swan's theories are brought in by the directors to explain the small calf brand and the small number of steers marketed. Losses in 1881 and 1882 were greater than had been estimated at those times and outside brandings did not, as imagined, compensate for such losses. It was apparent that unknown losses had been carried in the books of the "native corporations" of Frank and Swan since 1881. "After consultation with Mr. Swan, they have accordingly deemed it prudent and proper to write off, in addition to the annual deduction, 200 bulls, 2,200 steers, and 5,500 cows."

A bitterly cold winter in January, 1885, struck the ranges and with streams frozen some cattle famished for want of water. Range cattle, left coarse and unfinished by the severe winter and snow, continued to flood the Chicago yards. Editor H. L. Goodall of *The Daily Drovers Journal* gave warnings but his advice could not stop the steady stream of thin, young, and underfed Texas steers to St. Louis, Kansas City, and Chicago.[188]

Competitors in the shipment of refrigerated beef had arisen in Russia and Germany to reduce the profits of American exporters. In August, 1885, came the president's order to remove the fences. States and territories

---

[188] *Daily Drovers Journal,* July 3, December 24, 1885.

were passing trail quarantine laws. The southwestern railroad strike was another straw. On October 5 and November 5 prices of range stock at Chicago staggered as low as $1.80 per hundredweight.[189]

Grass and corn-fed cattle of one shipper who had bought them for $4.75 in May, 1885, were marketed in the following December for $4.25. "Three years ago," wrote a Montana stock journal late in 1885,[190] "there was a large number of states cattle – yearlings – shipped into Montana at an expense it is claimed, of $25 per head. This fall they were sold in Chicago at an average of $3.30 the top cattle bringing $3.60 and the poorest grade at $3.00. They weighed 1,100 pounds on an average, which would give $36.30 gross for each animal, and as the shipping expenses were at least $9 per head, there is $1.30 per head margin left for the transaction, which is not enough to pay for the loss."

An equally gloomy report covering the operations of the Western Ranches, Limited, for 1885 was made to its stockholders at their annual meeting in Edinburgh.[191] The severe winter in Indian Territory had done bad work. Hard frosts, alternating with rain and snow, had left the ranges covered with ice. The yearling herds, unable to get food, were reduced by cold and hunger, and the northerly drive in June to the northern ranges had disclosed a loss of 2,515 head or seven per cent of the capital of the company. Depressed prices caused a further loss of $25,000.

But even darker days were in store for the company. Not a single additional animal was placed on the ranges

---

189 *Idem,* October 5, November 5, 1885.

190 Quoted from *Rocky Mountain Husbandman* in *idem* of November 26, 1885.

191 *Annual Reports of The Western Ranches, Limited.*

during the parching summer of 1886. Two thousand yearling steers were contracted for at $14 per head but not to be delivered until the next year. The average price of the 3,170 steers sold was $27.25. The calf brand of 1886 was, however, an increase of thirty per cent over that of the previous year. A dividend of only four per cent was recommended.

Another array of figures framed in explanations and apologies came in the annual Swan Company report of March 12, 1886.[192] At the beginning of the year 1885 the cattle of the company numbered 109,893, and the deductions from strays, sales, and deaths were put down as 18,775. At the end of the year the books showed 123,460 cattle valued at $3,176,793.85. The natural increase of the herd was reported as 9,571 valued at $179,545 which was placed in a "reserve fund." The dividend reduced to six per cent was payable in March, 1886. A "special deduction of 3,000 for steers" seemed like a penance alongside the solemn declaration that "our range count should tally with our book numbers." The shipment of 1,834 steers and bulls to Omaha to be fattened on distillery grains at the Willow Springs Distillery seemed like more evidence of an overstocked range.

More optimistic are the reports on improvements. Two ditching machines drawn by six or eight mules or horses extended, widened, and improved various old watercourses. Thirty-five miles of laterals tapping a large ditch fed by Medicine Creek furnished irrigation for 4,000 acres. Another ditch bringing water from Richard's Creek to a plateau between that stream and Hunton's Creek was improved with thirty-five laterals.

[192] *Annual Reports of The Swan Land & Cattle Company, Ltd., 1883-1912.*

About 5,000 acres were made usable for meadows and winter grazing. At various ranches – Bates Creek, on the Little Medicine, and at the 07 headquarters – log-houses and corrals were built for the spring and fall round-ups.

To take up the annual installment of $60,000 in notes held by the Union Pacific Railroad Company the directors recommended that a new issue of preferred shares be authorized. This payment was considered as urgent because bills introduced in congress contained stringent clauses against the acquisition of lands by aliens or by alien corporations. The directors did not believe such contemplated laws would become retrospective but they were eager to use money to complete the purchase of the lands of the railroad before the possible passage of such hostile legislation. A year before W. W. Corlett of Cheyenne, one of the resident solicitors of the company, had assured the directors that a foreign corporation could legally hold lands and transact business in the Territory of Wyoming.

A dismal report for the year 1886 records the loss by death and strays at 10,371. Only 4,800 cattle were sold and the inventory of cattle, horses, lands, and – future hopes – was set down as $3,819,000 on December 31. It had been a disastrous year, ran the report. The moist autumn of 1885 had interfered with the curing of the grass and other territories and states had felt the scarcity of food and water. Enforced sales and crowded markets resulted. The Chicago yards alone received 2,000,000 cattle. The lessened demand due to industrial depression, strikes, the dry summer, a diminished corn crop, a lack of ready money, and commercial failures caused a loss of $135,000 to the company. After this chapter of lamentations the stockholders were prepared for the news that no dividend was to be paid in 1887.

But optimism and penance appear in another part of the report. The hotel and store had brought a profit of $3,199 and the irrigation works of the last three years were yielding good returns. The annual outlay of $30,520 since the year 1883 for barns, houses, and corrals was henceforth to be "largely reduced" and the necessity for the "strictest economy had been impressed on the new manager."

An alarming theory was raised in another paragraph. "Diminished sales and smaller calf brand raise the important question: do the number of cattle on the books tally with the numbers on the range? The directors are of the opinion that the losses of the year, although considerably over an average, will be covered by the deduction of 10 per cent from range bulls, and 8 per cent from the remainder of the range herd and from Grades and Texas, and such deductions have accordingly been made. The annually recurring failures to gather the expected number of mature steers, and the reduced calf brand, imply that some shortage still exists, not sufficiently provided for by previous deductions, and the directors hope, during the present year, to be able to ascertain its extent." The board believed, in brief, that existing shortages in the herds and the special deductions made in the years past were attributable to dishonest counts made by Swan and Frank in the original sale in 1882. On this subject the law agent of the company and "eminent American counsel" were preparing a "memorial" and an "opinion." [193]

Swan Brothers failed in May, 1887, and Finlay Dun, one of the directors and a man sadly inexperienced in handling cowboys, cattle, and vast pastures, was sent

---

[193] Report of the directors, December 31, 1886, in *Annual Reports of The Swan Land & Cattle Company, Ltd., 1883-1912.*

out as manager. From June 7 to August 13 he attempted
a count under the heads of cows, two-year-old heifers,
yearling heifers, bulls, three-year-old steers, yearling
steers, and Texas steers. No branding irons were used
but barrels and barrels of paint were smeared upon
29,008 terrified cattle before the farce had run its
course.[194]

An "interim report" of December 7, 1887, recounts
the defalcations of A. H. Swan and the heavy winter
losses found by Finlay Dun in the Laramie Valley. The
summer drought, the scarcity of money, the short corn
crop, overstocked markets, and the three weeks of rain
in August caused the prices of cattle to fall lower than
any time since 1878.[195]

But neither Finlay Dun's paint nor the fantastic arith-
metic of this report could save the shrinking assets or the
drooping faith of the stockholders. A committee of five
representing the shareholders and appointed at the meeting of December, 1887,[196] made a report that the management "appears to have been of the most careless and
reckless character" and that it was unfortunate that "our
deputations" to the ranges failed to detect "deceptions
practiced by the manager."

The deficiency in the herd from 1886 to 1887 was
estimated at 40,000 or 50,000 although a visit of a committee in the former year brought another "satisfactory"
report. The Reel herd costing nearly $70,000 and ap-
pearing on the books at 2,000 was found by actual count

194 Clay, *My Life on the Range*, 209, 210.

195 "Interim Report" dated December 7, 1887, in *Annual Reports of The Swan Land & Cattle Company, Ltd., 1883-1912.*

196 "Report by Committee of Shareholders Appointed at Meeting on December 20, 1887," in *Annual Reports of The Swan Land & Cattle Company, Ltd., 1883-1912.*

to contain only 672. The committee, stating that it had no confidence in the present board, recommended the appointment of John Clay as manager of the Wyoming properties and provided that he should devote all his time to the task. It suggested also that an official be appointed to have charge of the books and accounts so that the manager could give undivided attention to range matters.

"If more attention had been paid to erecting shelter," ran the report, "and providing a supply of hay for winter feed, instead of expending so much on extravagant purchases of land and cattle, the company would have been in a different financial position today. For this the board are much to blame."

John Clay, who assumed charge of the Swan Company in February, 1888, became its firm and guiding spirit for eight years. Financial disorganization of the company was apparent; foremen were too numerous; an expensive office in Cheyenne was a severe drain; and the bank account of the company, as well as its credit, was gone. "On the range," he said, "it was much the same thing. After going over the different ranches carefully, it seemed to be running full steam in spending money and eating grub. They had seven cooks with helpers at two places, nine men in all, at $40 a month. . . They had to have a general headquarters, a farming ditto, a cattle ditto, then one foreman did not care to live with another, and so on. Meantime the Swan Company paid the bill." [197]

On returning from Europe in August, 1887, he had first heard of the terrible slaughter of the preceding winter which had been even more destructive than those

[197] Clay, *My Life on the Range,* 214.

of 1871-1872 and 1879-1880. The repeated hurricane blizzards, the heavy falls of snow, and the blood-chilling rains had combined to kill off about one-third of all the northern range cattle. It is possible that the buffalo and other plains animals had suffered equally severe storms in the remote past. But unfettered by human mismanagement and equipped with more hardened constitutions they escaped the wholesale tragedies of the Swan Company herds.[198]

Over large areas of the Territory of Montana, the western Dakotas, and the Territory of Wyoming the winter losses ran as high as seventy-five, eighty, and even ninety per cent of all the cattle. It is doubtful whether the directors or the Scottish shareholders of the Swan Company saw or could even imagine the horrors of the northern ranges which "swarmed with bands of starving cattle, stiffly wandering from one temporary place of refuge to another, on legs that were partly frozen, and by the ice-coat of the snow stripped of hair to the knees, their ranks fast being thinned by the dropping out of those that could go no farther." [199]

At Edinburgh in March, 1888, the stockholders of The Western Ranches, Limited, also listened to the cold and mournful chronicle of the previous winter tragedy on the ranges.[200] Mr. John Clay estimated the herd in the previous December at 17,887. The winter losses he placed at 5,361, the loss of the bulls at 275 or 60 per cent, and the loss of 800 calves constituted 60 per cent of the crop. The directors placed the winter losses in a "suspense account" of nearly £35,000. The 22,400

[198] *Idem*, 178, 179; *Prose and Poetry of the Live Stock Industry*, 700-709.
[199] *Prose and Poetry of the Live Stock Industry*, 707.
[200] *Annual Reports of The Western Ranches, Limited.*

shares were reduced from £5 fully paid up to £3½ fully paid up.

The Swan Company as well as a score of other cattle companies had been spreading its cattle in reckless numbers over the West and Northwest. Such overstocking even with the mildest of winters was found to prove murderous to herds.

Its four formative years ended in disasters from which changes in range management and the transition from the open to the closed range were to emerge. Tempered and chastened by its misfortunes and mistakes the company, unlike many others, survived. Its convalescence under John Clay's new policies was slow because its ills had been great. "The cattle cyclone like an Alpine avalanche was no respecter of persons. It hit the just and the unjust. It was the protest of nature against the love of gain, against greed, mismanagement, and that happy-go-lucky sentiment which permeates frontier life. And yet what would the West have been without the trapper, the miner, and the cowpuncher, the pioneers of that wondrous country which pours wealth through its products into an already overflowing reservoir?" [201]

The era of great cattle companies with their golden visions and wild extravagance ended with the heart-breaking disasters of 1885 and 1886, although ominous signs had appeared as early as 1884. Overstocking, frenzied financing, mismanagement, the invasion of settlers and sheepmen, storms, declining markets, and the falling off of exports of cattle – these factors had combined

---

[201] Clay, *My Life on the Range*, 207, 208. "For years [after 1886-1887] the Swan Company considered itself a range company, till gradually it was left alone, a solitary ship surrounded by rocks and quicksand in the form of small ranchmen, sheepmen and farmers." *Ibid.*, 211.

to topple over the cattle companies grown huge in so short a time and on foundations of sand.

"Like other highly inflated booms, this one claimed as toll more than it had received for grinding, and therefore the stockman of the range who was not either badly crippled or cleaned out entirely, financially, was the exception. . . The depreciation of values was appalling, and it came so swiftly that ruin was upon thousands of cattlemen before they realized what had happened. Many a stockman who, notwithstanding his indebtedness that was running at perhaps two per cent a month, had considered himself wealthy in his herds that were feeding on the 'free grass' of the range he held under his transitory 'rights,' did not comprehend at first how the calamity could take from him even the half of his fortune." [202]

Although millions of cattle were marketed in these boom years it is doubtful whether any cattle companies realized profits over this period. Unlike the great fur companies of earlier days, they could not move on to fresh fields. The era of free grass was gone. The exuberant spirit of the cattle boom of the early eighties had neither forerunner nor guide. Born of freedom, it had flourished for a few years on the frontier where nature and the march of events did not permit it to grow to seasoned maturity. But a history picturesque and tragic in its ending is one of its legacies to the West.

---

[202] *Prose and Poetry of the Live Stock Industry*, 673.

Economics and Finances of the
Cattle Ranges

Economics and Finances of the Cattle Ranges

Some alluring examples of financial success were furnished by several notable individuals or partnerships prior to the rise of the great cattle companies. In the early seventies ranges were not overstocked and a great stream of cattle grazed into the West from Texas. Prices were fair and instances of enormous profits contained no warning against blizzards and snow or of the approach of the nesters and small ranchmen who, like a glacier, were to spread over the estates of the cattlemen.

Freighters, travellers, army officers, and scientists saw ranches flourishing and increasing in numbers before 1870. Conrad Kohrs, perhaps the mightiest cattleman of the Northwest, had begun his career as a butcher during the mining rush to Alder Gulch in the Territory of Montana and by 1866 had laid the foundations of his great herds. From his Sun River Range in that territory large herds were driven to the Union Pacific station at Cheyenne until the opening up of the Northern Pacific Railway in 1883.[203]

R. C. Keith had begun cattle raising in Nebraska in 1867 with five American cows which were increased by the purchase of about two hundred the next year. Each year the purchase of Texas cattle added to the herd. Wages of from $30 to $50 per month for the two herds-

---

[203] *Dillon* [Montana] *Examiner,* April 9, 1924. Tom Stout, editor, *Montana: its Story and Biography,* vol. I, 393, 394.

men, interest, the outlay for buildings and corrals, and the cost of cattle purchases made a total expenditure of $51,000 down to 1873. At the end of six years he estimated his cash profits at $12,000 besides a herd valued at over $109,000. Such striking figures were possible only during years of enormous demands for beef which had been produced where there was neither land, fences, or food to be paid for.[204]

In a fine pasture about one hundred miles long and thirty miles wide in the Laramie Valley in the Territory of Wyoming there were grazing before 1870 the great herds of Thomas Alsop, Charles Hutton, and Edward Creighton, the pioneer banker of Omaha. An extensive system of corrals, houses, and stables had been built. But their graded cows and beef herds numbering in all about 9,000 had easily survived the winters in the shelter of the bluffs and hills. Many herds of contemporaries were browsing in the grassy valleys of numerous streams. Reynolds, John Hitson, and the Patterson brothers ran their herds containing about 8,000 cattle on the left bank of the South Platte. The latter owned ranches on the Arkansas river and in the Territory of New Mexico. Before 1870 their transactions in cattle amounted to hundreds of thousands of dollars.[205]

But in grand scale and profits in the early history of the western cattle ranges the operations of John Wesley Iliff seem to lead all the rest. This former student of Delaware College in Ohio had migrated to Colorado where in 1859 he began his career in buying cattle. For fourteen years – until a few years before his death in

---

[204] Edwin A. Curley, *Nebraska, its Advantages, Resources, and Drawbacks*, 363, 364.

[205] F. V. Hayden, *U.S. Geological Survey of Wyoming and Adjacent Territories*, 248-257.

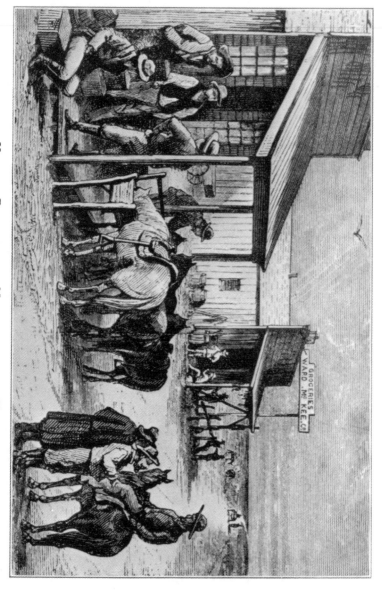

HALTING PLACE ON THE NINNESCAH RIVER, KANSAS
From a contemporary sketch drawn in 1874.

GROCERIES
WARD MᶜKEE.Cᵒ

1878 at the age of forty-eight – he was a dominating figure on the range. His stock grazed in valleys of the territories of Wyoming and Colorado and in Nebraska. At one time his 35,000 fed on his water fronts and meadows which extended for thirty miles along the north bank of the South Platte river. These thousands of acres he had acquired title to by buying out settlers – many of whom had been his cowboys or other employees who had homesteaded or preëmpted in order to sell him their holdings.

His cows numbered from 6,000 to 7,000. Shorthorn bulls costing from $60 to $80 were bought in Iowa and Illinois. During the first summer they were pastured on reserved ranges and during the first winter were fed on hay in sheds in order to adjust them to the climate. In July of each year he would purchase from 10,000 to 15,000 Texas steers going on two and three years. When bought at prices from $11 to $15 they weighed from 600 to 800 pounds and when sold these steers would weigh 1,000 pounds and bring from $38 to $50.

About forty men were employed during the summer and about a dozen during the winter. Two hundred horses, all from Texas, were required for these cowboys who, in addition to their board, received wages of from $25 to $30 per month. The cattle never tasted corn but in severe weather were given a little hay. Between the north and the south forks of the Platte river his cattle mingled with the herds of Carey Brothers, Swan Brothers, Sturgis and Lane, and Searight. These outfits worked on the same general lines but none were so careful in obtaining good sires.

Mr. Iliff had a deep faith that the trans-Missouri region would defy all competition in the production of horses, mutton, and beef. Employing a careful manager he carried on an extensive correspondence with bankers and commission men in Omaha and Chicago. Great quantities of hides were shipped, beef herds were sold at Indian agencies, and his steaks and tongues were enjoyed at the mess tables of various western army posts. Unarmed he rode from one ranch to another. And, it was said, he could ride a week over his great pastures and each night sleep at a different ranch. Unquestionably his labors in the saddle many hours a day in all sorts of weather in the direction of his properties hastened his early death but they were also prime factors in his success.[206]

Immense numbers of cattle were being sent in 1870 from the Territory of Colorado to the territories to the west and the estimated number to the Territory of Montana alone was 20,000. An observer at Cheyenne the next year pointed out the great demand and "enormous prices" for beef in these markets. The government alone was purchasing thousands of cattle for the Indian reservations and the army posts. "I should not want to begin with less than $6,000," he advised a prospective ranchman. "It will cost as much to take care of $6,000 or one thousand worth as it will of $10,000." [207]

"The amount of money handled by bankers along the base of the mountains from Cheyenne to Trinidad [Colorado] is enormous," wrote a western railroad surgeon

[206] Letter of Dr. H. Latham, June 5, 1870, reprinted in *idem*, 253; James Macdonald, *Food from the Far West or American Agriculture*, 95-97; General James S. Brisbin, *The Beef Bonanza; or How to Get Rich on the Plains*, 78, 79, 204; personal interview with William S. Iliff of Denver, Colorado, the son of John W. Iliff.

[207] Letter of Joseph M. Carey, May 22, 1871, in *Carey Letter Book* (Cheyenne), vol. I, 65-70.

in 1870.[208] "I have no data from which to calculate the amount, but it cannot be less than $1,250,000. Every settler who comes into any of these mountain territories, every mine that is opened, every Indian who goes onto reserves and is fed, every soldier who is brought into the country, creates an additional demand for stock cattle and beef."

Increasing numbers of Texas trail herds spread out as well as filled in the cattlemen's frontier of the seventies. "Two years ago," wrote a surgeon of the Union Pacific Railroad in 1870, "our beef and cattle were shipped from the East. Today cattle buyers from Chicago and New York are at every station on our railroads, and buying cattle in all our valleys for eastern consumption. It is safe to predict that 15,000 head of beeves will be shipped from our valleys east the present season." A former army officer in 1876 listed about seventy ranches in the Territory of Wyoming whose "horned cattle" over one year old numbered over 55,000.[209]

A writer in *Harper's Magazine* in 1879 advised that the minimum capital for beginning cattle ranching in Colorado be $5,000. An investment of $126,000 would net a profit of $114,651 during the first three years. But this optimism was tempered by the admission that there were "chances and contingencies of possible disaster." [210] "The statement has been repeatedly made, and, to my knowledge, never questioned," wrote A. T. Babbitt,

---

[208] Letter of Dr. H. Latham in the *Omaha World Herald,* June 5, 1870, as reprinted in Hayden, *U.S. Geological Survey of Wyoming and Adjacent Territories,* 256.

[209] *Idem,* 250-255. J. H. Triggs, *History of Cheyenne and Northern Wyoming,* 53, 55.

[210] A. A. Hayes, "The Cattle Ranches of Colorado," in *Harper's New Monthly Magazine* (1879), vol. LIX, 877-895.

the general manager of the Standard Cattle Company in 1884, "that the history of this business records *no cases of failure* where reasonable care has been bestowed, together with the employment of capital adequately proportioned to the volume of business carried on." [211]

The gospel of Babbitt in 1884 became the book of lamentations in 1886 and 1887.

An offer of the J. M. Carey cattle ranch in the Territory of Wyoming in June, 1882, for $525,000 affords a valuation of the property of a successful cattleman. The 20,000 cattle running on the Casper Range, another herd of 2,000 on Horse Creek and bearing the CY brand, and the branded and unbranded calves of these herds were listed. About 200 saddle horses, ranch implements, wagons, mules, machinery, 600 acres of land, range rights, and good will were included in the offer. One half in cash was asked, $100,000 after the next sale of the beef cattle, and the balance in one and two years with interest at ten per cent. Or, in lieu of this the vendor was willing to take $500,000 in cash and one-sixth of the stock in a cattle company with $600,000 capital. In November the property, somewhat augmented in the number of cattle, was priced for sale at $750,000. [212]

In March, 1884, the inventory of Carey and Brother showed 32,287 cattle and 436 horses. The expected calf brand was 7,500 "which can be sold as fast as they are dropped at $20 a head." In two years, it was expected, the annual calf brand would be 12,000 and the dividend

211 Copy of article by A. T. Babbitt on "The Grazing Interest and the Beef Supply," dated March 10, 1884, and found in the Bancroft Library, California. See also *supra* note 10.

212 Letters of J. M. Carey to P. E. Frederick at Cheyenne, dated June 28, 1882, and to Kent and Arnold at Cheyenne dated November 10, 1882, in *Carey Letter Book*, vol. II, 259-261, 300-303.

return from twelve to sixteen per cent. "We will take for the herd, horses, ranches, equipments & good will $1,200,000." [213]

The sale of a fine group of ranches in western Nebraska in 1883 was the beginning of the Nebraska Land and Cattle Company, Limited, a British corporation. For some years two Irishmen, John F. and Mark M. Coad, had been acquiring land and cattle as well as enjoying good profits near Scotts Bluffs and on Pumpkin Creek. Mark was the active overseer on the range and among the stock, but his brother, remaining in Cheyenne, devoted his talents to the cash books and ledgers of the partnership. The contract of sale drafted by himself is a credit to his business acumen.[214] The document is a type of the agreements by which scores of ranch holdings became converted into the assets of cattle corporations.

The Nebraska Land and Cattle Company agreed to pay for the properties the sum of $912,852.82 of which three installments of $200,000 each were to be paid within three months after the date of the contract. The balance was to be secured to Coad Brothers by a mortgage to bear six per cent interest and to mature on December 1, 1887. Proceeds from the sales of cattle and moneys received (but not paid on the installments) from the sales of capital stock or debentures of the cattle company were to be applied towards the liquidation of the mortgage.

Ten pastures were listed in the inventory of which Coad Brothers held title to 527 acres, titles to other land

[213] J. M. Carey to Alexander B. Davis, March 14, 1884, in *Carey Letter Book*, vol. III, 272.

[214] The contract dated March 30, 1883, is in possession of John F. Coad's son, Attorney Ralph C. Coad, of Omaha.

were in process of being obtained, and to four enclosed pastures aggregating about nine townships they held only a possessory title. To this total of about 56,000 acres was listed "a large open and unenclosed ranche with almost unlimited boundaries and located on and south of Pumpkin Creek."

The cattle transferred numbered 21,829 "as shown by the records of the same." The balance of the personal property – 180 saddle horses, wagons, work horses, saddles, machinery, 1,000 tons of hay, cooking stoves and camp kits, and an assortment of blacksmith and carpenter tools – indicates the general type of equipment for ranches in the first years of the eighties.

During the life of the mortgage John F. Coad was to be the "general manager" of the "ranche" at a salary of $5,000 a year. The contract vested him with full power in the management and control of the property except that he was not permitted to sell in any one year more than $225,000 worth of cattle. At every stage the contract amply protected the interests of Coad Brothers in a transaction, which, if made three years later, would likely not have amounted to more than $300,000.

The pioneer cattlemen labored in the golden and profitable age of ranching – an age which knew little of Texas fever, illegal fencing, overcrowded pastures, and such destructive storms as later marked the eighties. It was a period of individual or joint ownerships and partnerships. Astonished at the great profits, foreign and American travellers made impressive reports. The terms "enormous profits," "pastoral marvels," "cattle kings," "cattle barons," and the "beef bonanza" created optimistic legends – legends which, during the tragedies of the range, had a greater power of survival than had the cattlemen and their herds.

With the shrinking of the areas of virgin pastures more land and more capital were required. Capitalists, investors, managers, book counts, stockholders, boards of directors, dividends, loans, shares, debentures, and cattle corporations – such became the language of the range cattle business. With most of these terms Iliff and many other pioneer cattlemen were not familiar. The words indicate the transition from the old order – the change from individual ownership and management to the advent of big business on the plains. It is safe to say that during the seventies Iliff spent more hours in the saddle at round-ups and brandings than many officials of cattle companies in the eighties spent at the Cheyenne Club.

Not many records remain of the numerous cattle companies incorporated in every territory and state of the cow country. Their ledgers, tally books, contracts, and cash books too often disappeared during the bad management and the disasters on the plains as did also their shares and dividends. Not many managers or officials in cattle corporations preserved documents and records for those years when they and thousands of investors reaped little except financial losses.

Methods in finances and illustrations in management have, however, been preserved in the history of the Union Cattle Company incorporated in 1883 in the Territory of Wyoming with a capital stock of $3,000,000 in 30,000 shares.[215] Two directors – William C. Lane

---

[215] *Corporation Record* (in office of county clerk, Laramie county, Wyo.), vol. XIX, 53, 54.

and Thomas Sturgis – were from Cheyenne but the directors contributing most of the capital were Boston men. Like so many other companies its beginnings were years of hope and optimism. But in October, 1886, the directors voted to issue 1,400 bonds of the denomination of $1000. By the terms of the indenture made with the International Trust Company of Boston the debentures were payable in ten years, bore seven per cent interest, and were to be retired by an annual sinking fund.

Storms and winter losses came during the next season and by January, 1888, the company claimed to be insolvent. A petition of that month to the district court of Laramie county signed by the leading stockholders and creditors asked for the appointment of a receiver. The petition recited the heavy winter losses of cattle, the fall in prices, the lack of confidence in business, and the inability of the company to raise money. The court was asked to appoint a receiver who should protect the creditors, carry on the business, and wind up its affairs. Accordingly, Judge Jacob B. Blair on January 17, 1888, appointed Gorham B. Goodall and Frederick P. Vorhees as receivers with respective salaries of $5,000 and $4,000.

The five year receivership of this company exhibits the economics and finances of an extensive ranching property during the years when the old range system was passing. The receivers' papers contain a mass of reports, inventories, accounts, certificates, vouchers, and a great variety of claims. In motions, petitions, affidavits, orders, and various other legal documents are also recorded the varied interests and the obligations of the Union Cattle Company.[216]

---

[216] The detailed history of the receivership is in the office of the clerk of the court, Laramie county, Wyoming, doc. 4, no. 436. The title of the action

Properties in twenty-seven different localities in Nebraska and in the territories of Dakota and Wyoming appeared in the receivers' inventory, besides houses, barns, machinery, tools, grain, provisions, corrals, fencing, harness, and other equipment. Various herds of cattle numbering in all 18,994 were valued at $430,653; the 540 "cow horses," the 42 work horses, and the 47 mules were priced at about $36,000; a miscellaneous assortment of hay and posts was put at $5,700; and the stock held and owned by the company in the Goshen Hole Irrigation Company, the owner of 31,173 acres of land, was placed at $575,000. The balance obtained by deducting all liabilities from the assets of $1,533,000 was $180,000. The expense of carrying on the business for the year was estimated at nearly $34,000. This included taxes, provisions, office expense in Cheyenne, the cost of the labor, feed, machinery and repairs for an irrigation outfit, and the wages for handling cattle on the various ranges.

But meanwhile some of the debentures issued in 1886 had become due and were unpaid. By the trust agreement the company was prohibited from raising funds by placing any lien or mortgage on the property. The marketable steers had been sold before the receivership but the younger steers were not yet ready for the market. From time to time the court permitted the receivers, therefore, to issue receivers' certificates. These bore interest at seven and nine per cent and were sold in series by Lee, Higginson, and Company of Boston.

Numerous reports by the receivers for the first two years show continued expenditures, little income, but

was, Jared Whitman, Alexander Agassiz, Quincy A. Shaw, Edward Page, Henry L. Higginson, Thos. Sturgis, Jr., F. K. Sturgis, Isaac Hinckley, William White, Ephraim Whitman, plaintiffs vs. Union Cattle Company, def.

steady progress on the various ranches. Two capable foremen at an annual salary of $1,500 each were employed. On the Fox Creek Ranch Foreman W. H. Ashby's vouchers for 1888 showed an expenditure for the first three months of $1,384 for the work of 14 cowboys. In July wages for 25 cowboys amounted to $801.15. In August 30 cowboys received $1,004 and in September 28 were paid $892. On the Beaver Creek Ranch, the foreman, E. F. Hall, employed in April, 1888, 11 cowboys whose wages were $419.50. This number rose during the summer up to 33 in September and the wages to $1,025. In October 31 men were employed on the Cheyenne River Range for $1,044, but in December this number was reduced to 6 who were paid $310. The highest wages went to the cowboys who were employed most of the year, but the temporary help – the floating cowboys – rarely received more than $50 per month.

But many other expenditures appear in the foremen's vouchers. Round-up expenses, transportation, seed, taxes, tools, repairs, advertising rewards for cattle thieves, recording deeds, and salaries made up some of the disbursements. In one month the provisions for the Cheyenne River Range outfit cost $731 and in two months $344 worth of provisions were consumed by the cowboys on the Fox River Ranch. Another careful voucher for $.25 was for "expenses on branding iron."

Outside of the receipts from the sale of receivers' certificates only rather small sums were added to the working capital. The sales of fencing, hay and hides, rents from various properties, and the occasional sale of old cows and bulls, strays, and ponies helped the Union Cattle Company during the lean years of the receivership.

However, balances were increasing as were the calf brands. Receivers' certificates were being paid. In March, 1890, the inventory showed nearly 31,000 cattle. Of these the sale of 6,792 that season brought in $119,544. In 1891 the 9,624 cattle marketed sold at $151,691. In October the receivers announced their belief that $168,000 could be distributed in dividends. Accordingly, in November, the court ordered the distribution of a dividend in that amount to the creditors of the defendant, the Union Cattle Company.

Meanwhile the resignation of Goodall had left Vorhees as the receiver in charge. Encouraged by a successful year and good sales he urged the court to order a second dividend. Judge Richard H. Scott, therefore, on December 9, 1892, ordered that $153,927.53 be distributed as the final dividend. The 5,750 shares of the Goshen Hole Irrigation Company were prorated among the creditors – one receiving nearly 1,400 shares and another as low as .30 of a share. Certain creditors petitioned to be permitted to participate in dividends on the bonds issued during the receivership and held by them as collateral security for the bonds of the company. This motion was, however, denied by Judge Scott as well as by the supreme court of the territory.[217] By another order of January 24, 1893, the receivership was terminated and the receiver and his bondsmen discharged.

A study of the thirty-five creditors reveals but little financing with western money and is further evidence of the dependence of cattle companies upon money from the East. "In the early eighties," wrote a banker of long experience on the cattle ranges, "the banks knew little

217 3 Wyoming 803.

about this range business. There was a glamour about it. Once a year the cattle owner deposited a big wad of money. He generally paid his debts and had a balance left. That was the old style, but as the business extended, as men saw opportunity, great properties were accumulated and the advent of the Easterners and British led on to great inflation in prices of ranch property."

Among the creditors of the Union Cattle Company were two banks and three trust companies of New England. Representative Henry Cabot Lodge, more conversant with bay state politics than with range financing, had loaned $15,000 to the company in 1887 which was paid with interest in the first dividend. In the second distribution his dividend was $1,791 and 66 shares in the Goshen Hole Irrigation Company. Jared and Ephraim Whitman were other creditors from Boston. Gorham B. Goodall and his ranch foreman, W. H. Ashby, were western men and smaller lenders to the company. A note for $50,000 dated 1887 was held by eastern men, H. H. and Joseph S. Fay. Over $60,000 was owed to Lee, Higginson, and Company of Boston.

Another creditor, Henry L. Higginson, was from Boston as was Quincy A. Shaw who held open cash accounts, bonds, and notes to the extent of over $368,000. To their brother-in-law, Alexander Agassiz, the great scientist of Harvard University, the company was indebted for cash advanced from bonds, on which the two dividends entitled him to over $52,000. But the wealth he and Shaw had already extracted from the Michigan copper mines was vastly more, and, any losses suffered by Alexander Agassiz in the Union Cattle Company, did not curtail his gifts of a million dollars to his university.

But the dividends distributed were not enough to

repay the loss of shares and unpaid dividends on them. The receivership had undoubtedly secured for the Union Cattle Company a more careful and responsible management. But like scores of other cattle corporations it could not survive the storm and the changing methods on a disappearing cattlemen's frontier.

Illegal Fencing on the Western Range

Illegal Fencing on the Western Range

Upon the vast plains of the trans-Mississippi West took place the great struggles for the last of the free lands in the decade beginning with 1880. The disappearance of Indian dangers, the completion of transcontinental railways, a lavish land policy, and the spreading immigration of land seekers severely strained the federal government in its administration of the public domain. The inclosure of government lands by vested interests was only one of the illegal and fraudulent methods of appropriating lands during this restless decade. The public domain was sinned against by both opposing groups – the great cattle companies or ranchmen and the small ranchmen and farmers. And federal officials and agents denounced about equally the illegal fencing of the cattlemen and the speculation, fraud, and illegal entries which flourished during the invasion of the settler armies.

Alert to the evils of illegal inclosures and not deaf to the protests against them, Commissioner N. C. McFarland of the general land office in 1882 announced that the illegal fences had become matters of "serious complaint." An increasing volume of letters from settlers and the reports by officers and agents of his office showed the great extent of the inclosed areas and the promise of "future serious trouble." Laws in some states, in levying a tax on inclosures, had tended to give local "possessory rights" to the fencers but not any right of entry to the great acres hemmed in by barbed-wire fences.[218]

The commissioner, however, hesitated to recommend the removal of the fences. By an old law of 1807 [219] the president could direct the marshal of the district to take down the fences. But the tearing down of hundreds of miles of wire could not be done with orders, or subpoenas, or stern proclamations. Three decisions of the supreme court [220] a few years before had had the effect of turning over large tracts of land to those who might want them and of giving the right of holding them against the United States or persons claiming under the government. And, if the land were in the possession of another who had made improvements the right of preëmption could not again be exercised upon this area. Settlers, however, could not understand the refinements of court decisions and, while McFarland was pondering and debating, they continued to gaze through the barbed-wire fences and their protesting letters accumulated in his office.

A long letter from Bent county, Colorado, early in 1882,[221] described how most of the assumed rights to lands were obtained. A cattleman employing a large number of cowboys instructed them to put a few boards on a quarter section and then file upon it. After the required time had elapsed they would swear to a residence and to full conformity to the law. These fraudu-

---

[218] *Annual Report of the Commissioner of the General Land Office for 1882,* 13, 14.

[219] *U.S. Statutes at Large,* vol. II, 445.

[220] Atherton *vs.* Fowler, 6 Otto 513; Hosmer *vs.* Wallace, 7 Otto 575; Trenmouth *vs.* San Francisco, 10 Otto 251.

[221] Francis E. Boyd, dated February 12, 1882, in U.S. Senate *Executive Documents,* 48th congress, first session, no. 127, vol. VI, 36-39.

lent patents were then deeded directly or through a third party to the employer. Not one in fifty complied with the spirit and intent of the law. Fictitious names were used and, continued this letter, "cases can be proved where parties so employed to swear to fraudulent residence, improvements, etc., who received and deeded over their lands, that have openly stated 'not only did they not *know* where their claims were,' but that 'they had never even *seen* them.'"

Wholesale purchases of such patents were then fenced in. One party began to inclose a tract of land forty miles long. Travel was diverted from a public road and the fence was persistently cut but repeatedly repaired. The owner of the fence even threatened to "turn the travel even if it takes $10,000 to do it." The prevailing feeling, complained the letter, was that it would be a waste of time and money to apply to the land office at Pueblo for redress.

Commissioner McFarland in 1883 again reviewed the growing evils of the illegal inclosure of huge pastures. His circular in April reminded the cattlemen that they were not allowed to fence in public lands and thus withdraw them from the settlement laws. The interior department, he pointed out, would not object to the destruction of these fences by *bona fide* settlers who might be prevented by barriers, threats, or force from lawfully acquiring lands. The notice was widely distributed by land officials and by special agents over the grazing districts.[222]

"Some morning," grimly warned the *Wyoming Sentinel,* "we will wake up to find that a corporation has run

[222] *Annual Report of the Commissioner of the General Land Office for 1883,* 30, 31.

a wire fence about the boundary lines of Wyoming, and all within the same have been notified to move." John Willits and Sons of Kingman county, Kansas, informed McFarland that they had been pioneering with a few milch cows in the Chicaskia river where they hoped to work into ranching. But all government land, they protested, "is likely to be taken from us by a company fencing the whole thing, which we don't like, you may bet." [223]

John Fleming's sheep ranch near the American Falls in the Territory of Idaho was close to that of a cattleman who claimed a range fifteen miles square. There men rode the range armed with rifles which they threatened to use if the sheepmen entered what the cattleman called his range. "A few days ago while driving on along the public highway I met in congress with five cowboys, and before the chaplain had time to offer prayer, the speaker commenced pounding me over the head with a large six-shooter, exclaiming at the same time, 'Move from my range today or I'll see that you do it tomorrow,' at the same time pointing his revolver at me." [224]

A few rich cattlemen, reported another settler at Huerfano, Colorado, had fenced in with barbed wire nearly all the government land. Their cattle grazed outside the inclosures until the grass was short and were then driven into the "monstrous pastures." The settlers gave up or sold out, their stock starved, and the settlers left their homes. Lands were preëmpted without houses, fences, cultivation, or any other improvements. From

<hr>

[223] U.S. Senate *Executive Documents*, 48th congress, first session, no. 127, vol. VI, 13, 18, containing letters of Posey S. Wilson to H. M. Teller, dated January 4, 1883, and of John Willits and Sons, dated January 6, 1883.

[224] *Idem*, 26, for letter of John Fleming to the secretary of the interior, dated January 8, 1883.

Fort Lupton in the same state another farmer wrote that the sheepmen were hemmed in by great fences, and while the cattlemen took the "cream" the sheep had to be driven back to the bleak hills for their food. The sheep interests of the state were suffering likewise by the inclosing of large bodies of land along the water courses.[225]

On the Musselshell Range in the Territory of Montana twenty cattle firms in 1883 declared the range already overstocked. "Therefore we positively decline allowing any outside parties or any parties locating herds upon this range the use of our corrals, nor will they be permitted to join us in any round-up from and after this date." [226]

A government mail carrier reported that in the Loup River Valley of Custer county, Nebraska, were large cattle ranges inclosing hundreds of acres of government lands with barbed wire and disregarding section or even township lines. "I must drive through such gates as they choose to put, in order to get to the post office; having often to leave unruly horses to open an[d] shut their so-called gates in all sorts of weather." [227]

From Plattsmouth, Nebraska, Deputy-surveyor George W. Fairfield in 1883 charged that the whole country included in his contract was "run by and occupied by capitalists." [228] Desirable lands and water

---

[225] *Idem*, 29, 30, for letters of B. A. Arnold dated February 17, 1883, and N. Weare dated March 31, 1883, to the secretary of the interior.

[226] *Idem*, 22.

[227] Letter dated April 23, 1883, submitted by Postmaster-general Walter I. Gresham to Secretary of the Interior Henry M. Teller, and found in the office of the commissioner of the general land office, Washington, D.C.

[228] Letter to Surveyor-general D. V. Stephenson, dated November 26, 1883, in U.S. House *Executive Documents*, 48th congress, first session, no. 119, vol. XXVI, part ii, 3.

courses were inclosed by wire fences. Settlers were "frozen out" and the cattlemen refused to employ any settlers or claimants to lands. Notices were posted frequently bearing vile, canine names and warning anyone opening the fence to "look out for his scalp." Fairfield also reported the wholesale destruction of timber, and thousands of logs were cut and hauled for the building of fences, corrals, branding chutes, and houses in Nebraska and the Territory of Wyoming.

Heavily armed with such complaints and information special agents of the general land office now visited the great inclosed pastures of the plains. Travelling over great spaces and everywhere meeting the hostility of the fencers of the public lands these agents, nevertheless, assembled data and descriptions for the great grazing areas. Colorado and Nebraska were the regions especially examined in 1883, doubtless in response to the unusually large number of complaints from those areas.

Special-agent F. D. Hobbs made a detailed report [229] on the Brighton Ranch in Keith county, Nebraska. For two and three-quarter hours his horses travelled at a steady trot after entering a gate and before arriving at the other line of the inclosure. Virgil Allyn, the manager, stated that the Brighton Ranch Company controlled fifty entries or 7,000 acres. The fencing extended for eleven miles one way and from twelve to fifteen the other. The entire area, reported the agent, comprised 125,000 acres and "they are still fencing."

Manager Allyn had sworn before a special agent in May, 1883, that the lands inclosed were unproductive and "valueless for agricultural purposes and only fit

[229] Letters to Commissioner N. C. McFarland dated June 29, July 7, and October 23, 1883, and printed in *idem,* no. 127, vol. VI, 4-12.

for stock and cattle raising." But Special-agent Hobbs contradicted this with a heavy package of affidavits and with his own statement that "he saw as fine crops in the South Loup Valley as in any other part of the state." The ranch itself had harvested a fine crop of millet and one man in 1880 had cut, raked, and bunched four tons of hay on the government land. This hay had been summarily seized by the Brighton Ranch Company. Eber Barber, another farmer, after cutting two tons of hay in the pasture attempted to haul it out but "Virgil Allen and his brother William ordered him to turn the teams back, and with club and pistol they drove him back, and Allen afterwards caused the hay to be hauled off for his own use."

Allyn had insisted that his inclosures were not to keep settlers out. But why, asked the agent, has he inclosed 125,000 acres for 6,000 head of stock when 24,000 acres are considered ample for grazing that number? Two settlers with a few hundred head of stock had homesteaded some lands with a view to securing a grazing outlet to the hills. Allyn caused one of his cowboys to make a homestead along the line of the bluffs and then built a fence which completely shut out the two farmers.

Fraudulent entries aggregating 3,200 acres inclosed by Allyn were revealed by the minute inspections of the agent. Names were lacking, one entryman was a boy, others did not comply with the law, and other applications contained the names of persons who had never made homestead entries. Each of these entries was directly traceable to Allyn, "fraudulent at their inception or one held without compliance of the law, and are consequently proper subjects for cancellation."

But names of other big fenced pastures appear in

Hobbs's reports. Great bales of wire were being hauled to the Kennebeck Ranch near the Brighton Ranch and "two gangs of men" were preparing to inclose 20,000 acres. The fenced ranch of M. C. Keith of North Platte in Nebraska embraced 12,000 acres: the inclosure ran along the Union Pacific Railway line and a public road had "generously" been left between the railway and the fence. Another firm west of Custer county owned twenty miles of fence and still farther west Coe, Carter, and Company, it was reported, had put in fifty miles of fence. The Rankin Live Stock Company west or north of Custer county had purchased $5,000 worth of fencing material. One Charles O'Rourke had made a homestead in the pasture of 3,500 acres inclosed by Ira Nichols and located in Lincoln county, but "being a man of some pluck and intelligence, he proposed to stay in spite of threats." In a sale of ranch property by Coad Brothers in western Nebraska in 1883 the inventory listed four inclosed pastures of which one, the "main pasture," contained about 143,000 acres "to which Coad Brothers have no title except a possessory title or right thereto." [230]

Diagrams, descriptions, denunciations – all are contained in the reports of special agents to examine illegal fences in Colorado. John White was closing up both ends of Mancos Canyon to prevent both egress or ingress of settlers. The Carlisle Cattle Company, it was reported, was inclosing large ranges in the western part of the state. C. W. Sanborn reported that stockmen were fencing in private individuals who did not have the means to stock their inclosed lands and even leasing

[230] Contract of sale between Coad Brothers and the Nebraska Land and Cattle Company, dated March 30, 1883. In possession of Attorney Ralph C. Coad of Omaha.

their illegally fenced estate to reap profits. Forty-three firms were named whose inclosures ranged from a minimum of 2,000 acres to areas of 1,000,000 acres. One-half of the stockmen, he estimated, wanted the ranges thus fenced thrown open. "Some fenced to protect themselves, but are willing and anxious to take their fences down." [231]

The vast fences of the Arkansas Valley Land and Cattle Company, Limited, were described in the reports of Edwin S. Bruce.[232] The predecessor of this company had been A. S. Holly & Company, which since 1880 had been inclosing thousands of acres in Bent county, Colorado, along the Arkansas river. By a regular system of fraudulent or incomplete preëmptions of quarter sections many thousands of acres had been embraced in their inclosures. All the lands and holdings were sold to the Arkansas Valley Land and Cattle Company on September 15, 1882. The post and wire fences were then extended until the company held 600,000 acres or thirty townships of the public domain, on the north side of the Arkansas river. With a board of directors of aggressive Englishmen the company established its headquarters at Holly's Station. It divided its pastures for winter and for summer grazing for its 30,000 cattle. But the stock of small farmers and ranchmen could only gaze wistfully through the barbed inclosures upon the grassy estates of this corporation.

[231] James L. McDowell, August 4, 1883, Jesse L. Pritchard, August, 1883, C. W. Sanborn, September 29, 1883, to Commissioner N. C. McFarland in U.S. House *Executive Documents*, 48th congress, first session, no. 127, vol. VI, 27, 29, 38.

[232] William T. Holt, August 10, 1883, and Edwin S. Bruce, July 23, November 1, 1883, and January 2, 1884, to Commissioner N. C. McFarland in *idem*, 38-41.

A settler with ten years of experience in stock raising wrote from Denver to supplement the reports from the special agents.[233] He pointed out that but three courses were open: to permit the stockmen to fence their own ranges, to have the "monster fences" removed, or to get out of the stock business. "The worst of the trouble," he explained, "comes not so much from the curtailment of the public range and its unfair monopoly for benefit of a few persons (often foreign corporations) as from the heavy losses entailed on stock outside these fences during the winter months by reason of all the water, for miles, being fenced up, and because the long lines of fencing of ten to forty miles at a stretch, prevent the cattle from seeking water elsewhere, and also from moving on in case of a storm to seek their accustomed shelter. Hundreds of cattle thus perish miserably every winter from thirst and famine, and exposure to storms and cold 'northers' (against which they will not turn back) wholly because of this illegal fencing."

By June, 1884, thirty-two cases of illegal fencing involving 4,431,980 acres had been examined – more than double the combined areas of Delaware and Rhode Island. Secretary Teller stated that the office force for this work was inadequate: accurate surveys were necessary to examine the "immense tracts," many of which contained several thousand acres; additional money was also required to carry on the inspections because a single agent with necessary outfit, surveyors, chainmen, flagman, and teams required an outlay of $650. In the general land office division "P" the special service division was created. Its squadron of twenty-five special agents

233 William T. Holt to Commissioner N. C. McFarland, dated August 10, 1883, in *idem*, 33, 34.

was then detailed to scrutinize "that pursuit of lands [which] has become a headlong race, overturning the slight obstacles of the settlement laws, and trampling under foot the slighter attempts, heretofore devised, of administrative regulation." [234]

More and more posts and barbed wire were put up in 1884 and the reports of special agents bore more proofs as well as more indignation.[235] Near Garden City in Kansas ranchmen were employing men to file upon and to prove up claims which were then sold to the cattlemen. In other cases a bonus of $50 was payable to the settler upon transfer and assignment of the land to the cattlemen. In Las Animas county, Colorado, Mexicans preëmpted lands, claiming settlement five years back. In six weeks or two months final homestead proofs were made and the lands transferred to cattlemen who were then ready to inclose the areas. The cunning of such practice as well as its extent baffled the agents of the land offices.

In Kansas, reported one agent, each herder was required to make a timber culture entry along streams. All the watering-places in a township were then occupied and the other areas thus rendered undesirable for settlement. If *bona fide* settlers were already on the ground they were "bought off or scared off" and fences were then extended.

"It seems to me," ran an inspector's report in describing such wholesale frauds by settlers and cattlemen, "there should be some way to distinguish between a fire

[234] *Report of the Secretary of the Interior for 1884*, vol. I, 17. *Annual Report of the Commissioner of the General Land Office for 1885*, 79.

[235] Report of register and receiver at Garden City, Kansas, November 30, 1884, and at Pueblo, Colorado, November 15, 1884, in *Annual Report of the Commissioner of the General Land Office for 1885*, 55-60.

guard of a few furrows placed around a quarter section
and a cornfield – some way to determine whether a description of a house '14x16' referred to inches or feet
square; whether the floor was *bored* or *board,* and
whether the 'shingle roof' meant more than two shingles,
one on each side."

The best lands, continued his indictments, are controlled by men who have no interest in the development
of the country, evade taxation, and in many cases owe
no allegiance to laws or government. They possess abundant physical power to enforce their schemes of spolia-
tion and to defy local people and authorities. "Settlers
avoid such localities as they would districts stricken
with the plague, and the tide of immigration turns back
to publish and magnify the evil." [236]

Insistent demands from settlers and the recommenda-
tions of the general land office could not stop the fencing
of the public lands nor could the damaging evidence of
the special agents prevent or even remove the barriers.
But by the federal law of February 25, 1885, the construction and maintenance of inclosures on the public
lands were forbidden. District attorneys were required
to institute suits and cases involving fencing were to be
given precedence on the court docket. Violators of the
law were subject to imprisonment for not more than one
year and a fine of $1000 for each offense. The president
was empowered to employ civil or military force if
necessary to remove or destroy such fences. Following
this law the proclamation of the president on August 7
ordered all unlawful inclosures to be removed and for-

[236] Inspector A. R. Greene to Commissioner N. C. McFarland, dated November 3, 1884, in *idem,* 50-53.

WESTERN FARMER RUNNING THE "FIRE GUARD"
From a contemporary sketch drawn by Theodore R. Davis in 1868.

bade any threats or intimidation against actual settlers on the public lands.[237]

An imposing array of names and figures on illegal inclosures was gathered by special agents and published in the annual reports of the interior department.[238] Although by no means complete or accurate, the facts portray in prosaic form the great struggle of the ranchmen for the immense pasture lands of the West. Of the 193 cases of illegal fencing brought to the attention of the general land office in 1885 about 130 were located in 12 counties of Colorado. The Prairie Cattle Company was listed with 1,000,000 acres inclosed and the Arkansas Valley Land and Cattle Company with 553,000. In the Territory of New Mexico 3,000,000 acres were "reported closed."

Prosecutions began not long after the passage of the law of 1885 against fencing. It was a laborious process to secure the locations and the descriptions for the miles and miles of fencing. Pages and pages described the fences in the bill of complaint against the Arkansas Valley Land and Cattle Company. The corporation made no defense against the bill and on June 10, 1885, Judge Moses B. Hallett of the circuit court of the United States for the district of Colorado, issued decrees for the abatement and removal of the fences from two of its pastures.[239]

By four similar decrees on the same day Judge Hallett ordered the removal and abatement of the fences from four pastures of the Prairie Cattle Company. Although

---

[237] *U. S. Statutes at Large*, vol. XXIII, 321-322, vol. XXIV, 1024.

[238] *Report of the Secretary of the Interior for 1885*, 470-473.

[239] *Records of the Circuit Court of the United States for the District of Colorado* (Denver), cases 1666, 1677.

the company did not defend in the action, the bill of complaint was burdened with long descriptions and maps and diagrams. The "Anderson Pasture" on Purgatory river was an inclosure of 23,500 acres; the "East Pasture" on the "J J Ranch" 2,400 acres; the "West Pasture" on the "J J Ranch" 1,200 acres; and the fourth inclosure was the "Portray Pasture" of 10,883 acres.[240] If suits had been instituted for every case of inclosure the courts would have staggered under the burden of litigation.

Another array of figures on illegal fencing came in 1886.[241] By October 375 cases had been brought to the notice of the general land office which involved 6,410,595 acres. The agents secured the removal of fences in many cases and in 13 court decrees over 1,000,000 acres were restored to the public domain. Nowhere were the agents and courts more active than in Colorado in the work of unfencing the great pastures. Only the lack of available agents had prevented the prosecution of the work in other areas.

But a new device for holding or controlling the ranges appeared at once. This was the incorporation of irrigation or ditch companies which could divert streams from their natural beds and thus obtain the exclusive use of watersheds and water for the cattle. Two weeks after the enactment of the law against fencing, the Goshen Hole Irrigation Company, some of whose trustees were stockholders of the Union Cattle Company, was formed in the Territory of Wyoming. It was given power to divert water from Fox Creek, Box Elder Creek, Cherry Creek, Mountain Lion Creek, and other streams.[242]

240 *Idem*, cases 1682, 1683, 1684, 1685.
241 *Annual Report of the Commissioner of the General Land Office for 1886*, 97, 455-464.
242 *Corporation Record* (Laramie county, Wyo.), vol. XIX, 311-318.

In May, 1886, a special agent reported that Pratt and Ferris by their articles of incorporation were appropriating all the water of Rawhide Creek, a stream about forty-five miles long in the Territory of Wyoming. By tapping the stream above their legitimate holdings a large area was rendered too arid for settlement purposes. The effect, explained the agent, was to prevent settlement and thereby insure an exclusive right to an immense grazing area. Similar practice was reported on the Crazy Woman and other creeks in the territory as well as on the Little Missouri and Belle Fourche rivers in Dakota.[243]

Seven million acres involving 465 illegal inclosures appear in the tables of the land office report for 1887 of which over 200 were in Colorado. Secretary of the Interior Lamar reported the progress of suits and also removals completed or in process, with the hopeful comment, "It is apparent that this wholesale appropriation of the public domain is a thing of the past." But more protests in 1888 and the industry of special agents caused the office to publish a list of 531 inclosures for 7,224,070 acres of the public domain in 15 states and territories. By the next year, however, voluntary removals, suits, and the persuasion of special agents greatly reduced the number and extent of illegal fences. Only 42 cases for the 418,000 acres inclosed remained on the docket of the general land office in 1889.[244]

Mr. John Clay nearly forty years later and after long experience in range finances deplored in his *My Life on the Range* the policy of the government against fenc-

<hr>

[243] *Annual Report of the Commissioner of the General Land Office for 1886*, 471, 472.

[244] *Annual Report of the Commissioner of the General Land Office for 1887*, 457-466; for 1888, 361-375; for 1889, 275-280.

ing semi-arid lands intended by nature for grazing. Settlers in the Sand Hills of Nebraska and on the gumbo lands north of Belle Fourche in South Dakota abandoned or sold their lands which then reverted to grazing areas. The West, unable to make use of its vast regions of semi-arid lands, was like a giant, prostrate and unable to rise. "Where you allow a settler to take up 640 acres and he disturbs the grazing in 6,400, where is the gain?" [245]

More emphatic had been the lament in 1884 of an old Texas cattle trail captain in recalling the open range of a decade earlier.[246] "In those days there was no fencing along the trails to the North, and we had lots of range to graze on." Fences and farmers had reduced the trail to a crooked path. Farms, inclosed pastures, and fenced-in water-holes were charged against farmers from Ohio, Indiana, and other states – invaders called by the politicians "the bone and sinew of the country."

"D–n such bone and sinew!" concluded the old trail driver. "They are the ruin of the country, and have everlastingly, eternally, now and forever, destroyed the best grazing-land in the world. The range country, sir, was never intended for raising farm-truck. It was intended for cattle and horses, and was the best stock-raising land on earth until they got to turning over the sod – improving the country, as they call it. Lord forgive them for such improvements! It makes me sick to think of it. I am sick enough to need two doctors, a druggery, and a mineral spring, when I think of onions and Irish potatoes growing where mustang ponies should be exercising, and where four-year-old steers should be get-

---

[245] Clay, *My Life on the Range*, chap. XXXVIII.
[246] Quoted in *Prose and Poetry of the Live Stock Industry*, 686.

ting ripe for market. Fences, sir, are the curse of the country!"

In the settlement of the trans-Missouri West the individual settler meant more than the corporation; his plow was of greater promise than a cattleman's fence; land office records contain more of constructive pioneering than the books of corporations that fenced. The thousands of plain settler folk constituted a greater asset than the non-resident shareholders of cattle companies; the great fences could never remain deeply fixed in the soil; only to citizens did the government give quarter sections but for years foreign corporations with alien shareholders inclosed and appropriated kingdoms. It was right and necessary that the era of free grass and fences should pass. "But," wrote Theodore Roosevelt,[247] "the homesteaders, the permanent settlers, the men who took up each his own farm on which he lived and brought up his family, these represented from the national standpoint the most desirable of all possible users of, and dwellers on, the soil. Their advent meant the breaking up of the great ranches; and the change was a national gain although to some of us an individual loss."

---

[247] Theodore Roosevelt, *An Autobiography*, 104.

A Decade on the Dakota Ranges

A Decade on the Dakota Ranges

Northerly migrations of cattle frontiers to Kansas, to the territories of Wyoming and Montana, and to Nebraska finally compelled the invasion of the Territory of Dakota. But such migrations were hastened by the discoveries of gold in the Black Hills during the seventies which Colonel R. I. Dodge pointed out as a grazing country which "cannot be surpassed." Gold-seekers, adventurers, freighters, bullwhackers, and stage drivers in crossing the southern plains of the territory saw its virgin grasses. Their reports of the ranges and the water as by-products of their stories of the gold mines helped to usher in the pioneer decade of the range cattle industry in the territory.

The great territory between Mandan and Miles City and between the Missouri river and the Platte divide was one of the last provinces of the West to be invaded by the cowman during the eighties. Captain J. W. Powell's report of his visit in 1875 had also praised the "thick growth of the finest wild grasses" in the Black Hills country of which only 600 square miles were destitute of ranges for stock. In the fall of the next year Erasmus Deffebach and his brother John drove cows costing $15 and steers costing $25 into the Black Hills. Sold for $100 to $125 each the animals provided the roasts and steaks for the swarms of miners and freighters of the gold areas. In 1877 or 1878 the brothers started one of the first ranches in the western part of the territory near the present city of Belle Fourche. Near Spearfish a ranchman named Roads had been tending 175 cattle against the heavy snowfall of March, 1878. In the following year Valentine and William Dickey started the first cattle herd on the Little Missouri river north of Belle Fourche.[248]

Editor Porter Warner of the *Black Hills Daily Times* pointed out the abundant water and especially the bunch grass on which the herds had become "rolling fat." "We are assured that they will need neither hay nor shelter, and that the percentage of loss from exposure will be far less than in Colorado and Wyoming. Large herds are on the way here and before another year passes Dakota, or at least this portion of it, will be one of the great stock sections of the West." [249]

For years various army posts and Indian agencies had been demanding beef. But the stampedes to the new El Dorado of miners, freighters, merchants, and adventurers had opened up new markets. This trade inspired

---

[248] During 1921-1927 Lewis F. Crawford, superintendent of the State Historical Society of North Dakota, secured numerous interviews with former ranchmen and settlers on the Dakota frontier. These unpublished, manuscript interviews are herein referred to as Crawford, *Notes*. Another source by Mr. Crawford is his unpublished article on *The Coming of the Big Cattle Outfits*. See Crawford, *Notes* on interviews with Erasmus Deffebach at Miles City, Montana, December 26, 1923, and G. E. Lemmon at Lemmon, South Dakota, January 7, 1927; Crawford, *The Coming of the Big Cattle Outfits;* the *Black Hills Daily Times,* April 9, 1878; and the *Black Hills Pioneer,* June 1, 1882.

The writer is deeply indebted to his former student, Professor Harold E. Briggs of the University of Miami at Coral Gables, Florida, for permission to consult and to use his extensive notes gathered from the above sources. Of special value and help in the construction of this paper has been his "Ranching and Stock Raising in the Territory of Dakota," in the *South Dakota Historical Collections,* XIV (1928), 417-465, and his "The Development and Decline of Open Range Ranching in the Northwest," in the *Mississippi Valley Historical Review,* XX, 521-536.

[249] *Black Hills Daily Times,* December 1, 1879.

editors to give extravagant praise to the various grasses and feeding grounds of the Dakota plains – a region still witnessing the retreat of the Indians and the disappearance of the buffalo.

On the Box Elder Creek and on the Little Missouri river near Stoneville (now Alzada, Montana) Hughes and J. H. Simpson, owners of the Continental Cattle Company, were starting their "Hash Knife" ranch with cattle trailed up from Texas from which the majority of the cattle of the territory came. Later their "Mill Iron" brand was added. With J. W. Buster as manager, a foreman, and a second foreman their ranches prospered and at one time contained from 35,000 to 40,000 cattle.[250] Most of their young stock was bred in Texas and in the Territory of New Mexico and then driven north to be fattened on the Dakota ranges.

Profits at this time (1880) seemed to warrant the strong optimism then abundant. One rancher with a purchase of 3,250 head of cattle costing $45,400 reported expenses and losses for three years at $8,950 but the profits from sales at the end of that time ran up to $25,800. About this time the "E6" ranch owned by Dorr Clark and Duncan C. Plumb and running from nineteen to twenty thousand cattle was started on the south branch of the Grand river. The "Turkey Track" brand managed by Tony Day of the Creswell Cattle Company browsed on the Jones Creek range west of Hettinger.[251]

A severe test on stock raising came in the cold and prolonged winter of 1880-1881. The stock passing

---

[250] Crawford, *Notes* on interview with G. E. Lemmon of Lemmon, South Dakota, January 7, 1927.

[251] *Black Hills Daily Times,* February 14, 1880; Crawford, *Notes* on interview with Erasmus Deffebach of Miles City, Montana, December 26, 1923; Crawford, *The Coming of the Big Cattle Outfits.*

through suffered the principal losses but cattle adjusted
to the climate showed an endurance that gave renewed
hope to the cattle interests. The year 1882 was a lean
season in cattle migration to the Dakota plains although
in that time the Northern Pacific Railway shipped eastward 1,392 cars [252] of cattle loaded at points east of Miles
City.

"Five years ago," reviewed a Deadwood editor, "the
cattle interests of the West centered along the Union
Pacific Railroad, with ranges extending north only
as far as the North Platte river, and south far into New
Mexico. . . From the Platte to the Yellowstone and
from the confluence of the Belle Fourche and Cheyenne
rivers to the Big Horn mountains is an excellent grazing
district. Valleys rich with nutritious grasses, abundantly
watered and so effectively sheltered that stock could
easily subsist by grazing throughout the entire season." [253]

The Black Hills Live Stock Association fully organized in 1880 advertised its brands in newspapers of
Deadwood and Rapid City.[254] The herds of its members
ranged on the Belle Fourche and Cheyenne rivers and
on Elder, Box Elder, French, Spring, and Battle creeks.
Secretary W. E. Smith offered a reward of $100 to any
person for the detection and conviction of persons who
should drive off or steal range cattle of any members
of this association.

An incomplete list of the holdings of the members
in 1882 gives a picture of the Black Hills stock region.

252 *The* [Huron, S. Dak.] *Tribune,* December 28, 1882; *Black Hills Pioneer,*
June 1, 1882.

253 *Black Hills Pioneer,* June 1, 1882.

254 *Black Hills Pioneer,* June 1, 1882; *Black Hills Journal,* November 13,
1880.

The sixty members were listed with 264,000 cattle valued at $5,000,000. The "R M K" brand of ninety was owned by Rosenbaum and Mankin and located on Hay Creek. The 45,000 bearing the "SG" brand of Sturgis and Goodall ranged on the Cheyenne river. The "E6" brand owned by Dorr Clark and Duncan C. Plumb had trailed its first herd from Sioux City to Valentine, Nebraska, from which it had been moved to its range in the Grand River Valley.[255]

The immense pastures of Lake, Tomb, and Lemmon Cattle Company ran from the Cedar Creek on the north and south about fifty miles to Thunder Butte. Its lands leased from the government at from three to five cents an acre constituted a tract enclosed by about two hundred miles of fence. Its 30,000 cattle were herded by thirty cowboys in summer and by about fifteen in winter. The expenses of operation were about $2.50 per acre. At another ranch near Jordan in the Territory of Montana the company had 12,000 cattle. Its breeding ranch north of El Paso in Texas contributed yearlings to be finished on these northern ranges.[256]

Henry Oelrichs of the Anglo-American Cattle Company ranged about 30,000 cattle on Horse Head Creek in Fall River county. The "O X" brand of W. A. Towers and Gudgell was at the mouth of Beaver Creek on the Little Missouri near Marmouth. The Weare Live Stock Company, in which Marshall Field was interested was located on the Belle Fourche river and managed by Henry G. Weare of Spearfish. The "Diamond C" brand of E. R. Messersmith near the Killdeer mountains on

[255] *Black Hills Pioneer,* June 1, 1882; Crawford, *Notes* on interview with G. E. Lemmon of Lemmon, South Dakota, January 7, 1927.

[256] Crawford, *Notes* on interview with James H. Lemmon, Lemmon, South Dakota, July 12, 1921.

Magpie Creek was sold to the Crosby Cattle Company. Bartlett, Richards, and Comstock were the owners of the "Flying Crow" brand or "Running Water" outfit. The "777" ranch of the Berry, Boice Cattle Company under the management of Henry Boice drove thousands of cattle up from Texas to the Little Missouri between Horse and Deer creeks.[257]

Clark and Plumb's purchase of 1,800 cattle from the Deffebach Brothers had been the beginning of the "E6" brand.[258] Located on the Belle Fourche river six miles from the city of that name this property became the nucleus of the "V V V" brand of the Western Ranches, Limited. "We spent the next three or four days riding over the range," described a visitor of 1882. "My mouth waters when I think of the feed in that region. The bottom lands of the Belle Fourche had grass three feet high, although it was November. It lay in great swaths amid the gigantic groves of cottonwoods, cured as well as the best hay in a stack. The divides were an ocean of surging grass, cropped only by a few cattle and a countless number of antelope." [259]

West of the Clark and Plumb herds were the two brands of William and Valentine Dickey. "What a wondrous country it was for grass!" exclaimed a critical buyer on a visit in 1883. "Away from the bottom lands, up long sweeping valleys to broken bad lands and level divide, there was nothing but grass and more grass, the blue joint with ripening heads, good as corn for fatten-

---

[257] Crawford, *The Coming of the Big Cattle Outfits;* Crawford, *Notes* on interview with G. E. Lemmon of Lemmon, South Dakota, January 7, 1927, on interview with August Beisigl of Lemmon, South Dakota, July 13, 1921.

[258] Crawford, *Notes* on interview with G. E. Lemmon of Lemmon, South Dakota, January 7, 1927.

[259] Clay, *My Life on the Range,* 44, 45.

ing, and mossy stretches of buffalo grass curling closely
to the ground and making unexcelled winter feed, and
then to think in three years from this time this fair land
should be as bare as Sahara!" [260]

Four areas of the territory had now been invaded by
the cattlemen – the Black Hills district, the Little Missouri region, the Souris (or Mouse) River Valley, and
the ranges of the Upper Missouri. To these new pastures
came ranchmen and cattle companies with stock imported from Texas, Missouri, Arkansas, Iowa, Nebraska, Oregon, and from the Territory of Wyoming.
Coming in by drives and by rail shipments the stock
remained for a few years to be matured and then was
moved to the packing centers at St. Paul, Kansas City,
Omaha, and Chicago. Corporations, partnerships, and
individuals representing shareholders and lenders from
far-flung areas were to exploit the grazing areas of the
territory.

Dickinson, platted in 1882, became in the middle
eighties the preëminent cow town [261] and was to the territory what Ogallala in Nebraska, Dodge City in Kansas,
and Cheyenne in the Territory of Wyoming had been
for several years. Dusty trails led to it from Texas and
the Northern Pacific Railway brought to it lean stock
from Iowa and Minnesota. These, after being fattened
on the ranges, were driven back to Mingusville and
Dickinson to be loaded on trains bound for the markets.
To Dickinson came buyers and sellers to bargain over
prices and ranchmen departed from it to seek virgin
pastures. Owners, range managers, foremen, and cow-

[260] *Idem*, 91.

[261] Lewis F. Crawford, "The Medora-Black Hills Stage Line," in *Collections of the State Historical Society of North Dakota*, VII, 309-323; *Dickinson
Press*, files for 1883 and 1884.

boys were visitors; and here congregated bullwhackers, stage drivers, old buffalo hunters, adventurers, and such nameless or forgotten characters as have constituted the lawless men and women of the frontier.

Within a few years Dickinson saw the buffalo frontier crowded out by the cattlemen's frontier and disappear. Texas longhorns browsed on buffalo grass ranges dotted with skeletons and staring skulls of buffalo. Buffalo hunters were already living in the past and cowboys galloped over their old preserves. A train of thirty-four yoke of oxen returned to Dickinson from Deadwood with the wagons loaded with buffalo bones picked up on the return trip. Hunters like Vic Smith still scoured the plains but to Dickinson lean cattle for the ranges or fattened cattle for the markets meant a new order, and the rumble of stock cars was more welcome than the odors from a pile of buffalo hides.

As the number of cattle increased, the buffalo ranges contracted and the slaughter became swifter and more relentless. Loads and loads of buffalo hides and the "mountainous wreckage" of buffalo bones became the mute evidence of the end of the buffalo on the Dakota plains and of their replacement by prosaic cows from Iowa and longhorns from Texas.

> So ends the buffalo. Five years since he tossed
> In great earth-shaking herds his shaggy mane;
> Now not one calf. Once furious bulls did roar
> The challenge moving terribly to fight.
> Dry bones — the price one dollar for a ton.[262]

The Continental Land and Cattle Company with about 30,000 cattle made Dickinson its principal station

---

[262] Edwin Ford Piper, "Dry Bones," in *Barbed Wire and Other Poems*, 3. Reprinted herein by permission of The Macmillan Company.

THE OLD BONE PICKER OF THE PLAINS

From a contemporary sketch drawn by R. F. Zogbaum in 1887.

for eastbound shipments. John N. Simpson, the manager, in a visit to Dickinson declared that the drive to this place was one of the best in the West but remarked that the yards were rather unhandy and too near the town. In this month (September, 1883) 1,000 cattle were shipped and fifteen cars more the next month. The advertisement of the company listed the "Hash Knife" and the "HS" brands and gave St. Louis as the principal place of business. In the next year the company imported 120 pure-blooded bulls from Missouri. Arriving at Dickinson in July of that year from Texas, Simpson made extensive shipments and the local editor estimated that the railway would carry 14,000 of its cattle to the eastern markets that season. A trainload of black steers was sent to the markets in September. By the next month Simpson had sent 7,550 cattle eastward and other herds fattened on the ranges were on the trails to Dickinson to be loaded on the Northern Pacific cars.[263]

Two well-known hunters, E. F. Chase and his brother, in 1883 were locating a range near the Killdeer mountains and were shipping Iowa cattle to Dickinson to be driven to these pastures. Another carload of cattle from Iowa came to Dickinson to be placed on another range near the Killdeer mountains by E. R. Messersmith. Henry G. Weare drove a small herd into Dickinson to be loaded for the eastern markets. Two capitalists from Texas arrived the next spring to locate a new pasture for their herd of 7,000 then on the trail from that state.[264]

Eight cattle firms in 1884 united at Dickinson in offering a reward of $250 for information leading to the

[263] *Dickinson Press,* July 7, September 22, October 27, 1883, June 1, July 5, September 20, October 11, 1884.

[264] *Dickinson Press,* May 6, July 21, September 22, 1883, May 31, 1884.

arrest of any person setting fire to grass on their ranges.
Dorr Clark received at Dickinson twenty bulls from the
East and planned to make it his shipping point for the
season. W. L. Crosby of La Crosse, Wisconsin, made
frequent visits to this cow town on his way to his ranges
near the Killdeer mountains. L. F. Adams, the manager
of the Vermont Cattle Company, was another visitor at
Dickinson and long lines of cars carried fatted cattle
from the Dickey Brothers' ranges, from the Weare Live
Stock Company herds, and from Driskell and Sons'
holdings.[265]

The Northern Pacific agent at Dickinson furnished
figures [266] for shipments from the northern cattle country; 11 cars at Gallatin, 48 at Springdale, 426 from
Billings, 30 from Livingston, 98 from Huntley, 49 from
Custer, 263 from Miles City, 11 from Fallon, 891 from
Mingusville, and 1001 from Dickinson. This outgo was
replaced annually by the calf crops on the ranges and by
importations from surrounding areas and Texas.

Theodore Roosevelt's ranching years on the Little
Missouri river have given the region a fame inversely
proportionate to their importance in the history of the
cattle frontier.[267] "The romance of my life began here,"
he remarked later. In success and magnitude of operations he did not match such men as M. C. Conners, Simpson, or Henry Boice. He helped to organize the Little
Missouri River Stockmen's Association and served as
a captain in one of its round-ups. Between round-ups
and hunting trips he found time to write the story of
these years. And the charm and freshness of his *Ranch*

265 *Dickinson Press,* June 7, 14, 28, November 15, 1884.
266 *Dickinson Press,* November 1, 1884.
267 Hagedorn, *Roosevelt in the Bad Lands.*

Notes and *Hunting Trips of a Ranchman* are undimmed by his losses of about $75,000 on the Little Missouri ranges.

Antoine de Vallambrosa, Marquis de Mores, a young Frenchman of twenty-five or twenty-six impressed the Little Missouri ranchmen with his money and his dreams. Arriving five months before Roosevelt he founded the town of Medora on April 1, 1883. In May he closed an agreement whereby the twenty-four settlers along the Missouri were to furnish him five hundred sheep annually for seven years. A few months later he paid $40,000 for a herd of cattle near Miles City. With Herman and C. E. Haupt he organized the Northern Pacific Refrigerator Car Company which advertised three cattle brands. Distressed at the wastefulness of high freight rates and by the losses from long shipments, the marquis embarked on a program of building slaughter houses and refrigerator plants along the line of the Northern Pacific Railway.

With millions at his command de Mores was stirring the hopes of the Little Missouri Valley. His fame spread even to the Black Hills where an editor believed that "a revolution or reform will at no distant day occur in the export trade; that instead of herding live cattle in cars for transportation to market, slaughtering will be done, on or near the range, and carcasses only will be shipped in refrigerator cars, to any market in the world."

The Marquis de Mores, continued the account, "has practically demonstrated the feasibility of such a plan, as, also, of the policy of packing and canning at the initial rather than at the intermediate point, and is erecting large and costly works at Miles City for that purpose. There would seem to be no good reason why the abattoirs of the world should not be located in the immediate vicinity rather than scattered throughout Christendom as at present; and we believe they ultimately will be."

Another editor saw visions of a tannery and soap, candle, and glycerin works built near the slaughter houses. Elsewhere it was announced that the marquis with more zeal than experience had "a plan to raise 50,000 cabbages on his ranch near the Little Missouri." His Medora *Bad Lands Cowboy* was established. His schemes and dreams in the cattle country for about three years cost his father-in-law over $300,000. When he left the Bad Lands the glory of Medora departed but it still cherished the memory of its founder.[268]

Meanwhile Pierre Wibaux [269] was starting the foundations of large herds between the Yellowstone and the Little Missouri rivers. Coming to the territory in the same year as did Roosevelt and de Mores, this young Frenchman was the third of a picturesque trio among the Dakota cattlemen. The son of a rich textile manufacturer, he learned of the great western ranches while studying in England. And, against his father's wishes but with the aid of about $10,000 he came to the new ranges of the Little Missouri Valley. Beginning with a small herd and with only two cowboys Wibaux was his own foreman for several years, studied brands, breeds, and markets, and performed the exacting duties of the range.

268 *Idem, Roosevelt in the Bad Lands, passim; Turner County Herald,* May 10, 1883; *Black Hills Daily and Weekly Pioneer,* extra edition, March 17, 1884; *Dickinson Press,* July 7, September 22, 1883.

269 Crawford, *The Coming of the Big Cattle Outfits;* Clay, *My Life on the Range;* Bertha M. Kuhn, "The W-Bar Ranch on the Missouri Slope," in *Collections of the State Historical Society of North Dakota,* v, 155-165.

A log house, fourteen by sixteen feet was built on the banks of the Big Beaver Creek but his wife and son, Cyril, spent only one winter in this home where a Christmas dinner was served which was long a tradition of magnificent hospitality. In 1886 he was a member of the Eastern Montana Stock Growers' Association and was appointed as one of its round-up captains. After the heavy losses of 1886-1887 he returned to France and borrowed half a million dollars with which he bought up large herds of strong steers – the survivors of that terrible winter. From the disasters of others he was enabled to accumulate a large fortune.

During the excellent grazing years he continued to accumulate cattle and at the close of the year 1888 he was reported to be the owner of 40,000 cattle – perhaps the largest number owned by any one individual in America. For ten years J. B. Lambs was his foreman and in 1890 he branded 12,000 calves and shipped an equal number of cattle. About three hundred saddle horses were required to herd his cattle which one writer placed at one time at 65,000. The principal brand, "W – Bar," was located at the confluence of the Little Missouri river and Cherry Creek.

His "White House" or "The Palace," a long, one-story structure, was built in 1890 from lumber hauled fifteen miles from the nearest railway station. With its large rooms, elaborate woodwork, wallpaper, fireplace, and sitting room, it became famed far and near for the Old World hospitality it could dispense in the cattle country. Guests played often in its billiard room and lingered long in the wine room. But the desire to have her son educated in France prevented his wife from spending more than the summers at the "White House," excepting one winter.

At Mingusville (later called Wibaux in Montana) he maintained an office and sleeping quarters. At his death in 1913 at the age of fifty-five he left an estate valued at over half a million dollars. "He was," said a contemporary, "a man of wonderful energy, indifferently honest, a bit of a Bohemian, but resourceful and successful." His happiest years were spent on Big Beaver Creek and his statue at Wibaux gazes in contemplation over the lands over which he rode and on which his great herds browsed.

From Texas, Iowa, and Missouri large herds were driven into the Dakota ranges in 1883 but the southern herds especially were unacclimated when winter set in. "Then, too," said an observer of the Black Hills, "the snowfall has been heavy, particularly upon the ranges north and west of Deadwood where the greatest no. of cattle are located. We understand that there is at present 10 feet of snow along the Box Elder and is unusually deep throughout the entire district. . . It is too early to estimate the losses." [270]

Steady drives of large herds brought about 100,000 to the territory in 1884. In the first five months of the year a Rapid City bank alone paid out $60,000 for such droves. Another estimate – not an assessor's count – placed the number of cattle in the Black Hills at 800,000. From Spencer, Iowa, in July, 1884, the 2,300 cattle belonging to the Iowa and Montana Cattle Company passed through Pierre on their way to the Montana ranges. The *Bad Lands Cowboy* advertised seven-

---

[270] *The Estelline Bell*, August 25, September 22, 1883; *Black Hills Daily and Weekly Pioneer*, extra edition, March 17, 1884.

teen brands. An atlas listed twenty-seven cattle firms for this year. "The proprietors live in various places but principally at Cheyenne, Wyoming, Spearfish, Sturgis, Rapid City, and Custer City, Dakota." [271]

By 1885 Pierre had become a flourishing town to which came shipments from the East and at which cars were loaded with matured cattle for the markets. "Pierre is full of cowboys, waiting to drive stock across to the ranges," is a news item of February. It was expected that 10,000 cattle would come from the East to be dispersed over the Dakota plains. Regular shipments were made to Chicago to make room for the younger stock. Several carloads for the Sioux City Cattle Company came from the East, were unloaded to be branded, and then started for their ranges. Eleven hundred cattle of the Weare Live Stock Company came in October of which about one-half were sent to Chicago and the balance driven down to Fort Thompson in fulfillment of an Indian beef contract with the government. [272]

Farther up the Missouri river Bismarck was also growing to maturity as a cattle distributing station. The Northern Pacific Railway as early as 1879 had established a ferry between that city and Mandan to carry the cattle across the river. In 1885 the company contracted to transport 40,000 cattle from the Territory of Washington to the ranges of eastern Montana and Dakota territories. [273]

[271] *Black Hills Daily and Weekly Pioneer*, extra edition, March 17, 1884; *The Huron Tribune*, November 16, 1883; *The Estelline Bell*, July 10, 1884; *Bad Lands Cowboy*, November 13, 1884; A. T. Andreas, *Historical Atlas of Dakota*, 115.

[272] *The* [East Pierre] *Weekly Free Press*, May 21, August 20, October 20, 1885.

[273] *Saturday Evening Journal*, April 25, 1885; quotation in Crawford, *Notes*, from *Yellowstone Journal*, September 29, 1879.

The noise of loaded stock cars from and into Pierre continued during the spring and summer of 1886. The farms of Iowa, Illinois, and Minnesota sent many carloads to be distributed from Pierre. "A large amount of blooded stock is being shipped to this country this spring," reported a Pierre resident. "It will be but a few years until this will be the most famous stock growing region of our continent." M. C. Conners from Spearfish continued his large shipments to his ranges. Sixteen carloads of the Dakota Cattle Company were branded at Pierre and then, combined with another lot of thirty-five cars, were driven to grazing grounds of the Belle Fourche river.[274]

More and more herds were being crowded upon the ranges of the territory. The Vermont Cattle Company increased its herd to 10,000; the Reynolds Brothers imported about 9,000 Texas cattle – "Pilgrims" – during the summer; later in the year it was reported that 13,000 were ranging along the Crow river north of Deadwood.[275] "Overstocking may cause little or no harm for two or three years," wrote Theodore Roosevelt in that fall.[276] "But sooner or later there comes a winter which means ruin to the ranches that have too many cattle on them; and in our country, which is even now getting crowded, it is merely a question of time as to when a winter will come that will understock the ranges by the summary process of killing off about half of all the cattle throughout the Northwest."

The Medora *Bad Lands Cowboy* a few months later

---

[274] *The Weekly Free Press*, March 18, September 30, 1886.

[275] *The Weekly Free Press*, December 30, 1886; *The Saturday Evening Journal*, September 15, 1886; *The Estelline Bell*, May 1, 1886.

[276] Theodore Roosevelt, *Hunting Trips of a Ranchman*, Hermann Hagedorn, editor, 290.

reported the decision of the Little Missouri River Stock Growers' Association that the ranges in its round-up district were overstocked and that cowboys would "refuse to work with any new outfits running horses or cattle." Farther to the northeast the Mouse River Live Stock Association was formed to protect its stock and its hay meadows.[277]

A parching summer was another plague to visit the land of cattle. Herds on Box Elder Creek were driven to better ranges and extremely dry weather was reported in the vicinity of Pierre. Timber and prairie fires swept over a region north of Belle Fourche. Every vigilance was urged to prevent the ravages of prairie fires and in one section a reward of $450 was offered for the detection of any person setting a fire. Cattlemen from the south forsook dried up pastures and, with hopes of finding greener and less crowded fields, moved numerous herds into the Dakota ranges. "Our neighbors," reported John Clay, "kept piling cattle onto the bone dry range. The Continental Cattle Co. drove up 32,000 head of steers. The Worsham Cattle Co., with no former holdings turned loose 5,000 head or thereabouts. . . Thousands of other cattle were spread over the western and northwestern country in the most reckless way, no thought for the morrow. Even with the best of winters it would have been a case of suicide. As things turned out it was simple murder, at least for the Texas cattle." [278]

Gloomy forecasts of storms and winter losses of stock came from the *Deadwood Pioneer*.[279] Early in November the storm began and continued with little break

---

[277] Quoted in the [Bismarck] *Daily Tribune*, December 9, 31, 1886.
[278] *The Estelline Bell*, August 23, 1886; Clay, *My Life on the Range*, 177, 178.
[279] Quotation in *The Weekly Free Press*, October 7, 1886, February 3, 10, 1887.

until the end of February. Heavy snowfall attended by temperatures from $-15°$ to $-40°$ were interrupted by occasional Chinooks. Then came a freezing cold which left a heavy crust of glistening ice until the next blizzard. "25 below zero this morning. The Chinook last Friday melted snow rapidly for a time but was of short duration. The storm yesterday is generally acceded to have been the most severe of the season." These are comments of a shivering observer of February, 1887.

Near Jamestown nine hundred antelope were huddled together and smaller numbers, gaunt and fearless, were roaming about in Lamoure county in quest of food.[280] Straw piles, one, two, and even three years old were eagerly bought up at $1.00 a load by the cattlemen. And day after day they hoped for milder weather to melt the snow and to uncover the scant grass so long hidden under it.

Bony carcasses welcomed only by buzzards and coyotes were disclosed after the spring thaws. In the spring four or five hundred men followed by eight wagons and representing the "E6," the "W-Bar," the "777," the "O X," and other outfits were looking for their cattle. In the round-up they covered the country up to the Missouri river down to Fort Yates and up the Grand river. Only about a dozen steers were rounded up – gaunt survivors from among the thousands that had perished.[281] The loss of the "Hash Knife" outfit was placed at over 8,000. A herd of about 1,000 owned by the Custer Trail Cattle Company was practically destroyed.

---

280 *The Weekly Free Press,* February 3, 1887.

281 Crawford, *Notes* on interview with Don Stevenson, Jr., Carson, North Dakota, April 3, 1922.

VICTIMS OF A PRAIRIE SNOWSTORM DISCLOSED AFTER A THAW
From a contemporary sketch drawn by Paul Frenzeny in 1882.

"We have been a long while waiting for accurate round-up reports but finally have them," reported a Mandan editor. "In the territories throughout, it is safe to say that 75 per cent is not too high an estimate of losses. It is not pleasant to say that the losses are known to be large, much larger in fact than we have been willing to admit until forced by known facts." [282]

[282] *Daily Pioneer,* July 23, 1887.

Contemporary Portraits of the Frontier

Contemporary Portraits of the Frontier

Stock raising, mining, and agriculture in the West after the Civil War became subjected to unending streams of books and pamphlets. Cheapness and fertility of the land are the recurring words for the settlers and rather hopeful figures of profits appeared in the prospectus for the mines. But the claims for the western grazing plains are matched only by the optimism over profits – the profits generally hoped for but rarely earned. Descriptions of American frontiers have been less elaborate than those devoted to institutions. De Tocqueville and Bryce pictured the American government and Olmsted and Martineau the institution of slavery. The varied and changing aspects of the frontiers did not mature many current, classic accounts and Dr. Josiah Gregg's story of pioneer transportation and Parkman's *Oregon Trail* are rather exceptional. There is no Herodotus or Thucydides for the cattlemen's frontier or for the outposts of settlement and religion. From old and generally unconscious narratives recorded on the cattlemen's frontier only an imperfect picture can restore its moving scenes.

On the cattlemen's frontiers the hard labor came first. Corrals and branding chutes were more important than books and libraries; line riding and herding left little time or thought for writing; much of the life on the range was humdrum and prosaic which a few contemporaries and a later generation transported to the realms of romance and fiction. Diarists were rare in the cattle country and the immense distances and expanses did not encourage descriptions from the occasional visitors and travellers. But not a few actors in their later and wistfully reminiscent years recorded scenes of which they had been a part. Accounts by travellers, participants, and actual observers have barely survived the dime novels, fiction books, legends, and motion pictures. The legends of the "romance" of the ranges, of the cowboys and "cattle kings" have become almost permanent folklore. To these legends the writings of contemporaries on the cattlemen's frontier cannot rise in rebuke but can offer only a recital of prosaic and unconscious protest.

Edwin A. Curley, a special commissioner from *The Field* of London, visited the plains of Nebraska and the Territory of Wyoming in 1873.[283] "It is," he explained, "the time of trashy travels, consisting of the tittle-tattle of the train, the table, and the tap, illustrated with old maps and borrowed engravings, and made to sell." A heavy volume of four hundred and thirty pages devoted two chapters to "Pastoral Marvels" as seen near North Platte, Ogallala and Laramie City.

For six years herds had been browsing in the peninsula formed by the North and the South Platte rivers until the numbers had risen to 30,000. "Making every allowance, it is very evident that Messrs. Keith and Barton's cattle business has been enormously profitable." At Ogallala — the germ of a future cow town — he found half a dozen buildings which afforded rude comfort. Tom Lonergan, the postmaster and judge of probate, was the storekeeper for the cattle drovers. The visitors found

---

283 Edwin A. Curley, *Nebraska, Its Advantages, Resources, and Drawbacks.*

CONTEMPORARY PORTRAITS OF FRONTIER 223

Lonergan's cattle among the hills and ravines where the long-horned, thin, scrawny Texans were uncovering the short dry grass under the snow. The longhorns as well as the better calves by American sires lived on this grass and Curley was convinced that "winter grazing, even in the snow, is not necessarily another name for slow starvation."

Astonished at the enormous profits, the English travel-ler believed that only few men equipped with sufficient capital, experience, and judgment should embark in the business of ranching. Although the county had less than one hundred population he predicted immigration, re-stricted pastures, fences, and shrinking profits. As his own experience extended from admiring the "wonderful beauty" of the clouds to analyzing the costs of ranching, so the stock raising of the future was destined to pass from primitive grazing to the competition and risks of a great business.

For about ten years Joseph G. McCoy saw the pag-eantry of Texas cattle herds as they were grazed north-ward to the Kansas plains and shipped to eastern mar-kets. In his *Historic Sketches of the Cattle Trade of the West and Southwest* are preserved the names of famous drovers who travelled up and down the Texas trails.[284] L. B. Harris turned from the New Orleans and Mexican trade to embark upon the new pastures of Kansas where he was credited with the sale of one herd of 7,000 for $210,000. James F. Ellison and J. M. Choate sent herd after herd to the Kansas pastures. Heavy tributes on the cattle of J. M. Dougherty who drove herds to south-west Missouri were levied by hostile settlers. The herds

[284] McCoy, *Historic Sketches of the Cattle Trade of the West and Southwest.*

of Robert D. Hunter were forced to dodge the Kansas settlers until they were loaded for shipment near St. Joseph.

Other drovers in maneuvering to flank hostile regions attempted to move their herds along the Arkansas line to strike a shipping point east of Sedalia in Missouri. The cattle driven over this route "became foot sore and miserably poor in flesh, and of course, when put on the St. Louis market, sold for mean prices and weighed very light; so that when the drover had sold out and paid up expenses, but little cash remained to swell his impoverished pocketbook." Other trail-drivers remained near Baxter Springs where "soon the frost came and killed the grass, which, after drying a few days, was set fire and the whole country burned over. This was a great calamity to the drovers."

With his shipping facilities established at Abilene, McCoy heralded its advantages to the drovers. To its Drovers' Cottage came buyers to bid for the great cattle caravans. J. L. Driskill with three years' experience in selling beef to the Confederate armies was received with welcome. H. M. Childress had a record of seven years on various cattle trails. For several years Captain E. B. Millet's herds had furnished food for hungry mouths at Upper Missouri Indian agencies. Colonel J. J. Myers, one of Abilene's first and foremost patrons, directed the movement of several herds annually. To Kansas came also J. W. Tucker, a lover of trail work and excitement. Willis McCutcheon had become a regular driver to Abilene. All Kansas frontier cattle towns coveted the patronage and influence of J. D. Reed. Major Seth Mabry, always popular, would "rather sell than buy, but would rather buy than do nothing." Such men were the scene shifters on one of the last of America's frontiers.

Abilene had become a synonym for Texas cattle. "Well I'll swar," observed the Texas drover, "I never seed such a little town have such a big name." Merchants, traders, cattle arriving for shipment, steers being weighed and yarded, cowboys, a floating population – from these elements there developed an immense and lucrative trade in camp supplies and outfits, from huge spurs and star-spangled boots to wagons. Farmers supplied grain, vegetables, butter, and eggs and carloads of additional provisions were imported to satisfy the demands of the Texas cattle trade.

McCoy soon saw various other frontier towns contending for a share of the profits of this trade and, discouraged by the opposition from the settlers near Abilene, he transferred his zeal to Wichita. A well-known Texas drover aided him by every advertising method to attract drovers and buyers to that point. "The success attained was beyond the most sanguine expectation. During the first season nearly four thousand cars, containing nearly eighty thousand head of cattle, were shipped." But only a moderate business was done at Newton "which gained a national reputation for its disorder and bloodshed. As many as eleven persons were shot down on a single evening and many graves were filled with subjects who had 'died with their boots on.' "

Meanwhile, the railways in transporting cattle from Texas, in dispersing them to the ranges, or in hauling them to the ranges were engaged in bitter competition for a share of the profits from this trade. The Kansas Pacific Railway, the "Texas Stock Route," promised good grazing, plentiful water, perfect shipping facilities, free yards, and low rates. Two daily, fast "Stock

Express" trains ran from seven Kansas towns to the markets at Fort Leavenworth and Kansas City. The Leavenworth, Lawrence & Galveston Railway Company claimed to be the "best, shortest, and cheapest cattle route" and stated that the rate from Coffeyville to Kansas City was not to exceed $25 per car. The Atchison, Topeka & Santa Fé Railroad pointed out its good stock scales at Granada, Great Bend, Newton, and Wichita and the resting and feeding yards at Hutchinson. One of the advertisements in McCoy's book for "the cheapest, shortest and most reliable live stock route" guaranteed shipments that would not injure or bruise stock. Meat from injured stock, it pointed out, the butchers were compelled to sell at reduced prices.

On McCoy's frontier appeared again and again the specter of Texas fever. He noted the coming of blooded cattle for the improvement of the Texas herds; the rise and fall of fortunes in the trade; the development of banking facilities at markets and shipping points; the depression caused by the panic of 1873; the intermingling of northern shippers and cattlemen with southern drovers. Now and then he pointed to those signs of a changing frontier – a frontier which had conquered the buffalo and which was itself destined to be overwhelmed by the more prosaic army of settlers.

Other aspects of the cattle industry were revealed by James Macdonald, the correspondent of the *Scotsman* who in 1877 travelled over 11,000 miles in visiting the western cattle ranges.[285] His letters were intended to give British farmers trustworthy information on American competition in the British markets. For sev-

---

[285] Macdonald, *Food from the Far West, or American Agriculture.*

eral years Yankee inventive genius had enabled Americans to export refrigerated beef to the British Isles. An "alarming increase" of such imports began in 1877 and speeches were made on the all absorbing topic of American beef which was cooled artificially and was threatening the welfare of British farmers. Macdonald was to report on the extent of danger feared over "the importation of dead meat from the far West."

In Colorado, he asserted, hand-feeding and house-shelter were unknown and its 80,000 cattle roamed about in "wild-horse freedom." In Nebraska he regarded stock raising as only slowly developed. Kansas cattle were of fair size, too leggy, too sharp on the back and too flat in the rib, showing as the Scotsman said, too much "timmer" and too much "daylight." Texas cattle had long horns, long legs, a thin, lanky body, and a light waist. The beef, "teasingly tough," was inferior and the animals had a high percentage of bone and muscle. An Indiana man's estimate was quoted who "could salt in its horns all the roasting beef an average Texan steer was capable of carrying."

Seeing no immediate danger in the competition of American beef he warned his readers, however, that there were unlimited fields for production in America and that the improvement of cattle and of their feeding was only a matter of time. Now, he pointed out, weight was more sought after than quality and plains cattlemen were insisting that their cattle were equal in beef to any in the world. "Evidently beef has no universal standard of quality."

But concern over the competition of beef from the western ranges was also felt by the British Royal Com-

mission on Agriculture.[286] Its agent, John Clay, Jr., a
name linked later with a great cattle company on the
Wyoming ranges, investigated the western herds and
pastures in 1879 or 1880. His report two years later did
not charm the Scottish investors as did the promoters'
pamphlets of gilded glory a few years later. The great
uncertainty was the climate of the cattle raising areas.
Already warnings of overcrowded pastures were current
and drought and severe winters made the range cattle
industry a precarious business.

The quality of beef, continued Clay, is so poor that
the British need fear little over the competition. "We
hear a deal about the vast herds of the western states,
but when seen they are a miserable class of scalawags,
an unthrifty race, and their effect on British agriculture
is small indeed. They, of course, fill a gap. They supply
a certain class of the population, and allow the better
class of stock to be exported, and of course this is sufficiently serious." Better beef, he advised, was needed for
these regions. Expansion on the plains should not be in
numbers but in the grading up and improvement of the
herds with a better strain of bulls.

Henry T. Williams's panorama or "travellers' guide"
of 1878 [287] for the Union and Central Pacific Railroads
was weighted with contributions from Clarence King,
F. V. Hayden, and Joaquin Miller. In his nine months'
travel of 2,500 miles, the plains around North Platte in
Nebraska impressed him with their adaptability for
stock raising. Repeated experiences showed that cattle

---

[286] *Royal Commission on Agriculture, Reports of the Assistant Commissioners,* vol. xv, dated January 20, 1882 (session of February 7-December 2,
1882).

[287] Henry T. Williams, *The Pacific Tourist, Williams Illustrated Guide to
Pacific R. R. California, and Pleasure Resorts across the Continent.*

and horses would pass through the severest winters known without hay or shelter except that afforded by ravines. And, again the habits of the buffalo in the past were cited.

In statistics he described the eastbound cars of cattle shipments from Julesburg, Pine Bluffs, Sidney, and Ogallala. From Cheyenne – once "a very fast town, and . . . not so very slow now" – over 10,000 cattle were shipped in 1874. "The development of the cattle and stock interests of this vast upland region," explained the tract, "is something never thought of nor entered the heads of the projectors of the railroad. In 1867, when the first railroad arrived, there was [sic] not probably a hundred head of all kinds owned in the whole territory outside of those belonging to contractors and stage lines. Now it is a leading interest and represents millions of dollars."

But not all can make cattle raising a success, ran one of his warning prophesies. Capital and care are required and a fortune cannot be made in a year. The business was liable to losses, severe winters, unfavorable seasons, and glutted markets. It was more sure than mining and more profitable than agriculture or dairy farming. But later tragedies in the cattle country indicated that the optimist rather than the cautious adviser ruled the ranges.

Enthusiastic, if not satisfying, are the guides and handbooks of Robert E. Strahorn which were issued with studied regularity during the seventies and eighties. Visiting the Black Hills and the Big Horn regions, he pointed out that an investment on stock raising of $10,400 with a reinvestment over three years would yield a net profit of $36,200. Figures were taken from the books of an experienced and thoroughly reliable, but unnamed, stock dealer in Cheyenne. Profits of forty per cent and fifty per cent had been realized, "but the writer who lays down such figures as an average is very liable to get his reputation involved." [288]

Along the Union Pacific Railroad and its branches he travelled two or three years later. The widely distributed book was an immigration tract. Thousands of eyes read the alluring chapters for Nebraska on "The Great Western Grazing Region," "Room for Thousands," "Wonderful Profits," and the array of dreamy figures and optimistic forecasts.[289]

Strahorn was at least writing optimistically if not accurately about western range conditions. "The Territory [of Montana] has no superior, and I doubt if an equal, as a grazing region," ran his pamphlet in 1881.[290] Of its 275,000 stock cattle probably not 1,000 had ever tasted hay or grain. About 38,000,000 acres of grazing were open to the prospective rancher. The sum of $12,330 would start a ranch with about a thousand cattle, horses, shanties, harness, wagons, cooking utensils, three men as herders, and three men to brand for twenty days. The writer did not estimate the outlays for the continued operation for such a ranch.

The cattlemen's frontier was not without its promoter who did not publish all he saw, nor perhaps see all he published or described. The secretary of the Territory of Dakota, Alexander Batchelder, had issued a

[288] Robert E. Strahorn, *The Hand-Book of Wyoming and Guide to the Black Hills and Big Horn Regions for Citizen, Emigrant and Tourist.*

[289] Robert E. Strahorn, *To the Rockies and Beyond, or A Summer on the Union Pacific Railroad and Branches.*

[290] Robert E. Strahorn, *Montana and Yellowstone National Park.*

fifty-six page booklet in 1870.[291] "Dakota is the finest field in the world for stock growing." It is preëminent in the production of grasses which, when cut green, are not dusty and are sweeter than tame grass. A young man from the East, he illustrated, sold his store for $300, and, after embarking in cattle ranching, soon owned a herd of three hundred, worth between $40 and $75 each.

Cereals, fruits, and trees, he promised, grow "more rapidly, stronger and with less care" than in New England. "Lay aside your collars and kid gloves," he addresses the East. "Work a little. . . The fountain of perennial youth is in the country, never in the city. . . Young men predominate in the West, while maidens are scarce; therefore I say to you, get yourself a wife and bring her with you. . . To the young woman I would say just a word. Out here

There is no goose so gray, but soon or late
Will find some honest gander for a mate."

Careful observations and reasoned comments on the range country appeared in 1882 in *Camps in the Rockies* [292] by the great English hunter, William Adolph Baillie-Grohman and in his various magazine articles. Intimately informed, through several visits, on the big game and geography of the West, the author consulted the genial open-handed cowboys for details. His accounts are faithful mirrors of the West when books and magazines were painting "the delightful life" on the ranges and advising how to treble capital in three years.

Stockmen, he found, were recruited from men of good family as well as from the lowest social rank. The middle

[291] George Alexander Batchelder, *A Sketch of the History and Resources of Dakota Territory.*

[292] William Adolph Baillie-Grohman, *Camps in the Rockies.*

class also contributed its share from those who had been
railway conductors, hotel keepers, western merchants,
petty civil servants, trappers, and Indian scouts. In the
last decade the ranchmen had helped to people new
countries and not a few western cities subsisted on the
stock business. Some of the "dreary unhabited steppe
deserts" of Wyoming and Montana would have remained unsettled but for the cattlemen. These ranchmen,
in edging the red man from his hunting grounds and in
replacing the buffalo and elk with "domestic kine,"
were enacting "a piece of frontier history."

Three ways of embarking in the stock business were
cited: to buy the stock on the range, to contract for the
purchases from large drovers, or to go to Oregon or to
Texas in person to select the herds to be moved to the
range. "You or I, reader, can today start for any of the
three or four last-named territories [Wyoming, Montana, Idaho, and New Mexico] pick out a good 'range'
or district for grazing, as yet unoccupied, drive on to it
a herd of 10,000 cattle, select a suitable spot near to a
convenient creek, and there build our ranche or farm-
house, fence in 50 or 100 acres for hay land . . . without
paying a penny for it, or outstepping any territorial
or United States statute, or doing what is not perfectly
lawful."

In the United States, he warned, where "tall" talk
was common, the almost universal attitude was to ex-
aggerate. All figures of profits were more or less over-
colored estimates of thirty to thirty-five per cent on a
three or four year average and forty per cent on a seven
year average. Usually one bad winter in seven visited
the ranges and Grohman recorded that in the severe
winters of 1871-1872 and 1880-1881 the ranchmen lost

about half their herds. The remarkable career of John W. Iliff was portrayed who in no way owed his success in range operations to luck. But, "in a country where human fortune fluctuates so strangely, and where men of all classes, grades, and character, are thrown to-gether – it is doubly incumbent upon the stranger to keep his eyes and ears skinned – in fact, to believe but what he himself sees."

Social equality he regarded as a main factor in the unusually rapid growth of the great West. "A man out West is a man, and let him be the poorest cowboy he will assert his right of perfect equality with the best of the land, betraying a stubbornness it is vain and unwise to combat." It was of ten-fold importance to avoid a social pride which might incur spite or injury. In no business as much as in stock raising in the West was a man so dependent upon his neighbors, so open to petty annoyances, or so helplessly exposed to vindictive injury to property.

A careful inventory of stock raising in the Territory of Montana with 400,000 cattle came from the corres-pondent of the *London Times* in 1882.[293] Taxes, interest, and other expenses made an annual outlay of $2 per head but marketing entailed the heaviest cost. Cattle were driven to Pine Bluffs and Cheyenne to be "railed" until the coming of the Northern Pacific Railroad reduced the distance for driving to one-fourth of the former course. The great herds of Conrad Kohrs roamed over thousands of acres to which his only right – generally respected – was that of priority of occupation. About eight hundred tons of hay were stacked for his breeding animals but no hay or fodder was cut for the other stock.

[293] "Stock Raising in Montana," in *London Times,* May 29, 1882.

To each animal a pound of salt per week and twenty or twenty-five acres for grazing were allotted. In winters the animals scraped the snow to eat the cured grasses but in severe winters they became so poor that "you can read your newspaper through their ribs." In three years Kohrs drove 1,500 to the Northern Pacific Railroad at an expense of $120 per car for the 1,100 miles to the Chicago markets.

Frequent journeys to the Territory of Montana by Alexander Stanley Hill, the managing director of the Oxley Ranch Company of Alberta, were recorded in glimpses of the northwestern ranges during the eighties.[294] Free ranging, he believed, was producing ruinous consequences in the grazing territories. Trailing over the territory from the Milk River Range, through the basins of the Teton, Judith, and Musselshell rivers, he found the herbage utterly destroyed by numerous herds. If stockmen, he pointed out, could be encouraged to develop without squandering the resources, the lands would long continue to be the meat producing areas and the natural complement of the corn growing regions of the Dominion.

One evening was spent with Baillie-Grohman who had been shooting big game in the Territory of Idaho. Poindexter and Orr drove in 1882 a herd of 4,500 cattle from the territory to the Canadian ranches in a journey of ninety days. They gave Hill the benefit of their experience of thirty years in breeding cattle and claimed that overstocking had destroyed the grass and had compelled them to move their herds. Hill strongly advised

---

[294] Alexander Stanley Hill, *From Home to Home, or Autumn Wanderings in the North-West, in the years 1881, 1882, 1883, 1884;* cf. also an account of the Oxley Ranch Company by James Roderick Craig, *Ranching with Lords and Commons or Twenty Years on the Range.*

coöperation in the cutting and storing of hay against the heavy storms and long winters.

To his English readers he gave advice on personal clothing and equipment for ranch work. Buffalo robes were excellent but were passing away; a flabby hat was recommended for summer and a fur cap in winter; flannel underclothing and worsted socks and stockings were named; felt boots and moccasins were best in winter and high boots in other seasons; buckskin gloves and mittens he regarded as an "absolute necessity"; a belt should be worn to carry the cowboy's knife and matches. "A six-shooter is, I am happy to say, no necessity with us."

A hotel landlord at Billings, he found, protested against the town's reputation for lawlessness by declaring that only three or four killings had taken place in it since the coming of the railroad ten weeks before. Among its 3,000 Hill saw drinking and faro and poker playing night and day but little disorder and lawlessness. Good and evil were more or less present in any of the cow towns and discoverable according to the visitor's inclinations. The scum of westward floating population was usually on the surface. The quiet, industrious workers of the frontier towns were not generally found at billiard tables and in poker rooms.

The atmosphere of the cattlemen's frontier pervades the accounts of his long stage and horseback journeys over the Montana ranges. Indians, whiskey traders, drinking, good and bad food, the long distances from his ranch to Fort Benton and to Miles City, squaws, Mexicans, and high prices receive his varying comments. "Bull dog flies," cowboy gambling, cattle stealing, "snow-blinding," Chinooks, low temperatures, fur-traders, prairie lands – these are other elements of the

picture during the eighties. He is equally impressed by
the quick healing of gunshot wounds and by the pro-
fanity of Montanans. "Do you think," ran one man's
protest against work on the Sabbath, "I am going to
work day and night, Sundays and week days like a '—
—' telegraph post."

"Pony Bill," a cowboy slender in size rather than in
range experience, offered advice on brands and branding
irons. Figures and letters were easily changed. "Did
it never strike you," he asked, "that H.K. can be juggled
up into B.R.?" Select a plain, simple brand that can
easily be seen at a distance. Register and advertise your
brand. Keep a note book and in it set down all brands
you have memorized. An animal with an unknown
brand appearing in a herd should invite immediate attention. After asking and asking about the mark, he
advised, try to discover the name of the owner, and mail
him a post card at once.

But such advice was, if observed, a severe tax on
memory and honesty in days when many thousands of
brands were owned. In the office of the secretary of state
of Colorado in 1885 were books bulging with about
12,000 brands. Two hundred and fifty combinations
were built on the letter "H"; one hundred and fifty on
each of the letters "C" and "D." The Prairie Cattle Company owned nearly forty brands. Other brands in endless
variety represented a turkey track, crow's feet, a spear,
a pitchfork, spades, an anvil, an arrow, a cannon, a boat,
and scissors. Trained eyes might recognize saddle-bags
or a pistol in brands but how could a man be expected to
see a wineglass seared on a steer's flank or hip? [295]

---

[295] *Daily Drovers Journal,* September 8, 1882; "Stock Brands" in the
Pueblo Chieftain in *Daily Drovers Journal,* October 23, 1885; *Colorado
Brand Book.*

Copper branding irons "Pony Bill" regarded as better than those of wrought iron because they retained the heat longer. The thinner the iron the more quickly it could be heated. The faces of the iron should be smooth and the edges sharp and square to make a more lasting and a distinct brand. Rusty irons should not be used nor time wasted in using those not hot. "The longer the handle the less apt you are to make a nasty fry out of your fingers."

Heat the iron to rich red glow, shake off the ashes, "and slap her on and let her burn. Rock the brand to and fro, bearing hard on it and setting in all sharp and square." The hip, the cheek of the rump, the jaw, the shoulder, and the neck were all good places for the scar, but no place afforded such a broad, smooth room for a brand as the hind quarter and the side near the backbone.

"Finally, regarding the branding, remember that the brand claims the brute, and indistinct brands lead to disputes, ill feeling, and sometimes to fighting and killing."

"There is not the slightest element of uncertainty in cattle raising." Thus wrote Walter Baron von Richthoven in his book, *Cattle Raising on the Plains of North America,* published in 1885 and dedicated to the cattlemen of Colorado where he had lived for many years.[296] He estimated that English capitalists alone had invested $14,000,000 in the range cattle industry. Six Scottish companies were named, with shares varying from 42,000 to 4,500. Losses in cattle came through sickness, killing by railroads, extreme cold and lasting snows, straying into other herds, and from theft. "There are no risks beyond losses arising from natural causes, which can be

[296] Richthoven, *Cattle Raising on the Plains of North America.*

calculated down to a percentage per annum, and none arising from speculation."

"The Existing Cattle Companies are Prosperous, and New Ones Are Constantly Being Formed" is the title of chapter X. Eleven Texas firms were named and in the dividend records of many cattle corporations the Powder River Cattle Company alone was without a dividend earned in 1885. The value of the grazing lands he put down at one and one-quarter million dollars. Seven factors producing "immense profits" were noted: the natural increase of cows, the increase of steers, the yearly advance in weight, profits from the improvement of the herds, the future increase in the value of the beef, the advance in the value of the pastures, and the profits in raising one's own bulls.

The baron also painted the virtues of Denver: "Western people are hospitable, open-hearted, and liberal. So one may find in those western plains the noblest examples of manhood." The president of the Colorado Cattle Growers' Association had invited foreign capitalists to come to the Colorado pastures. "The cattle business and land ownership," he wrote, "may become land monopolies, as railroads and telegraph monopolies are now." And at this point the baron quoted the famous advice of Horace Greeley.

The book was an immigration tract, a volume with the language of a chamber of commerce with adroit figures and illustrations. It had more of gullibility than of deception. The book contained little about the comparative merits of agriculture or mining and there is no vision of the impending exhaustion of the plains grasses. The author painted nothing of the "romantic" or picturesque side of stock raising nor of the colorful side of the life of the herders. It is a description prosaic and material without any hints of the coming avalanche of settlers or of falling markets.

Reginald Aldridge, influenced by accounts of the western ranges in the English magazine, *The Field,* embarked in the ranching business for about six years during the seventies and eighties.[297] His herds were pastured successively in Kansas, Colorado, the Indian Territory, and in Texas. He was a type of Englishman who combined ranching, hunting, travel, and outdoor adventures. Just before him had passed the buffalo bone pickers but on his ranges he felt the increasing pressure from the farmers and small stockmen.

A holiday, sportive vein runs through his story. One winter was spent in a Kansas dug-out with a fireplace. The winter of 1879-1880 for over three months was unusually severe and Aldridge saw long lines of cattle "in single file travelling along before the wind." The monotony of line-riding was broken by calf-branding. Prairie fires, stampedes, range-straying, "cutting out," shipments to Kansas City, and long journeys to get provisions at frontier towns are noted in his account. On winter evenings "we used to pile up the blazing logs, sing songs, and forget the weather outside. I cannot say there was any great musical talent displayed, but the performers enjoyed these extempore concerts, and there was no audience to criticize."

A herd of sleek steers browsing in lush grass and guarded by a faithful cowboy with a background of picturesque scenery is the frontispiece of General James S. Brisbin's *The Beef Bonanza; or How to Get Rich*

[297] Reginald Aldridge, *Ranch Notes in Kansas, Colorado, the Indian Territory and Northern Texas.*

on the Plains.[298] The picture gives the tone to the volume
and its title the purpose. The general had for twelve years
been a resident of the plains and gave his "impressions,
which shall at least have the merit of being honest."

The book, issued in 1881, is a curious jumble of dull
inventories of stock, the successes of "cattle kings," long
lists of Texas drovers, testimony quoted from governors
and army officers, and psalm-like descriptions of resources and scenery. Figures and calculations over five
and six year periods all resulted in the high percentage
of "profits." As Erasmus Beadle's dime novels contributed little to the factual side of western history, so
the general's book added little to the economics of the
cattle range industry.

Theodore Roosevelt's *Hunting Trips of a Ranchman*
and *Ranch Life and the Hunting Trail* are descriptions
of his experiences of two or three years on the ranges
of Dakota and eastern Montana.[299] These accounts, even
without the later high fame of the author, retain the
qualities of first hand observation, honest effort, youthful
devotion, and an almost idyllic love for the scenes. In
the first issue in 1885 he saw ranching as a phase of life
as "fascinating as it is evanescent." In the other his pleasure has been tempered with the lament of prophecy: "In
its present form stock raising on the plains is doomed,
and can hardly outlast the century."

Grass, water, and shelter, he advised, were the three
essentials for a range. Profits were sometimes great but
the chances for large losses were great also. Texas fever,
prairie fires, the granger, the sheep owner, overstocking,

298 Brisbin, *The Beef Bonanza; or How to Get Rich on the Plains.*
299 Roosevelt, *Hunting Trips of a Ranchman* and *Ranch Life and the Hunting Trail.*

and hard winters – all were felt and noted by Roosevelt. Writing in the fall of 1886 of the overstocking of the ranges of the Little Missouri he predicted a winter that would understock the northwestern ranges by killing off about one-half of the cattle. His fear was realized that winter in losses that became historic to the cattlemen as well as tragic to the herds.

Two Texas cowboys once spent a few days with Roosevelt as noted in his book. Although unknown to him even by name, they had learned of his strayed horses, and, after a twenty-four hour search, had returned to him the missing animals. Both boys complained of the severe winter and longed to return to the South. But their cloudy account of a "small civil war" in a New Mexican county indicated why they remained in the Bad Lands and why Roosevelt never learned their names. Around the camp fire glow their conversation touched only the routine subjects of cow camps. A bunch of steers – a few Hash Knife four-year-olds and some young immigrant cattle had been seen; a stray horse with a blurred brand had joined the saddle ponies; the red F.V. cow mired in the mud had been pulled out and then charged upon her rescuers; Sawback, an old mule, was recovering from the effects of a rattlesnake bite; Bronco Jim had been bucked off by a big, bald-faced, sorrel Oregon horse, and his face smashed in; a rumor was current that the vigilantes had given notice "to quit" to two men whose horses included a large number of different brands – most of them blurred. Then the conversation became more personal and Roosevelt agreed to post their two letters – "evidently the product of severe manual labor." Each was addressed to a girl, and for the final hour the bearer of the two love tokens was given an unreserved account of the girls' charms and virtues.

Of the frontier types that thronged the cow towns, Roosevelt regarded the cowboy as the most important. In the small towns the cowboy balls were held as the round-up passed near. Conducted with decorum the ball was directed by a master of ceremonies "chosen with due regard to brawn as well as brain." Roosevelt once opened such a ball with a partner whose husband, in dancing the lanciers, knew all the steps far better than did the young New Yorker.

But long hours and the dreary monotony of day-herding and line-riding made up much of the life on the ranges. "Ranching is an occupation like those of vigorous, primitive pastoral peoples, having little in common with the humdrum, workaday business world of the nineteenth century; and the free ranchman in his manner of life shows more kinship to an Arab sheik than to a sleek city merchant or tradesman."

The many rooms of Roosevelt's home ranch house of hewn logs were filled with pelts and other hunting trophies. Before the burning pine logs in the fireplace his men played checkers or chess or possibly read books from the shelves filled with the works of Parkman, Irving, Cooper, Lowell, and Poe. Nearby stood hay ricks, sheds, and a stable, and a fenced-in garden furnished potatoes and other vegetables. Unlike most other ranches his ranch kept two or three milch cows and some hens. At his table were served elk meat, bread, bowls of milk, eggs, venison, antelope steak, prairie chicken, butter, plums, and tea or coffee. Occasionally the wall-eyed pike and the catfish varied the fare.

Such facilities and conveniences were somewhat exceptional as they were on the ranch of Henry S. Mudge, another Harvard graduate.[300] His ranch established in 1880 not far from Dodge City in Kansas, had twelve miles of fencing and contained about 10,000 acres. An editor on a visit noted four pastures, range cattle, milch cows, pure bred and graded Durham bulls, millet and bluestem hay, sorghum, and sacks of wheat, rye, and oats. The ranch house resembled a club house with its dairyman, a bookkeeper, and two cooks. A Chickering piano, a fireplace, pipes, tobacco, cigars, English and American magazines and newspapers, and a well-stocked library – these articles indicated a ranching establishment marked by pleasure and comfort rather than by the rough work of the business.

In contrast to the leisure and charms of the ranch on the Little Missouri and on that of Mudge, is the picture of a ranch as depicted by a Kansas herder.[301] Buffalo grass and blue joint furnished the food for the cows, the two-year-olds, yearlings, and calves during the day until they were driven into the corral for the night. The ponies were picketed with long ropes and saddles, blankets, and bridles were hung on pegs near the corral bars. An early breakfast for the herders consisted of corn-dodgers or baking-powder biscuits, fried bacon, and strong coffee without milk or sugar. Then the corral bars were let down and the cattle filed out over the trails to their feed grounds where they spread out. The animals when sated at ten o'clock were browsed toward the watering place. After lying down to rest for two or three hours the stock spread out again to feed. As the

[300] *Kansas Cowboy*, October 18, 1884.

[301] *The Garden City* [Kas.] *Paper*, June 5, 1879, as reprinted from the *New York Sun*.

sun got lower the herd was turned to graze toward the corral. At dusk the bars were put up, the ponies were staked, supper was cooked and eaten, and the herders went to bed.

During the long hours of herding the cowboys some-times played "seven-up," staking the pennies of one pocket against those of another. On the range the herders built piles of stones for watch towers. On these they could stand to gaze over a swell in the prairie or into a ravine and thus save long rides to detect strays from the herd. This routine, unrelieved by hunting or by reading, was broken by the round-ups, the branding work, and by in-frequent visits to the frontier towns.

Most of the contemporaries of the frontier pictured the American cowboy but a lesser number did justice to his constructive influences. Later, nearly all annalists of his era enlarged the picture but many transgressed reali-ties to make him the Alkali Ike of the paper backs, or without his consent, the hero in fiction and tragedy and on the screen. Perhaps no other frontier personage – save the American Indian – has received descriptive adjectives in such numbers, and, in such innocence. Roosevelt, who knew the cowboy and would not have disavowed his place in cowboyship, variously employed thirty terms to denote the starkly masculine qualities he saw in this frontier type.[302]

But very different traits were exposed by George W. Romspert after his long wagon tour over the plains. In his book issued by the United Brethren Publishing Company,[303] he is astonished at the "almost unexcep-

---

302 *Cf.* Branch, *The Cowboy and his Interpreters.*

303 George W. Romspert, *The Western Echo: a Description of the Western States and Territories of the United States as Gathered in a Tour by Wagon.*

tionably bold, bestial, and immoral character of these creatures of the broad western plains." These "savages," he warned, "will run a dirty cook out of camp." "There are many social glasses drank" and in the feuds there were seldom less than four or five killed. "But oh! how those cowboys curse the tenderfeet." After inducing a tenderfoot to mount a bucking horse, "the boys are usually slow about going to help a walloped tenderfoot, for fear he will not die if he is helped."

But neither Robin Hood nor Buffalo Bill attained the marksmanship conceded to the cowboy by Romspert. "They will make him stand still and hold out his hand, and then try to shoot between his fingers, or shoot a hole through his ears, or see how closely they can shoot to the top of his head by shooting through his hat. . . There is not much danger until they get pretty full and want to make *too fine* a shot, such as shooting between the flesh and skin, and then the thing is too fine to be pleasant."

To Joseph G. McCoy the early Texas cowboy was far from a romantic figure. He lived hard and worked hard; he had little, if any, taste for reading but enjoyed the blood and thunder stories. "He enjoys a coarse practical joke or a smutty story; loves danger but abhors labor of the common kind; never tires riding, never wants to walk, no matter how short the distance he desires to go. He would rather fight with pistols than pray; loves tobacco, liquor and women [more] than any other trinity. . . He enjoys his pipe, and relishes a practical joke on his comrades, or a corrupt tale, wherein abounds much vulgarity and animal propensity." [304]

[304] McCoy, *Historic Sketches of the Cattle Trade of the West and Southwest,* 10, 11.

The creditable exceptions to the hard drawn pictures of the cowboys in the cow towns were many. "We are a melancholy-looking crowd when at dawn one chill October morning, we turn our backs on the seductive charms of Dodge City, with swollen heads and shrunken purses. We have nothing before us but the long dreary winter months, which will be spent in cheerless dugouts, line-riding, repairing fences and corrals, killing wolves, and turning the heavy drift of cattle, which must inevitably take place, as much as possible off our range."[305] But the twenty-four hours spent in saloons, in gambling dens, and in dance halls with wretched music brought not only insolvency to the cowboy but ill repute to his kind for the other days of the year.

Observers were almost unanimous in mentioning the low wages and the improvidence of cowboys. McCoy in 1874 gave the monthly wages of Texans as from $15 to $20. A higher scale prevailed in the north and William T. Hornaday declared that on the Montana ranges the wages should be $200 instead of $40. In a later year the manager of the Oxley Ranch Company related that Jess, one of the cowboys, paid $85 for a saddle, $20 for a bridle, $15 for spurs, and $15 for a lariat. "I have seen some of my men with sombreros costing $85. These would come from San Francisco, rigged out with a heavy silver cord, etc." To Alexander Stanley Hill, the dark and sad feature in the lives of cowboys was the sudden loss of a year's earnings to a professional gambler. Hundreds of dollars were squandered in the poor excitement of an evening at euchre, faro, or draw poker. With his ready money gone "he has

[305] John Baumann, "On a Western Ranche," in the *Fortnightly Review* (1887), vol. XLVII, 516-533.

nothing to live upon but 'jawbone,' i.e. credit, and to 'call his jaw,' i.e. live on credit, till he has got further employment and wages." [306]

That the food was bad on the ranges became almost a proverb to eye-witnesses and mouth-witnesses. McCoy testified that corn bread, mast-fed bacon, and coffee made up nine-tenths of the diet of Texas cowboys. Each drank one or two quarts of the strongest, inky colored coffee without sugar or cream. One rider listed a daily fare of bread, coffee, sow-belly, larrup (treacle), and onions. Hornaday found a brief note left in a dug-out on the Montana ranges. "May 6th. – Arrived here. Lonesome as ——, but a good supper. Buffalo hump and onions." A trail foreman of a later period expended his allowance for provisions for delicacies along the trail but charged the outlay to potatoes. But a rigid inspection of his figures indicated that each cowboy had consumed a daily ration of twenty pounds of that vegetable! "Almost every known law of physiology and hygiene," commented a Colorado doctor on the cowboy's life and fare, "may be persistently violated, and yet the transgressor seems to thrive thereby." [307]

The old cattlemen's frontier was submerged by the great waves of settlers, small farmers and ranchmen, sheepmen, and homesteaders. These advancing in the eighties and nineties, engulfed the cattlemen who had

[306] McCoy, *Historic Sketches of the Cattle Trade of the West and Southwest*, 10, 11; William T. Hornaday, "The Cowboys of the Northwest," in the *Cosmopolitan* (1887), vol. II, 219-233; Craig, *Ranching with Lords and Commons*, 89; Hill, *From Home to Home*, 255-256.

[307] McCoy, *Historic Sketches of the Cattle Trade of the West and Southwest*, 10; Baumann, "On a Western Ranche," in the *Fortnightly Review* (1887), XLVII, 516-533; Hornaday, "The Cowboys of the Northwest," in the *Cosmopolitan* (1887), vol. II, 219-233; J. Evetts Haley, *The XIT Ranch of Texas and the Early Days of the Llano Estacado*, 142.

been but the spray thrown far in advance of the crest of these tides. Transitory as it was, the cattlemen's frontier was the most picturesque and perhaps the most American of America's frontiers, and the horsemen who invaded this vacant empire dismounted not without regret.

"We who have felt the charm of the life," wrote Roosevelt about fifty years ago, "and have exulted in its abounding vigor and its bold, restless freedom, will not only regret its passing for our own sakes, but must also feel real sorrow that those who come after us are not to see, as we have seen, what is perhaps the pleasantest, healthiest, and most exciting phase of American existence." Forty years later an old cowboy was driving and walking about the streets of Cheyenne. He pointed to sites where had been enacted the life and scenes of a bygone era. "Yes," he mused, "the cowboy is gone. The old range life has disappeared and will never return. If I knew a country where it would, I'd go there if I had to go in a canoe."

The old range rider voiced the lament of his departed youth and – his memories of a vanished American frontier.

Appendix

CATTLE BRANDS

OWNED BY MEMBERS

OF THE

WYOMING

Stock Growers' Association.

Left Ear.		Right Ear.

CHICAGO:
The J. M. W. Jones Stationery & Printing Co.
1882.

This book of brands, published pursuant to a resolution of the Wyoming Stock Growers' Association, by subscription, embraces the membership of that association with the exception of a small number who have failed to respond to the applications of the Committee. Nearly sufficient funds have been subscribed to cover the cost of a second edition which will probably be issued in the Spring of 1884. It is suggested that in the interval those desiring their brands included in the next edition should file with the Committee their applications. The delay in the issue of this edition has been occasioned by the tardy response of a considerable number of the subscribers to the work. In consideration of difference of usage as to the reading of Earmarks, we designate on the title page the usage adopted in this publication.

A. T. BABBITT,
F. E. WARREN, }Committee.
PHILIP DATER,

CHEYENNE, September, 1882.

SPARKS & TINNIN (Nevada Brands).

P. O. Address,
Range, Goose Creek and Thousand Springs Valley, Nev.
Brand, same as cut, left side;
left hip; **J DS R**
any part of animal.

SPARKS & TINNIN,

P. O. Address,
Range, Lodge Pole Creek, Wyoming and Neb.
Brand, Cattle, same as cut, on left shoulder,. high up on animal.

Horses branded on left thigh.

JOHN SPARKS.

P. O. Address, Cheyenne, Wyoming.
Range, Lodge Pole and vicinity
Brand, Cattle, same as cut

on either side or hip.
Horses branded on left thigh.

MARSH & COOPER.

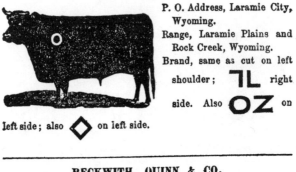

P. O. Address, Laramie City, Wyoming.

Range, Laramie Plains and Rock Creek, Wyoming.

Brand, same as cut on left shoulder; **7L** right side. Also **OZ** on left side; also ◇ on left side.

BECKWITH, QUINN & CO.

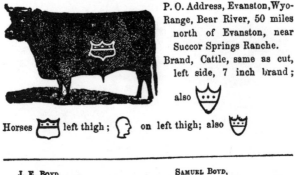

P. O. Address, Evanston, Wyo—

Range, Bear River, 50 miles north of Evanston, near Succor Springs Ranche.

Brand, Cattle, same as cut, left side, 7 inch brand; also

Horses ⛨ left thigh; ☺ on left thigh; also ♛

J. E. BOYD,
Omaha, Neb.

SAMUEL BOYD,
Fort Fetterman, Wyo.

Range, Antelope and Cheyenne, north of North Platte River.

Brand, same as cut on left side.

SWAN & FRANK LIVE STOCK CO.

A. H. SWAN, Supt.

P. O. Address, Cheyenne, Wyoming.

Range, Sabile, Chug and Laramie Plains.

Brand, same as cut, on left side and hip. Earmark, also,

NATIONAL CATTLE CO.

A. H. SWAN, Supt.

P. O. Address, Cheyenne, Wyoming Ter.

Range, North Chug.

Brand, same as cut, left side,

earmark

also

W. C. IRVINE & J. H. FORD.

P. O. Address, Cheyenne, Wyo.

Range, Old Woman Creek.

Brand, same as cut, on left side.

LUKE VOORHEES & CO.

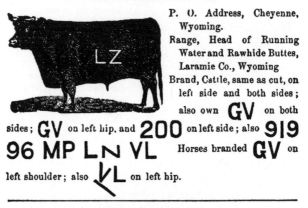

P. O. Address, Cheyenne, Wyoming.

Range, Head of Running Water and Rawhide Buttes, Laramie Co., Wyoming

Brand, Cattle, same as cut, on left side and both sides; also own **GV** on both sides; **GV** on left hip, and **200** on left side; also **919** **96 MP L N VL** Horses branded **GV** on left shoulder; also  **VL** on left hip.

CHAS. D. MOTLEY.

P. O. Address, Laramie City, Wyoming.

Range, Laramie Plains.

Brand, same as cut, also **X** **N E** Jockey Saddle on some Cattle and Horses.

H. B. KELLEY.

P. O. Address, Chugwater, Wyoming.

Range, Chugwater.

Brand, Cattle branded same as cut on any part of animal; also owns **T P** **31**

Horse brand, **H** on left shou der.

STURGIS, GOODELL & CO.

P. O. Address, Cheyenne, Wyoming.

Range, Goshen's Hole and Cheyenne River.

Brand, same as cut, on left hip; **G** on right; wattle on left side of neck; **J**

on left hip and side, wattle on nose; **CK** on left side and hip

STURGIS & LANE.

P. O. Address, Cheyenne, Wyoming.

Range, Goshen's Hole and Cheyenne River, Wyo.

Brand, same as cut on left side.

Earmark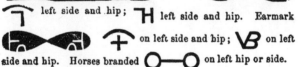

7 left side and hip; **H** left side and hip. Earmark

◄■► **T** on left side and hip; **VB** on left side and hip. Horses branded **O——O** on left hip or side.

GOLDSCHMIDT & FISHER.

P. O. Address, Cheyenne, Wyo.

Range, Bridger's Ferry, Shawnee Creek and Lost Springs. north side North Platte River.

Brand, same as cut. Horses branded same as cut on

left hip. Also owns cattle branded **◄——** and **(K)D**

Earmarks of young stock, crop the left, overslope the right.

JAMES A. JACKSON.

P. O. Address, Rawlins, Wyo.
Range, Sweet Water, Wyo.
Brands, same as cut on left
side; **2Ƶ** on right
side; both on same ani-
mal; also ⅃ on both
sides.

RAND, BRIGGS & CO. and BOSTON LIVE STOCK CO.

P. O. Address, Cheyenne,
Wyoming.
Range, Snake River and Ban-
nock Creek, Idaho, and
Sweetwater and Platte
River.
Brands, same as cut on right

side; also **OX** on left side, and ——————— on right side;

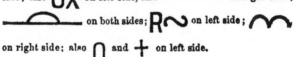 on both sides; **R~** on left side; ⌒⌒

on right side; also ∩ and + on left side.

CREIGHTON & CO.

P. O. Address, Antelope,
Nebraska.
Range, Horse and Pumpkin
Creeks.
Brands, same as cut, **ℐ**

HARRIS & CLEVENGER.

P. O. Address, Wm. Harris,
M. D., Laramie City, Wyo.,
or J. M. Clevenger, Buff-
alo, Wyoming.
Range, Clear Creek and Crazy
Woman, Wyoming.
Brand, Cattle, same as cut,
on any part of animal.

Earmark   Horses ⋏ on left hip.

BENJAMIN, WEAVER & CO.

P. O. Address, Fort Fetter-
man, Wyoming.
Range, North Platte River,
Sage, Lightning and Box
Creeks.
Brand, same as cut, on any
part of animal.

Earmark

Also own 𝓗 ᒍH ᒍH TT and V

Horses and Mules branded ⩦ on left shoulder, or 𝓗 on
left hip.

STODDARD, LAPHAM & HOWARD.

P. O. Address, Buffalo,
Wyoming.
Range, Powder River and
Crazywoman, and Clear
Creek Forks of Powder
River.
Brands, same as cut, H-X

MORETON, FREWEN & CO.

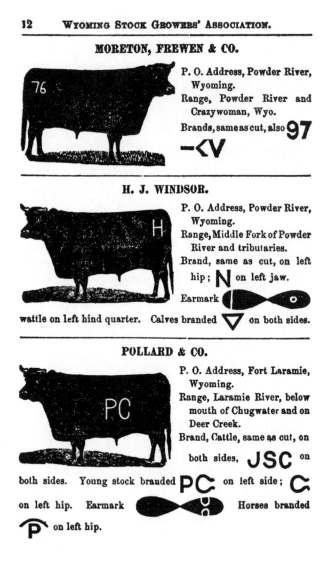

P. O. Address, Powder River, Wyoming.

Range, Powder River and Crazywoman, Wyo.

Brands, same as cut, also 97

−<V

H. J. WINDSOR.

P. O. Address, Powder River, Wyoming.

Range, Middle Fork of Powder River and tributaries.

Brand, same as cut, on left hip; N on left jaw.

Earmark

wattle on left hind quarter.   Calves branded ▽ on both sides.

POLLARD & CO.

P. O. Address, Fort Laramie, Wyoming.

Range, Laramie River, below mouth of Chugwater and on Deer Creek.

Brand, Cattle, same as cut, on both sides, JSC on

both sides.   Young stock branded PC on left side; C

on left hip.   Earmark   Horses branded

P on left hip.

CONVERSE CATTLE CO.

P. O. Address, Cheyenne, Wyoming.

Range, Lance Creek and vicinity.

Brand, all young Cattle are to be branded same as cut on left side,

CW on left side LW on left shoulder, side or thigh, waddle left jaw; on left side or hip

behind left shoulder,

OTO on left side, Y behind shoulder, YY on hip, left side, *old stock.* Y on neck, Y behind shoulder, Y on hip, left side, young stock behind shoulder, \ on thigh, left side, F on left side; —— on left shoulder or thigh,

J on left side or hip, X—7 on left side or hip

WESTERN LIVE STOCK CO.

P. O. Address, F. S. Lusk, Gen'l Manager, Denver, Col.

Range, Indian Creek and Running Water.

Brand, same as cut, left side and hip.

Earmark

and chin wattle.   Also own

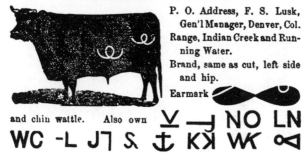

E. L. BAKER.

P. O. Address, Fort Fetterman, Wyoming.
Range, La Prelle Creek, near Fort Fetterman, Wyoming,
Brand, same as out, left side.

Earmark,

Horses branded hip or shoulder.

HARDIN, CAMPBELL & CO.

P. O. Address, Bingham, Tongue River, Wyoming.
Range, Tongue River and Wolf Creek.
Brand, Cattle, same as cut, on any part of animal. Horses branded **O4** on left shoulder.

HUNTER & BERGMAN.

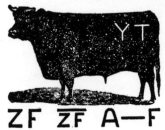

P. O. Address, Cheyenne, Wyoming.
Range, Skull and Beaver Creeks, Laramie Co.
Brand, same as cut. Earmark

GEO. A. KEELINE.

P. O. Address, Council Bluffs,
Iowa, and Fort Laramie,
Wyoming.
Range, North side Platte
River, between Forts Lar-
amie and Fetterman.
Brand, same as cut.   All
Cattle branded both sides.

GEO. KEELINE & SON.

P. O. Address, Council Bluffs,
Iowa, and Fort Laramie,
Wyoming.
Range, North side Platte
River, between Forts Lara-
mie and Fetterman.
Brand, same as cut.   Ear-
mark,
All cattle branded both sides.

GEO. KEELINE & SONS.

P. O. Address, Council Bluffs,
Iowa, and Fort Laramie,
Wyoming.
Range, North side of Platte
River, between Forts Lara-
mie and Fetterman.
Brand, same as cut, called
hog eye.

Earmark   All Cattle branded both sides.

JOHN M. ADAMS.

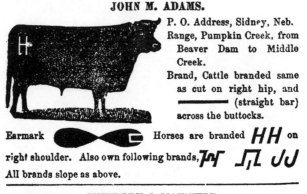

P. O. Address, Sidney, Neb.

Range, Pumpkin Creek, from Beaver Dam to Middle Creek.

Brand, Cattle branded same as cut on right hip, and ———— (straight bar) across the buttocks.

Earmark ●◄►● Horses are branded *HH* on right shoulder. Also own following brands, *TH* *JL* *JJ* All brands slope as above.

SHEIDLEY & MAYFIELD.

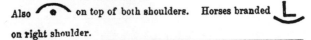

P. O. Address, Camp Robinson, Neb.

Range, White River and Runningwater.

Brand, Cattle branded same as cut, generally on right side; some few of old stock branded on left side.

Also ◠• on top of both shoulders. Horses branded L on right shoulder.

EMERSON BROTHERS.

P. O. Address, Livermore, Colorado.

Range, La Prelle Creek, near Fort Fetterman.

Brand, same as cut; also

JL W left side.

Earmark  Horses branded ♉ left shoulder.

A. B. BALLOU.

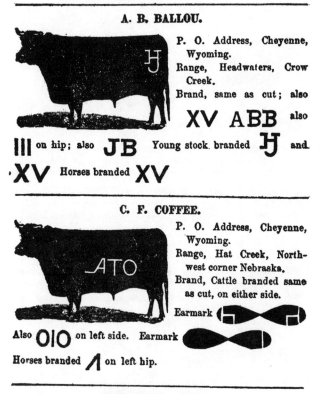

P. O. Address, Cheyenne, Wyoming.
Range, Headwaters, Crow Creek.
Brand, same as cut; also

XV ABB also

||| on hip; also JB Young stock branded Ҷ and

XV Horses branded XV

C. F. COFFEE.

P. O. Address, Cheyenne, Wyoming.
Range, Hat Creek, Northwest corner Nebraska.
Brand, Cattle branded same as cut, on either side.

Earmark

Also OIO on left side. Earmark

Horses branded Λ on left hip.

ANDREW GILCHRIST.

P. O. Address, Cheyenne, Wyoming.
Range, Crow Creek, Wyó.
Brand, same as cut; also

OV Λ̂ Â

HENRY A. BLAIR.

P. O. Address, Cheyenne, Wyoming.

Range, Powder River, Wyoming.

Brands, Cattle branded same as cut, on left side. Young stock from 1882 branded on both sides.

Also own **IC** on left side, near shoulder; **U** on left thigh.

Cattle in **U** brand have waddle on nose. **44** on left side.

Cattle in this brand also branded **B4** Earmark on ⌷

brand  Horses branded **U** on left hip.

J. L. ATKINSON.

P. O. Address, Evanston, Wyoming.

Range, Bear River, south of Evanston, Wyoming.

Brands, Cattle, same as cut. Horses and Mules, **A** on left shoulder.

GEORGE W. BAXTER.

P.O. Address, Fort Washakie, Wyoming.

Range, Grass Creek, Sweetwater Co., Wyoming.

Brand, same as cut; also,

7L LU

Earmark

ALLERTON & SPENCER.

P. O. Address, J. C. Spencer, Custer City, Dakota.

Range, Jenny's Stockade, on old Cheyenne and Deadwood Stage Road.

Brand, same as cut; also,

ΛKL   LΛY

LΛK Latter on right side only, but claim brand on any part of animal. Increase branded **L** on right hip, **Λ** on right side, and **K** on right shouldor.

GUTHRIE, HORD & CO.

P. O. Address, Cheyenne, Wyoming.

Range, La Bonte and Wagonhound, Wyoming.

Brand, Cattle, same as cut, on both sides; **O** left side and hip; **Q** left side and hip; **◇** left side.

W. L. WHIPPLE.

P. O. Address, Cheyenne, Wyoming.

Range, Cottonwood Creek and Laramie River.

Brand, same as cut, Cattle and Horses.

EDGAR B. BRONSON.

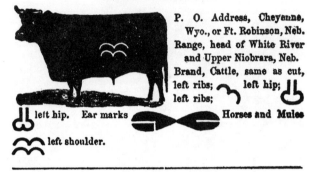

P. O. Address, Cheyenne,
Wyo., or Ft. Robinson, Neb.
Range, head of White River
and Upper Niobrara, Neb.
Brand, Cattle, same as cut,
left ribs;   left hip;
left ribs;

left hip.   Ear marks   Horses and Mules

left shoulder.

WHIPPLE & SAWYER.

P. O. Address, Cheyenne,
Wyoming.
Range, Cottonwood Creeks
and Laramie River.
Brand, same as cut, on both
sides, or any part of animal.
Ear-
mark.
Horses branded
on shoulders.

ATKINSON & MAJORS.

P. O. Address, Evanston,
Wyoming.
Range, Platte River, south of
Fort Steele.
Brand, Cattle, same as cut, on
both sides. All cattle sold
vented on left shoulder.
Horses branded   on
left shoulder.

C. A. CAMPBELL.

P. O. Address, Antelope
Springs, Wyoming.

Range, Antelope Springs,
Wyoming.

Brand, same as cut, on left
hip or side.

Earmark

Horses branded on left
hip or side.

MARK M. COAD.

P. O. Address, Camp Clark,
Nebraska.

Range, Pumpkin Creek, Neb.

Brand, Cattle, same as cut
on left side and hip, with
straight bar or rail under
said brand on the side.

BARTLETT RICHARDS.

P. O. Address, Spearfish,
D. T

Range, Donkey Creek and
Little Powder River.

Brand, same as cut, both
sides.

Earmark

Also **85** Earmark

BUCK & WAITE.

P. O. Address, Poor's Ranche,
Sioux Co., Neb.
Range, Gordon Creek.
Brand, same as cut, on left
side.

Earmark

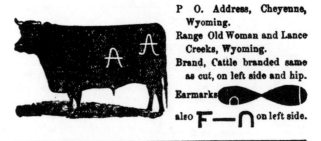

J I+H

J. HOWARD FORD.

P O. Address, Cheyenne,
Wyoming.
Range Old Woman and Lance
Creeks, Wyoming.
Brand, Cattle branded same
as cut, on left side and hip.

Earmarks

also F—∩ on left side.

PICKERING & LEWIS CATTLE CO.

P. O. Address, Cooper, Wyo.
Range, Laramie Plains, Albany Co.

Brands, same as cut, and

on left hip and right side;

on or near left loin. All

animals so branded are also road branded either Ω (mule shoe)
or letter E also claim ≡ on one or both sides; ⅗ on left
side.

A. W. HAYGOOD.

P. O. Address, Granite Canon, Wyoming.
Range, Granite Canon, Wyo.
Brand, same as cut.

S. F. EMMONS.

P. O. Address, care B. E. Brewster, Cheyenne, Wyo.
Range, Hat Creek Basin, Sioux County, Nebraska.
Brand, Cattle branded same as cut.

Earmark

Horse Brand, **S-Ɛ** on either left shoulder or hip.

BLYDENBURGH BROS. & MORGAN.

P. O. Address, C. E. Blydenburgh, Rawlins, Wyoming, and Samuel Morgan, Warm Springs,
Range, Jack Creek and Upper Platte.
Brand, Cattle branded same as cut on both sides; also **BM** **oT** both on any part of animal.

Horses branded **3** on left shoulder.

JOHN HUNTON.

P. O. Address, Bordeaux, Wyoming.

Range, Chugwater Creek, Wyoming.

Brands, Cattle or Horses, same as cut, any part of animal; 2 Cattle or Horses, any part of animal, also

CLARK & HUNTON.

P. O. Address, Bordeaux, Wyoming.

Range, Antelope and Dry Cheyenne.

Brand, same as cut, on Cattle and Horses, on any part of animal.

BULLOCK & HUNTON.

P. O. Address, Bordeaux, Wyoming.

Range, Chugwater Creek, Wyoming.

Brand, same as cut, Cattle and Horses, on any part of animal.

HANNA & McCAULEY.

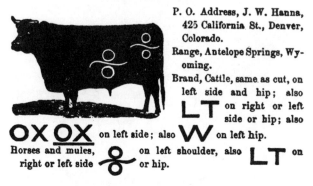

P. O. Address, J. W. Hanna,
425 California St., Denver,
Colorado.
Range, Antelope Springs, Wyoming.
Brand, Cattle, same as cut, on
left side and hip; also
LT on right or left
side or hip; also

OX OX on left side; also **W** on left hip.
Horses and mules, **&** on left shoulder, also **LT** on
right or left side or hip.

S. D. HUNTER.

P. O. Address, Greeley, Col.
Range, White River, Neb.
Brand, same as cut.
Earmark

B. S. HOPKINS.

P. O. Address, Cheyenne,
Wyoming.
Range, Heads of Crow Creek.
Brands, same as cut; also
JL

MARSH & COOPER.

P. O. Address, Cheyenne, Wyoming.
Range, Rock Creek, Laramie Plains, Wyoming.
Brand, same as cut, with double dewlap cut down.
Earmark

Also own

Horses branded **12** left shoulder.

G. H. CROSS.

P. O. Address, Fort Fetterman, Wyo.
Range, between La Bonte and La Prelle Creeks.
Brands, same as cut, on any part of animal. Horses branded same on left hip.

COGGESHALL & WARNER.

P. O. Address, Cheyenne, Wyoming.
Range, Cheyenne River, Wyo.
Brand, Cattle, same as cut, jingle bob left ear, wattle under chin.

Horses **Z4**

MILWAUKEE & WYOMING INVESTMENT CO.

P. O. Address, Cheyenne, Wyoming.
Range, Laramie River.
Brand, same as cut,

Earmark

Also **BP JD 17**

REEL & ROSENDALE.

P. O. Address, Cheyenne, Wyo.
Range, on Hams Fork, Muddy, Green River and tributaries, Uinta and Sweetwater Counties.
Brand, same as cut.
Earmarks on young cattle,

R. S. VAN TASSELL.

JAMES F. BRYSON, Foreman.
P. O. Address, Cheyenne and Rawhide Buttes, Wyoming Ter.
Range, Rawhide Creek and Running Water.
Brand, same as cut, left side and hip, V left side of

jaw, **VT** both sides.   Earmark

Horses branded **VT** left flank, and V left jaw.

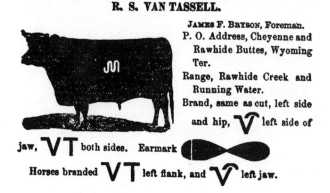

E. L. BAKER.

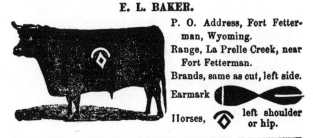

P. O. Address, Fort Fetter-
man, Wyoming.
Range, La Prelle Creek, near
Fort Fetterman.
Brands, same as cut, left side.

Earmark

Horses,   left shoulder
or hip.

JNO. R. POOR.

CLARK HOWARD, Foreman.
P. O. Address, Poor's Ranch,
Sioux County, Nebraska.
Range, Niobrara River, 20
miles west of Snake River.
Brands, same as cut, left side
and hip.   Horses same
brand left hip.

707 left side.

E. S. NEWMAN.

P. O. Address, Pine Ridge,
Dakota.
Range, Running Water, Neb.
Brands, same as cut, right
hip; left; also
on both sides, and on
left side.   Earmark of
calves,   Point of left horn sawed off.   Horses
branded left hip.

PLUNKET, ROCHE & CO.

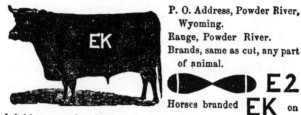

P. O. Address, Powder River, Wyoming.

Range, Powder River.

Brands, same as cut, any part of animal.

Horses branded **EK** on left hip ; vented under brand or on shoulder.

E. R. THAYER.

P. O. Address, Greeley, Weld Co., Colorado.

Range, Pawnees, Weld Co., Colorado.

Brand, same as cut, **ZZ**

Earmark

JOHN F. COAD.

P. O. Address, Cheyenne. Wyoming.

Range, Scott's Bluffs, North Platte River, Nebraska.

Brand, Cattle branded same as cut, on side ; on hip; waddle on left hind quarter on range stock.

Horses branded **C** on right shoulder.

JOHN W. CONNOR.

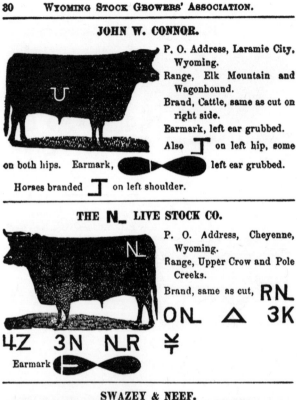

P. O. Address, Laramie City, Wyoming.
Range, Elk Mountain and Wagonhound.
Brand, Cattle, same as cut on right side.
Earmark, left ear grubbed.
Also ⌐ on left hip, some on both hips.   Earmark,  left ear grubbed.

Horses branded ⌐ on left shoulder.

THE N_ LIVE STOCK CO.

P. O. Address, Cheyenne, Wyoming.
Range, Upper Crow and Pole Creeks.
Brand, same as cut, RN_
ON_   △   3K
4Z   3N   N_R   ⅄

Earmark

SWAZEY & NEEF.

P. O. Address, Warm Springs, Carbon Co., Wyoming.
Range, Upper North Platte.
Brand, same as cut, left side;
also own ET and JF on left side.

Horses branded ⅄ on left shoulder.

F. TILLOTSON.

P. O. Address, Fort Fetterman, Wyoming, and Ur-
bana, Ohio.
Range, North Platte River,
Carbon Co., Wyo.
Brand, same as cut,
also,

J. M. TOMPKINS.

P. O. Address, Cheyenne,
Wyoming.
Range, Platte River and Horse
Shoe.
Brand, same as cut, also,

Z—X

DICKEY BROTHERS.

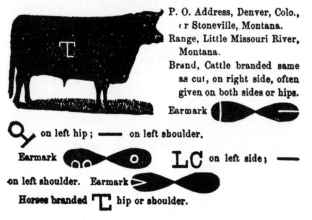

P. O. Address, Denver, Colo.,
or Stoneville, Montana.
Range, Little Missouri River,
Montana.
Brand, Cattle branded same
as cut, on right side, often
given on both sides or hips.
Earmark

on left hip ; —— on left shoulder.

Earmark   LC on left side ; ——
on left shoulder.   Earmark

Horses branded   hip or shoulder.

STANDARD CATTLE CO,

A. T. BABBITT, Gen'l Manager.   R. M. ALLEN, Ass't Manager.

P. O. Address, Cheyenne, Wyoming.

Range, headwaters Chugwater and Horse Creeks, Wyoming.

Brands, same as cut, on left shoulder and hip, or any part of animal.

Earmark,   Also own following brands;

Z ʒ DS IOI HM U̲ VK   Horses

branded O̅ on left shoulder. Also, Range on Belle Fourche and Little Powder Rivers, Wyoming.

P. O. Address, A. T. Babbitt, General Manager, Cheyenne, or John Winterling, Foreman, Sun Dance, Wyoming.

Brand, IOI Texas cattle, left side, loin or hip. Earmark,

Increase same brand on both sides. Also,

own following brands : ♂̃ on left side, and SB on left jaw.

Increase branded IOI HZ Increase branded IOI

In part earmarked   Some fine bulls

branded Z̲ Horse brands, Z IOI

JESSE KNIGHT.

P. O. Address, Evanston, Wyoming.

Brand, same as cut, on right shoulder, and bar ▬ across rump, under tail.

Earmark

PRICE & JENKS.

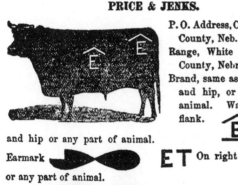

P. O. Address, Chadron, Sioux County, Neb.

Range, White River, Sioux County, Nebraska.

Brand, same as cut, left ribs and hip, or any part of animal. Wattle in right flank.  Left ribs

and hip or any part of animal.

Earmark  **ET** On right and left ribs, or any part of animal.

Earmark

HACKNEY, WILLIAMS & CO.

P. O. Address, Cheyenne and Buffalo, Wyoming.

Range, Crazy Woman and Clear Fork of Powder River, Wyoming.

Brand, Cattle branded same as cut, and ——— on left stifle; also, ⟋ on left shoul-

der. Horses branded ╫ on left shoulder.

TOM SUN.

P. O. Address, Rawlins, Wyo.

Range, Sweet Water, Wyo.

Brands, same as cut, both sides. Horses, left hip

E. J. REID.

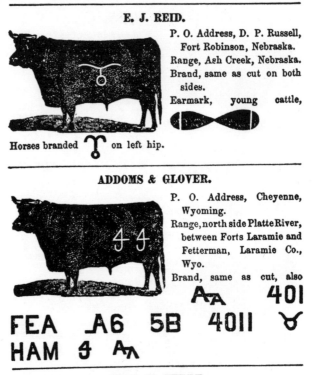

P. O. Address, D. P. Russell,
Fort Robinson, Nebraska.
Range, Ash Creek, Nebraska.
Brand, same as cut on both
sides.
Earmark, young cattle,

Horses branded ⅄ on left hip.

ADDOMS & GLOVER.

P. O. Address, Cheyenne,
Wyoming.
Range, north side Platte River,
between Forts Laramie and
Fetterman, Laramie Co.,
Wyo.
Brand, same as cut, also

AA 401

FEA ⅃6 5B 4011 Ծ
HAM ᘿ Aʌ

CHAS. H. TERRY.

P. O. Address, Cheyenne,
Wyoming.
Range, Laramie County,
Wyoming.
Brand, same as cut.
Ƴ Horses and mules
only.

HOLDEN & STEVENS.

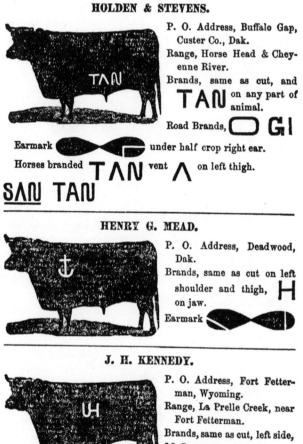

P. O. Address, Buffalo Gap, Custer Co., Dak.

Range, Horse Head & Cheyenne River.

Brands, same as cut, and **TAN** on any part of animal.

Road Brands, ☐ GI

Earmark ☒ under half crop right ear.

Horses branded **TAN** vent **∧** on left thigh.

SAN TAN

HENRY G. MEAD.

P. O. Address, Deadwood, Dak.

Brands, same as cut on left shoulder and thigh, **H** on jaw.

Earmark ☒

J. H. KENNEDY.

P. O. Address, Fort Fetterman, Wyoming.

Range, La Prelle Creek, near Fort Fetterman.

Brands, same as cut, left side, **IX** left side.

Horses, **UH IX** left hip.

MATHER & ROBINSON CO. (Limited.)

C. A. GUERNSEY, Supt.

P. O. Address, Hat Creek,
Wyo. Ter.
Range, Cheyenne River.
Brands, same as cut (three
nines), one each on left
shoulder, side and hip.

Wattle right thigh.   Horses branded ⌃ left hip.

G. H. GOBLE.

P. O. Address, Evanston,
Wyoming.
Range, 50 miles north of
Evanston, on Bear Creek.
Brand, same as cut.

F. EARNEST.

P. O. Address, Fort Fred
Steele, Wyo.
Brands, same as cut on left
side; young stock on both
sides; ⌐ right hip;
young stock both hips;
ℛ on right hip; ▬

across haunches; Ð left side.
Horses, ⚲ ⋀ 6

N. R. DAVIS & CO.

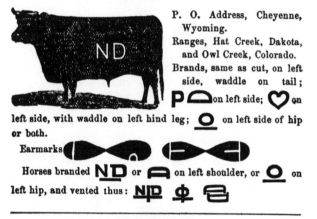

P. O. Address, Cheyenne, Wyoming.

Ranges, Hat Creek, Dakota, and Owl Creek, Colorado.

Brands, same as cut, on left side, waddle on tail; on left side; ♡ on left side, with waddle on left hind leg; ○ on left side of hip or both.

Earmarks

Horses branded **ND** or ⌂ on left shoulder, or ○ on left hip, and vented thus: **ND** ⌽ ⊟

SCOTT & HANK.

P. O. Address, Mandel, Wyoming.

Range, Tongue and Little Powder Rivers.

Brand, same as cut, left side. dewlap in throat.

Horses branded same.

J. F. PERRY.

P. O. Address, Fort Fetterman, Wyoming.

Brand, same as cut, left side.

Earmark

R. A. TORREY.

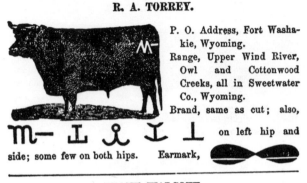

P. O. Address, Fort Washakie, Wyoming.

Range, Upper Wind River, Owl and Cottonwood Creeks, all in Sweetwater Co., Wyoming.

Brand, same as cut; also, on left hip and side; some few on both hips.   Earmark,

FRANK WALCOTT.

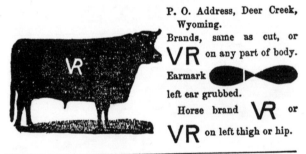

P. O. Address, Deer Creek, Wyoming.

Brands, same as cut, or VR on any part of body.

Earmark left ear grubbed.

Horse brand VR or VR on left thigh or hip.

CLARK & PLUMB.

P. O. Address, Deadwood, Dakota.

Range, Belle Fourche and Crow Creek.

Brand, same as cut, left shoulder, side and hip.

Earmark

For horses,  V on left shoulder.

DURBIN BROS.

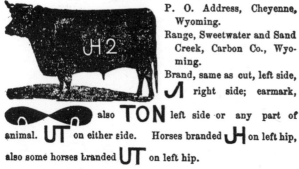

P. O. Address, Cheyenne, Wyoming.

Range, Sweetwater and Sand Creek, Carbon Co., Wyoming.

Brand, same as cut, left side, right side; earmark,

 also TON left side or any part of animal. UT on either side.   Horses branded H on left hip, also some horses branded UT on left hip.

PETERS & ALSTON.

P. O. Address, Powder River, Wyoming.

Range, Powder River and Beaver Creek.

Brand, Cattle. same as cut on hip, neck and jaw.

Earmark, double swallow-fork left ear;

Also F U VU UA

Horses branded, KC on left hip; also C on left shoulder.

ANDERSON BROS.

P. O. Address, P. Anderson, Fort Collins, Colorado.

Range, Antelope Springs, Wyoming.

Brand, same as cut, on left side and jaw. Same brand for horses and mules.

SEARIGHT BROS.

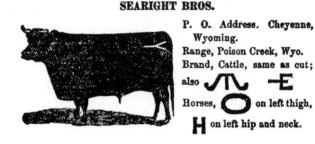

P. O. Address. Cheyenne, Wyoming.
Range, Poison Creek, Wyo.
Brand, Cattle, same as cut; also on side, hip, or thigh.
Horses, on left thigh, on left hip and neck.

GILLETTE, STERLING & CO.

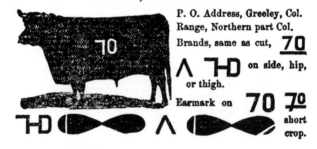

P. O. Address, Greeley, Col.
Range, Northern part Col.
Brands, same as cut, 70
on side, hip, or thigh.
Earmark on short crop.

BOSLER BROTHERS & CO.

P. O. Address, Sidney, Neb.
Range, North Platte, north of Ogallala.
Brands, same as cut, and tip of right horn off;
wattle on left side of neck;
wattle on right side of neck;
left ear off.

J. M. CAREY & BRO.

P. O. Address, Cheyenne, Wyoming.

Range, North Platte River, Carbon and Albany counties.

Brand, same as cut, anywhere on neat Cattle, and on left hip of horses; also ⊦

behind left shoulder on Cattle, and on left hip of Horses.

Marks of Cattle, underslope both ears and jug handle in brisket.

CAREY COMPANY.

P. O. Address, Cheyenne, Wyoming.

Range, Pole and Horse Creeks, Laramie Co.

Brand, same as cut, anywhere on neat cattle; on left hip of horses; also own CT TO cattle bought of Chas. Terry.

FERDON & BIDDLE.

P. O. Address, Spearfish, Dak.

Range, Belle Fourche and Little Missouri.

Brand, same as cut, left side,

Earmark

Horses branded ⌐ O left hip.

SMITH & ASH.

P. O. Address, Rawlins, Neb.
Range, Big Bend of Muddy
and Platte Rivers.
Brand, same as cut, on left
hip, **W** on right side,
on right side.

WM. DOLAN.

P. O. Address, Egbert, Wyo.
Range, Muddy Creek, Wyo.
Brand, same as cut.

E. B. GRAHAM & T. B. SNYDER.

P. O. Address, Cheyenne,
Wyoming.
Range, Running Water, Neb.
Brands, same as cut, left
shoulder and hip;

left side and hip, wattle on
left fore leg; **M** both sides, wattle on left side of neck, **O-LL**

both sides; $\frac{N}{N}$ left side and hip; **7L** left side and hip, wattle

left shoulder; **79** left side; **Q** left side and right hip; **2Y**

left side; **O4** on right side; ◇ left hip, and **O4**

left side;

THOMAS & PAGE.

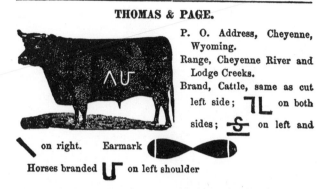

P. O. Address, Cheyenne, Wyoming.
Range, Cheyenne River and Lodge Creeks.
Brand, Cattle, same as cut left side; on both sides; on left and

on right. Earmark

Horses branded on left shoulder

U. S. INDIAN BRANDS, PINE RIDGE AGENCY, DAK.

V. T. McGILLICUDDY, Agent.
P. O. Address, Pine Ridge Agency, Dakota.
Range, Pine Ridge Reserve, Dakota.
Brands, same as cut; also

 ID △

R. A. TORREY.

P. O. Address, Fort Washakie, Wyoming.
Range, Upper Wind River, Owl and Cottonwood Creeks, Sweetwater Co., Wyo.

Brand, same as cut, M—

Brands mostly on left hip and side; some few on both hips, and some of the running 𝑚— on right hip.

F. M. PHILLIPS.

P. O. Address, Fort Lara-
mie, Wyoming.
Range, Laramie River, mouth
of Chug.
Brand, same as cut.
Earmark

PRATT & FERRIS CATTLE CO.

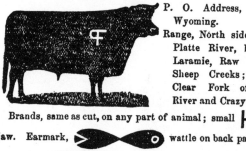

P. O. Address, Cheyenne,
Wyoming.
Range, North side of North
Platte River, below Fort
Laramie, Raw Hide and
Sheep Creeks; also on
Clear Fork of Powder
River and Crazy Woman.

Brands, same as cut, on any part of animal; small ⊢ on left

jaw. Earmark, ➤   ○ wattle on back part of right

ham. Also ⊐╪ on any part of animal. Double dewlap

and ear marked ◖▶◀◗   Also own ⴘ ╪⊏

⋔ ⴘ or K Y any part of animal. Horses branded ⅌

left shoulder or ⴘ left hip.

RANKIN BROS.

P. O. Address, Rawlins, Wyo.
Range, Carbon Co., Wyo.
Brand, same as cut.

TAYLOR & COFFEY.

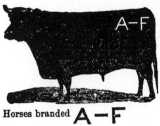

P. O. Address, Cheyenne, Wyoming.
Range, Hat Creek Valley and Cheyenne River.
Brand, Cattle, same as cut, anywhere on animal.

Earmark

Horses branded **A-F**

WYOMING & MONTANA CATTLE CO.

JOHN H. CONRAD, President.

P.O. Address, Fort McKinney, Wyoming.
Range. Tongue River to Goose Creek, Wyoming, to Little Big Horn, Montana.

Brand, same as cut, 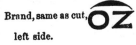 left side.

Earmark

E. W. BENNETT.

P. O. Address, Rawlins, Wyo.
Range, Jack's Creek, Upper North Platte, Carbon Co.
Brands, Cattle, same as cut, left shoulder.

Horses, **ԴՐ** left thigh.

T. H. McGEE.

P. O. Address, Cheyenne.
Wyoming.
Range, Crow Creek.
Brand, same as cut, left side;
————— left thigh. Ear-
mark, jingle-bob on left ear
and swallow fork right ear.

E. NAGLE.

P. O. Address, Cheyenne,
Wyoming.
Range, Sabille and Laramie
Rivers.
Brand, same as cut, on side,
and Ω mule shoe on left
hip.

Earmark [image] Owner of steers branded

ЛЛ left side; also of herd cattle branded M left hip

also herd cattle branded 7| left hip; also following brands,

74 75 76 76 or 78 on side and Ω on hip.

CRAWFORD, THOMPSON & CO.

P. O. Address, Evanston,
Wyoming.
Range, north from Evanston
on Bear River, and North
Wood, Johnson Co., Wyo-
ming.
Brands, | | on both sides on
loin; also | on

both sides on loin on cattle in Johnson County.
Horses branded same as Cattle on left shoulder.

WAID & HURLBUT.

P. O. Address, Cheyenne, Wyoming.
Range, Sand and Dewell's Creeks, north side of North Platte.
Brands, same as cut, left side. (Cattle were previously branded 〇 〇 〇 left shoulder or hip. Ear-

Horses branded **FL**

mark ⊂⊃

B. E. BREWSTER.

P. O. Address, Cheyenne, Wyoming.
Range, Duck Creek, Laramie Co., Wyoming.
Brand, Cattle branded same as cut, right hip; Ol left hip.

Horse brand, 10 left shoulder.

B. BREWSTER & CO.

P. O. Address, Cheyenne, Wyoming.
Range, Hat Creek Basin, Sioux County, Neb.
Brand, Cattle, same as cut and 10

Ear mark ⊂⊃   Horses 10 left shoulder.

J. H. KENNEDY.

P. O. Address, Fort Fetterman, Wyoming.
Range, La Prelle Creek, near Fort Fetterman.
Brand, same as cut left side ; **IX** left side.

Earmark,   Horses, **UH IX** left hip.

ANDREWS & HUDSON.

P. O. Address, Dry Cheyenne, via Fort Fetterman, Wyo.
Range, Duck Creek, Dry Cheyenne River.
Brands,   same   as   cut ;

small

crop off left ear; also **E3**

and **E3**

EMERSON BROS.

P. O. Address, Livermore, Colorado.
Range, La Prelle Creek, near Fort Fetterman. Brands,

same as cut; also **JL**

JW left side.

Horses branded   left shoulder.

W. L. KUYKENDALL.

P. O. Address, Warm Springs, Carbon Co., Wyo.

Range, Spring Creek, Carbon Co., Wyoming.

Brand, same as cut, on both sides and left hip; claim right to brand on any part of animal; also **HI** on left hip; **COB** on left side; **SU** on left side or any part of body. Horses branded **SU** on right shoulder; also **H** on left shoulder.

MAY GOLDSCHMIDT.

P. O. Address, Cheyenne, Wyoming.

Brand, same as cut; claims **AVH** any parts of animals, both Cattle and Horses.

HARKNESS & CO.

P. O. Address, Hat Creek, Wyo.

Range, Lance Creek.

Brand, same as cut, left side and hip. Horses branded **V5** on left shoulder.

DATER & CO.

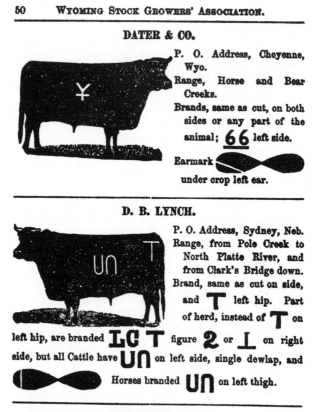

P. O. Address, Cheyenne, Wyo.

Range, Horse and Bear Creeks.

Brands, same as cut, on both sides or any part of the animal; **66** left side.

Earmark under crop left ear.

D. B. LYNCH.

P. O. Address, Sydney, Neb.

Range, from Pole Creek to North Platte River, and from Clark's Bridge down.

Brand, same as cut on side, and **T** left hip. Part of herd, instead of **T** on left hip, are branded **LCT** figure **2** or **⅃** on right side, but all Cattle have **UN** on left side, single dewlap, and Horses branded **UN** on left thigh.

WM. GUITERMAN.

P. O. Address, Cheyenne, Wyoming.

Range, Hat Creek and Cheyenne River.

Brand, same as cut.

E. W. WHITCOMB.

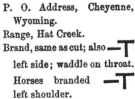

P. O. Address, Cheyenne, Wyoming.
Range, Hat Creek.
Brand, same as cut; also —⊤ left side; waddle on throat.
Horses branded —⊤ left shoulder.

M. H. & W. A. MURPHY.

P. O. Address, Ft. McKinney.
Range, Piney Fork of Powder River.
Brand, same as cut, left side; hock; under tail.
Earmark

Horses branded ⌒ on left hip.

TRABING BROS.

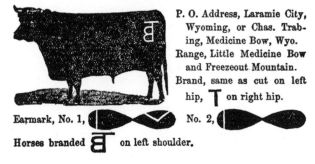

P. O. Address, Laramie City, Wyoming, or Chas. Trabing, Medicine Bow, Wyo.
Range, Little Medicine Bow and Freezeout Mountain.
Brand, same as cut on left hip, ⊤ on right hip.

Earmark, No. 1, No. 2,

Horses branded ℈ on left shoulder.

C. HECHT & BRO.

P. O. Address, Cheyenne, Wyoming.

Range, Hat Creek and Old Woman.

Brands, same as cut and CR

22 RH

Earmark, young stock,

INTERNATIONAL CATTLE CO.

HARRY OELRICHS, Manager.

P. O. Address, Cheyenne, Wyoming.

Range, South Fork, Cheyenne.

Brand, same as cut, and

TOT   TOT

⊢O⊢   -4L

SEABURY & GARDNER.

P. O. Address, Cheyenne, Wyoming.

Range, Bear Creek.

Brand, same as cut, and $\frac{4}{E}$

HC $

Earmark   also handle LOP LOB

OELRICHS BROTHERS & CO.

P. O. Address, Cheyenne, Wyoming.

Range, Rawhide, Wyoming.

Brand, same as cut, left loin; either or both sides;

left side;

left side; left side; left side.

Earmark

Horses branded **WH** left shoulder.

TESCHEMACHER & DE BILLIER.

P. O. Address, Cheyenne, Wyoming

Range, Bitter Cottonwood and Wagonhound.

Brand, same as cut; also

LU ∩U 66

Earmark

SUDDITH & MONTGOMERY.

P. O. Address, Laramie City, Wyoming.

Range, Laramie Plains and Clear Fork, Powder River.

Brand, same as cut, on Laramie Plains Cattle; wattle on left jaw young cattle on Powder River Cattle; link on ribs both sides, and wattle right jaw.

WATSON, JOHNSTON & McCREA.

P. O. Address, Spearfish, Dakota.
Range, Head of Little Powder.
Brand, same as cut. Earmark on increase

BALCH & BACON.

P. O. Address, Laramie City, Wyoming.
Range, Laramie Plains.
Brand, all Cattle branded prior to 1878 have "block," same as cut, on left side. All Cattle branded during 1878 have "block" on left side and right hip. All cattle branded since 1878 have "block" on left side and right thigh. Have some Cattle branded ∪ on left loin and some branded ⟵ on left side. All of above brands are supposed to have dewlap mark in brisket. Have some Oregon Cattle branded ⅂ on left hip. Horses branded S on left shoulder or thigh.

BLYTH & PIXLEY.

P. O. Address, Evanston, Wyoming.
Range, 55 miles north of Evanston, on Bear River.
Brand, same as cut, on right side.

JOHN C. KINGMAN.

P. O. Address, Cheyenne,
Wyoming.
Range, Crow Creek, Wyo.
Brand, same as cut, on left
hand shoulder. All horses
vented **B9** on left hip.

C. W. WRIGHT.

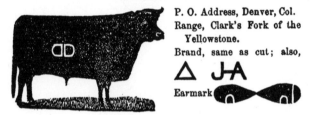

P. O. Address, Denver, Col.
Range, Clark's Fork of the
Yellowstone.
Brand, same as cut; also,

△ JHA

Earmark

M. E. CARTER.

P. O. Address, Fort Bridger,
Wyoming.
Range, Stinking River east
of Yellowstone Park and
Smith's, Black's and Hen-
ry's Forks of Green River.
Brand, same as cut, on left

hip and left thigh, and *C* on left jaw.

Earmark  None but grown steers sold.

WIEDEN, MABRY & CO.

W. E. JOHNSTON, Manager.

P. O. Address, Boiling Springs Ranch, Sioux Co., Nebraska.

Range, E. S. Newman's to Boiling Springs Ranch, on Running Water, distance 40 miles.

Brands, Cattle, same as cut, both shoulders and left side; right ear grubbed both sides or twice on left side and wattled with jug handle on the neck.

Horses left hip or thigh and on left side of neck; and left thigh or cushion.

HUNTER, EVANS & HUNTER.

P. O. Address, Pine Ridge Agency, Dakota.

Range, Running Water, Neb.

Brands, same as cut, left side; left side, and left hip; also some with on left side and hip;

left jaw; also same branded with bail brand. left side; jingle bob in each ear; also same swallow fork in each ear. Horses branded with Cattle brand on left hip. Also same with on left shoulder; left hip; right hip.

ORGAN & DRAPER.

P. O. Address, Cheyenne, Wyoming.
Range, North Platte and Rawhide.
Brand, same as cut; also,

Earmark

POST & WARREN.

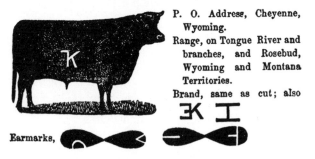

P. O. Address, Cheyenne, Wyoming.
Range, on Tongue River and branches, and Rosebud, Wyoming and Montana Territories.
Brand, same as cut; also

Earmarks,

J. H. DOUGLAS WILLAN.

P. O. Address, Laramie City, Wyoming.
Range, Little Laramie River.
Brand, Horses branded same as cut; also,

J R on left shoulder.

DORR CLARK.

P. O. Address, Deadwood, Dakota.

Brand, same as cut, on left hip.

McGINLEY & STOVER.

P. O. Address, Fort Collins, Colorado.

Brands, A OK 73 VL /⊂▽ ⊥ 人

BALDWIN & COWLES.

P. O. Address, Pine Bluffs, Wyoming.

Range, Pine Bluffs, Pole Creek and South Platte.

Brands, ƎⱵ also JP 333 NF Ⱶ ℧℧

Ɐ IT XYZ 04 ℧ U CⱯL ꟼL S̄S̄

⌐ right hip.

Horses ⌐ on left shoulder.

STURGIS, GOODELL & LANE.

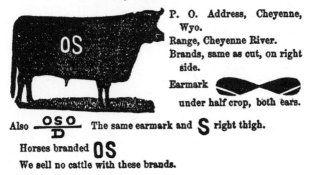

P. O. Address, Cheyenne, Wyo.

Range, Cheyenne River.

Brands, same as cut, on right side.

Earmark under half crop, both ears.

Also   O S O / D   The same earmark and **S** right thigh.

Horses branded **OS**

We sell no cattle with these brands.

G. H. & J. S. SNYDER.

P. O. Address, Cheyenne, Wyoming.

Range, South Platte.

Brand, _ᴶ_ Cattle and Horses.

INDEX.

Bibliography

Bibliography

This bibliography is not intended to be exhaustive. Only those manuscripts and books are listed that have been utilized in the preparation of this volume.

ALDRIDGE, Reginald. Ranch Notes in Kansas, Colorado, the Indian Territory and Northern Texas (London, 1884, second edition).

ALLEN, Lewis F. "Improvement of Native Cattle," in Report of the commissioner of agriculture for the year 1866 (Washington, 1867).

ASSESSMENT BOOK FOR LARAMIE COUNTY, Territory of Wyoming, for 1877 (unprinted records in court house).

ATHERTON vs. FOWLER, 6 Otto 513.

BABBITT, A. T. "The Grazing Interest and the Beef Supply," dated March 10, 1884, and found in the Bancroft Library of California. Printed in the Daily Drovers Journal, Chicago, April 10, 1884.

BAD LANDS COWBOY (Medora, North Dakota), 1884.

BANCROFT, Hubert Howe. History of Nevada, Colorado and Wyoming (San Francisco, 1890).

BARRINGTON, Mrs. Russell, editor. The Works and Life of Walter Bagehot (London, 1915), 10 vols.

BATCHELDER, George Alexander. A Sketch of the History and Resources of Dakota Territory (Yankton, 1870).

BAUMANN, John. "On a Western Ranche," in the Fortnightly Review (London, 1887), vol. XLVII, 516-533.

BENTON WEEKLY RECORD (Ft. Benton, Montana), 1881, 1882.

BLACK HILLS DAILY AND WEEKLY PIONEER (Deadwood, South Dakota), 1884.

BLACK HILLS DAILY TIMES (Deadwood, South Dakota), 1879, 1880, 1882.

BLACK HILLS JOURNAL (Rapid City, South Dakota), 1880.

BLACK HILLS PIONEER (Deadwood, South Dakota), 1882.

BOWLES, Samuel. Across the Continent (Springfield, Mass., and New York, 1865).

BRANCH, Douglas. The Cowboy and his Interpreters (New York, 1926).

BRAND BOOK CONTAINING THE BRANDS OF THE CHEROKEE STRIP (Wilmot Proviso Brush, publisher, Kansas City; Isaac Poore, printer and binder, 1882). In Congressional Library, Washington, D. C.

BRANDS AND MARKS, Book A (unpublished, in the office of the live-stock commission at Helena, Montana).

BRIGGS, Harold E. "Ranching and Stock Raising in the Territory of Dakota," in South Dakota Historical Collections, XIV (1928), 417-465.

——— "The Development and Decline of Open Range Ranching in the Northwest," in the Mississippi Valley Historical Review, XX, 521-536.

BRISBIN, General James S. The Beef Bonanza; or How to Get Rich on the Plains (Philadelphia, 1881).

BRITISH ROYAL COMMISSION ON AGRICULTURE. Reports of the assistant commissioners, vol. XV, dated January 20, 1882 (session of February 7-December 2, 1882).

BUREAU OF ANIMAL INDUSTRY, Second Annual Report (Washington, 1885).

CALDWELL [KAS.] POST, 1882.

CABLE, Alexander C. Manuscript letter to William A. J. Sparks dated February 4, 1887, in office of the commissioner of the general land office.

CAREY LETTER BOOKS, in the office of J. M. Carey and Sons, Cheyenne, Wyoming. These contain business correspondence, inventories, reports, and financial statements of various cattle companies from about 1868 to 1892.

CATTLE BRANDS OWNED BY THE MEMBERS OF THE WYOMING STOCK GROWERS' ASSOCIATION (Chicago, 1882). Prepared by A. T. Babbitt, F. E. Warren, and Philip Dater and containing the names and brands of about one hundred and sixty stockmen.

CLAY, John. My Life on the Range (privately printed, 1924).

——— "My Life on the Range," in Live Stock Markets (Chicago), vol. XXXII, no. 32, November 16, 1922. Published by John Clay & Company live stock commission.

COLORADO BRAND BOOK (Denver, 1887). In Public Library at Denver.

COLORADO FARMER AND LIVE STOCK JOURNAL (Denver), 1877, 1878.

COMMERCIAL INDICATOR (Kansas City, Missouri), 1878, 1879.

COMMISSIONER OF THE GENERAL LAND OFFICE, Annual Report for 1882-1889.

CRAIG, James Roderick. Ranching with Lords and Commons or Twenty Years on the Range (Toronto, 1903).

CONTRACT OF SALE of the Nebraska Land and Cattle Company dated March 30, 1883, in possession of Attorney Ralph C. Coad of Omaha.

COOK, James H. "Trailing Texas Long-Horn Cattle through Nebraska," in Publications of the Nebraska State Historical Society (Lincoln), XVIII, 260-268.

CORPORATION RECORD, vol. XIX in office of county clerk of Laramie county, Wyoming.

CRAWFORD, L. F. Notes based on interviews with former ranchmen and settlers of Dakota Territory. The author is under obligation to his former student, Professor Harold E. Briggs of the University of Miami at Coral Gables, Florida, who made a detailed examination of these records of Superintendent L. F. Crawford of the State Historical Society of North Dakota.

——— "The Medora-Black Hills Stage Line," in Collections of the State Historical Society of North Dakota (Bismarck), VII, 309-323.

CRAWFORD, Samuel J. Kansas in the Sixties (Chicago, 1911).

CURLEY, Edwin A. Nebraska, its Advantages, Resources, and Drawbacks (London, 1875).

DAILY DROVERS JOURNAL (Chicago), 1882-1887.

DAILY GLOBE-DEMOCRAT (St. Louis), November 18, 1884.

DAILY PIONEER (Mandan, North Dakota), 1887.

DALE, Edward E. The Range Cattle Industry (Norman, Oklahoma, 1930).

DICKINSON PRESS (Dickinson, North Dakota), 1882-1884.

DILLON EXAMINER (Montana), April 9, 1924.

DUFFIELD, John, editor. "Driving Cattle from Texas to Iowa, 1866," in Annals of Iowa (Des Moines, Iowa), third series, vol. XIV, 246-262, April, 1924.

ESTELLINE BELL (Estelline, South Dakota), 1883, 1884, 1886.

FORD COUNTY GLOBE (Dodge City, Kas.), 1878, 1879, 1880, 1882.

GARDEN CITY PAPER (Garden City, Kas.), June 5, 1879.

GORDON, Clarence W. "Report on Cattle, Sheep, and Swine" (10-31), in tenth census of the United States, III, 965-985.

GRAINFIELD [KAS.] CAP SHEAF, 1886.

GREELEY, Horace. An Overland Journey from New York to San Francisco (New York, 1860).

GRESHAM, Postmaster-general Walter I. to Secretary H. M. Teller dated April 23, 1883, and found in the office of the commissioner of the general land office.

HAGEDORN, Hermann. Roosevelt in the Bad Lands (Boston and New York, 1921).

HALEY, J. Evetts. The XIT Ranch of Texas and the Early Days of the Llano Estacado (Chicago, 1929).

HARGER, Charles M. "Cattle Trails of the Prairies," in Scribner's Magazine (New York, 1892), XI, 732-742, June, 1892.

HARRINGTON, W. P. History of Gove county, Kansas, to the Organization of the county in 1886 (published privately, 1920, unpaged).

HAYDEN, F. V. U.S. Geological Survey of Wyoming and adjacent Territories (Washington, 1871).

HAYES, A. A. "The Cattle Ranches of Colorado," in Harper's New Monthly Magazine (New York, 1879), vol. LIX, 877-895.

HENRY, T. C. "Thomas James Smith," in Transactions of the Kansas State Historical Society, 1905-1906 (Topeka).

HILL, Alexander Stanley. From Home to Home (New York, 1885).

HORNADAY, William T. "The Cowboys of the Northwest," in the Cosmopolitan (Rochester, 1887), vol. II, 219-233.

HOSMER vs. WALLACE, 7 Otto 575.

HUNTER, J. Marvin, editor. The Trail Drivers of Texas (second revised edition, Nashville, 1925). This volume reproduces with minor changes the material in vol. I (San Antonio, 1920) and vol. II (San Antonio, 1923). References in this work are to the second revised edition of one volume.

INTERNATIONAL TRUST CO. vs. UNION CATTLE CO., ET AL., 3 Wyoming 803.

JARED WHITMAN, ET AL. vs. UNION CATTLE COMPANY, doc. 4, no. 436 in office of the clerk of the court of Laramie county, Wyoming.

KANSAS COWBOY (Dodge City, Kas.), October 18, 1884.

KENDRICK, John B. "The Texas Trail," in the Cheyenne [Wyo.] State Leader, December 10, 1916.

KUHN, Bertha M. "The W-Bar Ranch on the Missouri Slope," in Collections of the State Historical Society of North Dakota (Bismarck), vol. V, 155-165.

LARAMIE STOCK ASSOCIATION MINUTE BOOK. These records begun by the secretary of the association, W. L. Kuykendall, are preserved in the office of the Wyoming Stock Growers' Association at Cheyenne. The name "Laramie Stock Association" is also used in these official minutes. Volume II of these records is unpaged and has the title of "Minute Book Wyoming Stock Growers' Association."

LETTERS FROM OLD MEMBERS and Friends of the Wyoming Stock Growers' Association (Cheyenne, 1923).

LIST OF MEMBERS, By-Laws, and Reports of the Wyoming Stock Growers' Association, and the Laws of Wyoming, for the Protection of Stock Growers, as Amended by the Ninth Assembly (Cheyenne, 1886).

LIVE STOCK JOURNAL (Fort Worth, Texas), 1883.

LODGE, Henry Cabot, editor. Selections from the correspondence of Theodore Roosevelt and Henry Cabot Lodge, 1884-1918 (New York and London, 1925).

LUMMIS, Charles F. "Pioneer Transportation in America," in McClure's Magazine (New York), vol. XXVI, 81-94.

McCOY, Joseph G. Historic Sketches of the Cattle Trade of the West and Southwest (Kansas City, 1874).

MACDONALD, James. Food from the Far West or American Agriculture (New York, 1878).

MAJORS, Alexander. Letter dated April 15, 1884, and printed in the Cheyenne [Wyo.] Sun, May 1, 1884.

——— Seventy Years on the Frontier (Denver, 1893).

MATADOR LAND AND CATTLE COMPANY, Annual Reports, 1883-1885, printed, unpaged, and bound. In office of John Clay and Company (The Rookery, Chicago).

MELINE, James F. Two Thousand Miles on Horseback; Santa Fé and Back; a Summer Tour Through Kansas, Colorado, & New Mexico in the year 1866 (New York, 1868).

MINUTE BOOK COLORADO CATTLE GROWERS' ASSOCIATION. Unprinted and covering the years 1867-1883 as found in the office of the [Denver] Daily Record Stockman.

MINUTE BOOK WYOMING STOCK GROWERS' ASSOCIATION. In office of Wyoming Stock Growers' Association at Cheyenne.

NIMMO, Joseph, Jr. "The Range and Ranch Cattle Traffic . . . of the United States" (bureau of statistics, Washington, 1886), in Report on the Internal Commerce of the United States, part III.

Printed also as House Executive Document no. 267, 48th congress, 2d session, serial number 2304.

OLMSTED, Frederick Law. A Journey through Texas; or, a Saddle-Trip on the Southwestern Frontier (New York, 1860).

OSGOOD, Ernest Staples. The Day of the Cattleman (Minneapolis, 1929).

PAXSON, Frederic Logan. "The Cow Country," in the American Historical Review, XXII, 65-82 (October, 1916).

PELZER, Louis. "The Shifting Cow Towns of Kansas," in Transactions of the Illinois State Historical Society for the year 1926, 41-51.

——— "A Cattlemen's Commonwealth on the Western Range," in The Mississippi Valley Historical Review, XIII, 30-49 (June, 1926).

——— "Financial Management of the Cattle Ranges," in the Journal of Economic and Business History, II, 723-741 (August, 1930).

——— "Trails of the Trans-Mississippi Cattle Frontier," in J. F. Willard and Colin B. Goodykoontz (editors), The Trans-Mississippi West, 139-161 (Boulder, Colo., 1930).

PIPER, Edwin Ford. Barbed Wire and Other Poems (Iowa City, 1927).

POWDER RIVER CATTLE CO. CATTLE BOOK, found in the office of J. M. Carey and Sons, Cheyenne, Wyoming.

PROCEEDINGS OF THE ADJOURNED MEETING of the Wyoming Stock Growers' Association (Cheyenne, 1916).

RECORD OF BRANDS, Book A, Laramie county, Wyoming, in office of recorder at Cheyenne.

RECORDS OF THE CIRCUIT COURT of the United States for the District of Colorado (Denver). Cases 1666, 1677, 1682-1685.

RECORDS OF INCORPORATION in office of secretary of state, Helena, Montana.

RECORDS OF INCORPORATION, Book H, in investment division of the secretary of state, Des Moines, Iowa.

REPORT OF THE BUREAU OF ANIMAL INDUSTRY for 1886 (Washington, 1887).

REPORT OF THE STATE BOARD OF AGRICULTURE, Kansas, for the years 1877-1878 (Topeka, second edition).

REPORTS OF KANSAS STATE BOARD OF AGRICULTURE. Fifth Biennial Report, 1885-1886, and Sixth Biennial Report, 1887-1888.

REVISED STATUTES OF WYOMING in force January 1, 1887.

RICHTHOFEN, Walter Baron von. Cattle Raising on the Plains of North America (New York, 1883).

ROLLINS, Philip Ashton. The Cowboy: his Equipment and his Part in the Development of the West (New York, 1922).

ROMSPERT, George W. The Western Echo: a Description of the Western States and Territories of the United States as gathered in a Tour by Wagon (Dayton, Ohio, 1881).

ROOSEVELT, Theodore. An Autobiography (New York, 1909).

—— Hunting Trips of a Ranchman (New York, 1923).

—— Ranch Life and the Hunting Trail (New York, 1926), National edition.

SANDERS, S. F. to Secretary H. M. Teller for a letter dated April 9, 1883, in the office of the commissioner of the general land office.

SATURDAY EVENING JOURNAL (Bismarck, North Dakota), 1885, 1886.

SECRETARY OF THE INTERIOR, Annual Reports for 1884-1889.

SESSION LAWS of Wyoming Territory, 1884.

SESSION LAWS of Wyoming Territory passed by the Ninth Legislative Assembly.

SMILEY, Jerome C. Prose and Poetry of the Live Stock Industry of the United States, with Outlines of the Origin and Ancient History of our Live Stock Animals. This was the only volume issued of the three planned and was prepared by authority of the National Live Stock Association and published by that body at Denver and Kansas City, copyright 1904 and 1905.

SPALDING, C. C. as quoted in Kansas Historical Collections (Topeka), vol. XI, 121, 122 from the Annals of the City of Kansas (Kansas City, Mo., 1858), 78, 79.

STEWART vs. WYOMING CATTLE RANCHE COMPANY, 128 U.S. 383.

STOUT, Tom, editor. Montana: Its Story and Biography; a History of Aboriginal and Territorial Montana and Three Decades of Statehood (New York, 1921), 3 vols.

STRAHORN, Robert E. The Hand-Book of Wyoming and Guide to the Black Hills and Big Horn Regions for Citizen, Emigrant and Tourist (Cheyenne, 1877).

—— Montana and Yellowstone National Park (Kansas City, 1881).

———— To the Rockies and Beyond, or a Summer on the Union Pacific Railroad and Branches (Omaha, 1879).

SWAN LAND & CATTLE COMPANY. Annual Reports describing range financing, meetings of boards of directors, shipments, management, profits, losses, purchases and the general operation of an extensive corporation. In office of John Clay and Company (The Rookery, Chicago). These printed, bound, but unpaged records cover the years from 1883 to 1912.

———— LIMITED *vs.* FRANK, ET AL., 39 Federal Reporter 456.

TENTH CENSUS of the United States, III (statistics on agriculture).

TEXAS LIVE STOCK JOURNAL (Fort Worth), 1883.

THE TIMES (London, England), May 23, 1882.

TRENMOUTH *vs.* SAN FRANCISCO, 10 Otto 251.

THE TRIBUNE (Huron, South Dakota), 1882, 1883.

TRIGGS, J. H. History of Cheyenne and Northern Wyoming (Omaha, 1876).

TURNER COUNTY HERALD (Hurley, South Dakota), 1883.

UNITED STATES Senate, Executive Documents, 35th congress, 1st session, no. 1, vol. I, 797.

———— Senate, Executive Documents, 35th congress, 1st session, no. 46, vol. XII, 2-4 (April 16, 1858).

———— Senate, Executive Documents, 40th congress, 2d session, no. 77, vol. II, chap. iii; contains "Captain Raynolds's Report and Journal."

———— Senate, Executive Documents, 48th congress, 1st session, no. 127, vol. VI, containing letter of Posey S. Wilson to H. M. Teller dated January 4, 1884, of John Willits and Sons to same dated January 6, 1883, of John Fleming to same dated January 8, 1883, B. A. Arnold to same dated February 17, 1883, and of N. Weare to same dated March 31, 1883.

———— House, Executive Documents, 36th congress, 2d session, no. 47, vol. VIII, 9-11.

———— House, Executive Documents, 39th congress, 1st session, no. 1, vol. III, part i, 112, 113, 251. Contains the report of Quartermaster-general M. C. Meigs, dated November 8, 1865.

———— House, Executive Documents, 46th congress, 2d session, no. 46. The report of the public lands commission containing resolutions and testimony of the Wyoming Stock Growers' Association.

—— House, Executive Documents, 48th congress, 1st session, no. 1, part v, containing report of Governor William Hale of the Territory of Wyoming dated November 10, 1883.

—— House, Executive Documents, 48th congress, 1st session, no. 1, part v, containing letter from Thomas Sturgis to E. S. Morgan, secretary and acting-governor of the Territory of Wyoming dated June 11, 1883.

—— House, Executive Documents, 48th congress, 1st session, no. 127, vol. VI; no. 119, vol. XXVI, part ii. These documents contain various letters on illegal fencing from inspectors, settlers, and government agents.

—— House, Executive Documents, 48th congress, 2d session, no. 7, vol. XX, part ii. This contains Joseph Nimmo's report on "The Range and Ranch Cattle Business of the United States."

—— Statutes at Large, II, XXIII, XXIV.

—— Yearbook of the United States Department of Agriculture for 1908.

WALKER, Robert, to Secretary H. M. Teller for a letter dated March 9, 1883, in the office of the commissioner of the general land office.

WARREN RECORD (Indianola, Iowa), September 10, 1874.

WEBB, Walter Prescott. The Great Plains (Boston, 1931).

WEEKLY FREE PRESS (East Pierre, South Dakota), 1885, 1886, 1887.

WESTERN CENTRAL KANSAS COWBOY (Dodge City, Kas.), 1883, 1884.

WESTERN RANCHES, LTD., Annual Report and Balance Sheet. In the office of John Clay and Company (The Rookery, Chicago) and for the years from 1882 to 1912. Printed and bound but unpaged.

WILLIAMS, Henry T. The Pacific Tourist, Williams Illustrated Guide to Pacific R.R. California, and Pleasure Resorts across the Continent (New York, 1878).

WRIGHT, Robert M. Dodge City the Cowboy Capital (Wichita, Kas., 1913).

YELLOWSTONE JOURNAL (Miles City, Montana), 1883.

Index

Index

of, 87; lack of interpretation of, 221

GALLARDO, Gregorio: bullfighter, 68
Gallatin: cattle shipments from, 206
Garden City (Kans.): cattle center,
45; mention of, 183
General Land Office: action of, on
illegal fencing, 178-180
Geo. Keeline & Sons: range of, 265
Germany: beef exports from, 141
Giants in the Earth, The: reference
to, 50
Gilchrist, Andrew: range of, 267
Gillette, Sterling & Co: range of, 290
Goble, G. H: range of, 286
Gold discovery: effect of, on cattle
migrations, 195
Goldschmidt, May: range of, 299
Goldschmidt & Fisher: range of, 259
Goodall, Gorham B: mention of, 164,
167, 168, 199
Goodall, H. L: editorials by, 141
Goose Creek Range: location of, 255
Gordon, Lord Douglas: 131, 132
Gordon Creek Range: 272
Goshen Hole Irrigation Company:
mention of, 165; shares of, 167, 168;
operations of, 188
Goschen Hole Range: 129, 259
Graham & Snyder: range of, 292
Grainfield [Kans.] *Cap Sheaf:* quo-
tation from, 77
Granada: 226
Grand river: 197, 214
Grand river valley: range in, 199
Granger: 110
Granite Cañon (Wyo.): range near,
273
Granville Stuart: cattle firm, 81
Grass: designation of, as "king," 80
Grass Creek Range: 268
Grazing: land for, 190
Great Bend (Kans.): as cow town,
57; mention of, 64, 226
Greeley, Horace: mention of, 238
Greeley (Colo.): range near, 275;
residents of, 279, 290

Green, W. R: office of, 126
Green Horn Association: 76
Green Mountain Stock Ranching
Company: headquarters of, 123
Green river: freighters bound for,
30; range on, 277, 305
Gregg, Josiah: writing of, 221
Grimes and Thornton: cattle firm, 129
Gudgell: cattleman, 199
Guernsey, C. A: office of, 286
Guiterman, Wm: range of, 300
Guthrie, Hord & Co: range of, 269

HACKNEY, Williams & Co: range of,
283
Hall, E. F: 166
Hallett, Moses B: decrees of, on fenc-
ing, 187
Hams Fork: range on, 277
Hanford Land and Cattle Company:
capital stock of, 123
Hanna, J. W: range of, 275
Hanna & McCauley: range of, 275
Hardin, Campbell & Co: range of, 264
Hardin, Jake: 110
Harkness & Co: range of, 299
Harper's Magazine: quotation from,
159
Harris, Jack: office of, 80
Harris, L. B: cattleman, 223
Harris, William: address of, 261
Harris & Clevenger: range of, 261
Harte, Bret: 50
"Hash Knife": losses of, 214
"Hash Knife" ranch: owners of, 197
Haskell, Cap: activities of, 128
Hat Creek (Wyo.): range near, 286,
299
Hat Creek Basin: range at, 273, 297
Hat Creek Range: 267, 287, 291, 300,
301, 302
Hat Creek Valley: 110
Hat Creek Valley Range: 295
Hatch, Rufus: 127
Haupt, C. E: cattleman, 207
Haupt, Herman: cattleman, 207
Hay Creek: 199

Pierre (Dak.): cattle mart, 211, 212;
references to, 210, 213
"Pilgrims" (cattle): 212
Pine Bluffs: cattle shipments from,
229; range near, 308
Pine Ridge (Dak.): brand inspection
at, 93; resident of, 278
Pine Ridge Agency (Dak.): 293, 306
Pine Ridge Reserve Range: 293
Piper, Edward: cattle driven by, 37
Piper, Edwin Ford: quotation from,
202
Plains: use of, for winter grazing, 28,
29
Plains grasses: food value of, 28;
factor of, in range boom, 121; quo-
tation on, 195-197; references to,
200, 201
Planters' Hotel (Denver): 73
Platte divide: 195
Platte river: 47
Platte River Range: 260, 265, 270,
281, 292, 294
Plattsmouth (Nebr.): 177
Pleuropneumonia: 139
Plumb, Duncan C: cattleman, 129,
199, 200; ranch of, 197
Plunkett, Roche & Co: range of, 279
Plunkitt, Horace: cattleman, 107; quo-
tation from, 138
Poindexter: cattle drive of, 234
Poison Creek Range: 290
Pole Creek: range near, 300
Pole Creek Range: 280, 308
Pole Range: 291
Pollard & Co: range of, 262
"Pony Bill": advice of, on brands,
236
Pools: see Cattle pools
Poor, Jno. R: range of, 278
Poor's Ranch: location of, 272, 278
Portray Pasture: 188
Post & Warren: range of, 307
Potts, Benjamin F: cattle interests of,
83
Powder river: 124; range on, 261;
reference to, 279, 289

Powder River Cattle Company: business of, 124; brand of, 124; references to, 107, 238
Powder River Range: 262, 268, 279,
283, 284, 289, 294, 301, 303
Powell, J. W: report of, on Dakota,
195
Prairie Cattle Company: organiza-
tion of, 125; Scottish interests in,
125; business of, 126; management
of, 126; ranch of, 187; fences of,
removed, 187; brands of, 236
Prairie fires: losses from, 213; refer-
ences to, 239, 240
*Prairie Snowstorm disclosed after a
Thaw, Victims of a* (illustration):
215
Prairie Traveler, The: 26
Pratt and Ferris Cattle Co: streams
diverted by, 189; range of, 283
Preëmption: 174, 176, 181
Prentice, George: 130
Price & Jenks: range of, 283
Pringle, Robert: activity of, 129
*Prose and Poetry of the Live Stock
Industry: see Live Stock Industry,
Prose and Poetry of*
Prouty, S. S: cattle paper managed
by, 80
Pryor, Ike T: cattle driver, 49, 50;
quotation from, 50
Public domain: use of, by cattlemen,
94-96; purchase of, 94, 95; plea
against public sale of, 94, 95; struggle for, 173; illegal appropriation
of, 173; regulation of fencing of,
173, 174; preëmption rights on, 174;
settlers' demands for, 174; rights
assumed on, 174, 175; fraudulent
patents on, 174, 175; lawlessness on,
176; diversion of water on, 188,
189; restoration of fenced areas to,
188; illegal inclosures on, 189
Public lands: see Public domain
Public Lands Commission: work of,
on ranches, 94
Pueblo: cattle pool at, 75, 76